Wade Sokolosky

Wade Sokolosky
and Mark A. Smith

"To Prepare for Sherman's Coming"

The Battle of Wise's Forks,
March 1865

Savas Beatie
California

Library of Congress Control Number: 2015946034

ISBN: 978-1-61121-266-2
First edition, first printing

e-book ISBN: 978-1-61121-267-9

SB

Published by
Savas Beatie LLC
989 Governor Drive, Suite 102
El Dorado Hills, CA 95762

916-941-6896
sales@savasbeatie.com
www.savasbeatie.com

MIX
Paper from
responsible sources
FSC
www.fsc.org   FSC® C011935

Savas Beatie titles are available at special discounts for bulk purchases in the United States by corporations, institutions, and other organizations. For more details, please contact Special Sales, P.O. Box 4527, El Dorado Hills, CA 95762, or you may e-mail us at sales@savasbeatie.com, or visit our website at www.savasbeatie.com for additional information.

Proudly published, printed, and warehoused in the United States of America.

Dedicated to
the American Soldier

Table of Contents

Table of Contents (continued)

List of Maps

List of Illustrations

List of Illustrations (continued)

List of Illustrations (continued)

Preface

Sergeant William Trousdale of the 48th Tennessee was killed on the final day of the battle of Wise's Forks. Trousdale and scores of other Confederates were buried in unmarked graves, where they remain to this day.

Like Trousdale and his fallen comrades, the battle itself has been largely forgotten for more than 150 years. Despite its significance within the larger context of the Carolinas campaign, Wise's Forks has received only a fraction of the attention paid to battles fought at Bentonville, Monroe's Crossroads, and Averasboro. John G. Barrett's *The Civil War in North Carolina* (1963) and Mark L. Bradley's *Last Stand in the Carolinas: The Battle of Bentonville* (1996) offer excellent basic narratives of the battle, but their coverage was deliberately limited.

In the last decade, two published works—Tom J. Edwards and William H. Rowland's *Through the Eyes of Soldiers: The Battle of Wyse Fork* (2006), and Timothy Auten's *The Battle of Wyse Fork: North Carolina's Neglected Battle* (2008) advanced the battle's scholarship. Both deserve praise for providing insight on this previously neglected chapter in North Carolina's Civil War history.

To Prepare for Sherman's Coming builds upon the excellent work done by earlier authors by using more sources and add a different perspective. It is important to understand the battle in the context of the Union's campaign-level objectives—a strategy implemented by Lt. Gen. Ulysses S. Grant in support of Maj. Gen. William T. Sherman's march through the Carolinas during the winter and spring of 1865. The engagement at Wise's Forks came about because the Federals needed a functioning railroad inland from the coast, as opposed to a desire on their part to defeat the Confederates in battle.

Acknowledgments

This study has benefited from the help and advice of many people. We are grateful to former Bentonville site manager John Goode for handing over his research files, which became our jumping-off point. We are particularly indebted to Mark L. Bradley for taking time to read the manuscript. Mark's guidance, professionalism, and mentorship (and most of all his friendship) helped us tell this story. Mark's tireless efforts and inspiration have made this study a better product, and words cannot describe our deepest appreciation.

We also extend our thanks to Eric Wittenberg for finding time in his busy schedule to read the manuscript. Eric is a true friend and mentor, and served as a motivator to keep us on task. His encouragement and insightful discussions over the years are greatly treasured.

Our gratitude extends to Donny Taylor, manager of the Bentonville Battlefield State Historic Site. Aside from reading the manuscript, Donny on several occasions took time out of his busy schedule to walk the battlefield with us. Donny grew up on the Wise's Forks battlefield and has studied the engagement for decades.

Special thanks to Dr. Charles Classen and Bill Ellis of Kinston, North Carolina, for granting permission to use Stephen McCall's painting titled *Kirkland's Brigade at Wyse Fork*, March 10, 1865 as our cover art. We are equally grateful to Lyle Holland of Kinston for his assistance in securing permission, and for always being available to answer questions. Thanks also to Dennis Harper of Kinston for sharing his extensive knowledge of the battlefield.

Skip Riddle assisted us greatly in casting a new light on the sacrifices and contributions of the 9th New Jersey. Skip's personal research proved invaluable. If he did not have the answers, he wasted little time in reaching out to his network of fellow historians. For this Skip, we are forever grateful.

We are indebted to Heidi Crabtree for sharing her years of research on Capt. George W. Graham. Heidi's forthcoming book, *Not a Soldier, But a Scoundrel*, will further our knowledge of the notorious captain's service in eastern North Carolina.

We extend our thanks to the staff at many libraries and archives. To Lt. Col. (Ret.) Pat Beatty, for his assistance in tracking down potential sources at Fort Leavenworth; to Victor T. Jones of the New Bern-Craven County Library in New Bern, North Carolina; to volunteers and staff at the History Place, Carteret County's Historical Society and Research Library in Morehead City; to Rebecca Elbert of the Winchester-Frederick County Historical Society; to Megan Maxwell of the Museum of the Cape Fear in Fayetteville; and to Marty Tschetter of the Wayne County Public Library in Goldsboro.

Special thanks to the many individuals who provided copies of diaries, letters, and photographs from their private collections. The contributions of the Army of Tennessee at Wise's Forks would have been incomplete without assistance from researchers around the county who have specialized knowledge of particular Civil War units, including Sidney W. Bondurant and Mike Griggs of the General Barton and Stovall Brigade History & Heritage Association. Richard Melvin, R. Hugh Simmons, Larry Stephens, O. Lee Sturkey, and Bryce A. Suderow went above and beyond in providing invaluable assistance.

We owe a debt of gratitude to our friend Col. Darrell Combs (Ret.), United States Marine Corps, for his outstanding illustrations of some of the key events pertaining to Wise's Forks. Darrell's interest in the Carolinas campaign stems from the fact that his great-great-grandfather fought at Averasboro as a member of the 82nd Ohio and was killed several days later at Bentonville.

This project would not have been possible without the help of special individuals. Heather Ammel and Travis Seymour provided excellent editorial assistance. Bentonville staff members Amanda Brantley and Derrick Brown provided technical help.

We were especially honored when George Skoch agreed to prepare the maps. A battle study requires plentiful maps to visualize troop movements and dispositions. The maps that grace this study attest to George's extraordinary skill and professionalism. His contribution has resulted in a far better book.

Special thanks to our publisher, Theodore P. Savas of Savas Beatie and his wonderful staff. Ted's approach to publishing military history is second to none. From the outset, he placed no limitation on the number of photographs and maps, trusting instead our judgment. *To Prepare for Sherman's Coming* is supplemented with a bounty of such illustrations to better tell the soldiers' stories. Developmental editor Mark A. Moore's help made this a much better book, and Production Manager Lee Merideth was a joy to work with and an excellent task master. This book would not have been possible without their patience, support, and guidance.

Our greatest thanks are reserved for our families, whose love and support is unfailing. Wade would like to thank his wife Traci for her faith, encouragement, and support throughout the many years it took to complete this project. Mark would like to thank his wife Tracey for her continued support: even while he forced her to read the many drafts of the manuscript: and for enduring the many evenings he spent working on this study at his computer.

Wade Sokolosky
August 2015, Beaufort, NC

Mark A. Smith
August 2015, Claysville, PA

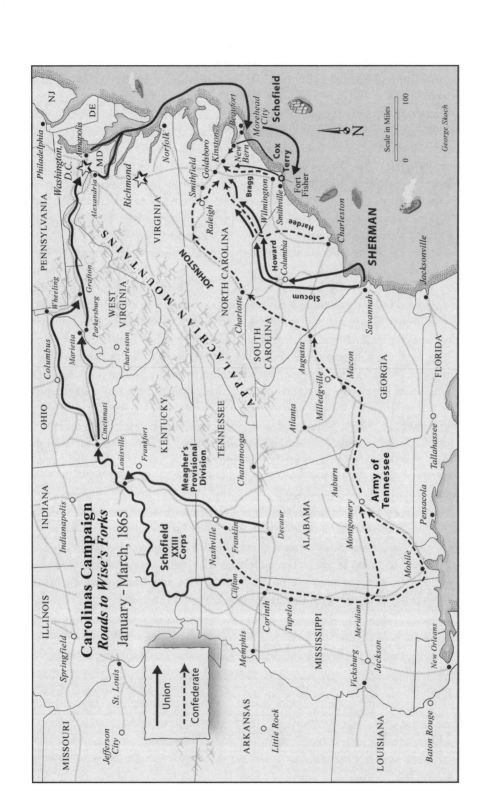

Carolinas Campaign
Roads to Wise's Forks
January – March, 1865

Union →
Confederate ⇢

Scale in Miles
0   100

George Skoch

SHERMAN

Schofield

Cox
Terry

Bragg

Hardee

Howard

Slocum

JOHNSTON

Meagher's
Provisional
Division

Schofield
XXIII
Corps

Army of
Tennessee

APPALACHIAN MOUNTAINS

ILLINOIS
INDIANA
OHIO
PENNSYLVANIA
NJ
DE
MD
WEST VIRGINIA
VIRGINIA
KENTUCKY
TENNESSEE
NORTH CAROLINA
SOUTH CAROLINA
GEORGIA
ALABAMA
MISSISSIPPI
ARKANSAS
LOUISIANA
FLORIDA
MISSOURI

Philadelphia
Washington, D.C.
Alexandria
Richmond
Norfolk
Annapolis
Beaufort
Morehead City
New Bern
Kinston
Goldsboro
Smithfield
Raleigh
Wilmington
Smithville
Fort Fisher
Charleston
Columbia
Charlotte
Augusta
Macon
Milledgeville
Atlanta
Savannah
Jacksonville
Tallahassee
Pensacola
Mobile
Montgomery
Auburn
Decatur
Corinth
Tupelo
Meridian
Jackson
Vicksburg
Memphis
Nashville
Franklin
Clifton
Chattanooga
Frankfort
Louisville
Cincinnati
Columbus
Marietta
Parkersburg
Grafton
Wheeling
Charleston
Indianapolis
Springfield
St. Louis
Jefferson City
Little Rock
New Orleans
Baton Rouge
Tallahassee

Chapter 1

"Prepare the way for my coming."
— *Maj. Gen. William T. Sherman*

Grant Plans a Campaign

E arly on the morning of January 29, 1865, the side-wheel steamer *USS Rhode Island* entered Beaufort Inlet, cruising past watchful Union sentries at Fort Macon as the vessel sought sanctuary in Morehead City Harbor. John Hedrick, the harbor's U.S. Treasury Department agent, noted the day was "exceedingly cold." Excitement over a certain *Rhode Island* passenger, however, eclipsed any concern about the weather. On board was Lt. Gen. Ulysses S. Grant, general-in-chief of the Union army, who, for the last six months, had engaged the army of Confederate Gen. Robert E. Lee in some of the bloodiest combat operations of the Civil War.[1]

Grant's purpose in visiting the coast centered on a broadening military strategy for North Carolina, which in the coming weeks would transform the state into a major operational theater of the war. By March 1865, the U.S. Army's execution of Grant's strategy would employ more than 85,000 Union soldiers in the Tar Heel State as part of the effort to defeat the Confederacy.[2]

---

1 *Official Records of the Union and Confederate Navies in the War of Rebellion*, 30 vols. (Washington, DC, 1900), Series 1, vol. 27, 710. Hereafter cited as *ORN*. All references are to series 1 unless otherwise noted; Judkin Browning and Michael Thomas Smith, eds., *Letters from a North Carolina Unionist: John A. Hedrick to Benjamin P. Hedrick 1862-1865* (Raleigh, NC, 2001), 250.

2 *The War of Rebellion: A Compilation of the Official Records of the Union and Confederate Armies*, 128 vols. (Washington, DC, 1888-1901), Series 1, vol. 47, pt. 1, 43. Hereafter cited as *OR*. All

Lt. Gen. Ulysses S. Grant
Library of Congress

Grant's rather sudden focus on North Carolina stemmed from the operational successes of Maj. Gen. William T. Sherman. In December of 1864, Sherman had presented the city of Savannah, Georgia, to President Abraham Lincoln as a Christmas gift. The fall of Savannah, an important port city for the Confederacy, dealt a tremendous blow to Southern morale, but it was Sherman's March to the Sea that severely damaged the Confederacy's ability to wage war. Sherman's march had sliced through the Confederate heartland and disrupted the vital resources that Georgia had provided to the Southern cause.[3]

Sherman's successful march to Savannah defined how he expected to conduct future operations in the Carolinas. As Sherman refitted his army in Savannah, he began a dialogue with Grant about what his army's next move should be. Grant initially considered transferring Sherman's army north by sea to Virginia to join Union forces confronting Lee's Army of Northern Virginia. Grant wrote, "I had no idea originally of having Sherman march from Savannah to Richmond, or even to North Carolina." The winter of 1864, one of the rainiest in memory, had turned roads into quagmires with no immediate prospect for improvement. Grant knew the torrential rains had rendered most

references are to series 1 unless otherwise noted. Prior to January 1865, roughly 12,000 Federal soldiers were stationed in eastern North Carolina.

3   Mark A. Smith and Wade Sokolosky, *No Such Army Since the Days of Julius Caesar, Sherman's Carolinas Campaign: from Fayetteville to Averasboro* (Fort Mitchell, KY, 2005), 1-2; Mark L. Bradley, *Last Stand in the Carolinas: The Battle of Bentonville* (Campbell, CA, 1995) 1-2; William T. Sherman, *Memoirs of W. T. Sherman by Himself*, 2 vols. (New York, NY, 1891), vol. 2, 181, 190, 219, 231, 227-228; Maj. Johnny W. Sokolosky, "The Role of Union Logistics: Sherman's Carolinas Campaign of 1865," Master's Thesis (Fort Leavenworth, KS: U.S. Army Command & General Staff College, 2000), 3.

roads impassable, and that terrible weather would cause Sherman's army much trouble on the march.[4]

Sherman, however, had a plan. As historian Mark L. Bradley observed, "Sherman realized that by marching his army through the Carolinas, he would inevitably cut Lee's supply lines to the Deep South and induce hundreds—if not thousands—of Lee's troops from that region to desert." His march through Georgia to the sea aptly demonstrated the devastating effect an army could have on an enemy's transportation and supply networks. If Sherman marched his army through the Carolinas, he would eviscerate what remained of the Confederacy, which was already on the verge of collapse. In Virginia, Lee's Army of Northern Virginia was desperately trying to prevent the capture of Richmond, the Confederate capital, and the vital rail junction at Petersburg. In the Western Theater, Gen. John B. Hood's Army of Tennessee had met with disaster at Nashville at the hands of Union Maj. Gen. George H. Thomas's Army of the Cumberland, leaving Hood's once-proud army a ghost of its former self.[5]

Two factors convinced Grant to approve Sherman's suggestion for a march through the Carolinas. First, Grant was confident enough in Sherman's abilities as a commander to permit his subordinate to embark on such a daring and risky undertaking. This confidence stemmed from their close personal relationship forged during several successful campaigns earlier in the war. Second, Grant soon

Maj. Gen. William T. Sherman
Library of Congress

4 Smith and Sokolosky, *No Such Army*, 2; Sherman, *Memoirs*, vol. 2, 25, 259-261, 269; Sokolosky, "The Role of Union Logistics," 9; Ulysses S. Grant, *Personal Memoirs of Ulysses S. Grant*, 2 vols. (New York, NY, 1885), vol. 2, 578.

5 Bradley, *Last Stand*, 2; Smith and Sokolosky, *No Such Army*, 1-2; Sherman, *Memoirs*, vol. 2, 224-225.

learned that due to a lack of transport ships, Sherman's army could march overland to Virginia more quickly than it could move by sea.[6]

On December 27, 1864, Grant instructed his trusted lieutenant to "make your preparations to start on your expedition without delay. Break up the railroads in South and North Carolina, and join the armies operating against Richmond as soon as you can." Having received Grant's authorization to proceed, Sherman began preparing for his army's ambitious movement.[7]

Grant initiated the first phase of his North Carolina strategy after approving Sherman's plan to march north from Savannah. On December 30, he ordered a combined army-navy operation to silence Fort Fisher, the Confederacy's largest bastion, thereby opening the door for the capture of Wilmington, North Carolina. Grant dispatched from Virginia Bvt. Maj. Gen. Alfred H. Terry and more than 9,000 soldiers from the Army of the James to reinforce Rear Adm. David D. Porter's naval force off Fort Fisher. On January 15, 1865, after a desperate struggle, the combined force seized Fort Fisher and began preparations for the capture of Wilmington.[8]

The fall of the seemingly impregnable Fort Fisher changed Grants opinion regarding the importance of eastern North Carolina, specifically the port city of Wilmington. Until that time, Grant had shown little interest in its capture, but thereafter sought to begin operations as soon as possible. Historian Chris Fonvielle Jr. noted, "Grant was so intent on capturing Wilmington he left the main theater of war in Virginia—a rare move for him—to travel to Cape Fear to confer with Admiral Porter and General Terry."[9]

The news of Fort Fisher's capture pleased Sherman. "I rejoice in it for many reasons, because of its intrinsic importance," he wrote to Grant several days before launching his new campaign into South Carolina, "and because it gives me another point of security on the seaboard." The capture of Fort Fisher proved to be the first success in the execution of a much broader strategy.[10]

---

6   Smith and Sokolosky, *No Such Army*, 2; OR 46, pt. 1, 45.

7   *OR* 44, 820-821; Smith and Sokolosky, *No Such Army*, 2; Sherman, *Memoirs*, vol. 2, 238.

8   Chris E. Fonvielle Jr., *The Wilmington Campaign: Last Rays of Departing Hope* (Campbell, CA, 1997), 193-198. A lengthy discussion of the Wilmington campaign strays far beyond the scope of this book. Fonvielle's superb study provides the most detailed examination of the campaign.

9   Fonvielle, *The Wilmington Campaign*, 19, 331.

10 OR 47, pt. 2, 102-104; Smith and Sokolosky, *No Such Army*, 7; Sherman, *Memoirs*, vol. 2, 258.

With Fort Fisher eliminated, Wilmington was now vulnerable. Significant as the South's last major open seaport, Wilmington served as a key transportation hub for three railroads—above all, the Wilmington & Weldon, which served as the logistical lifeline for Lee's army in Virginia. The Union army now valued the railroad because of its access to the sea and its proximity to the town of Goldsboro, Sherman's ultimate destination in North Carolina.

To reinforce efforts in North Carolina and to prepare for other contingencies, Grant ordered the transfer of Maj. Gen. John M. Schofield and his XXIII Corps from Tennessee to the Tar Heel coast. Concern that the Confederacy might attempt to halt Sherman's advance convinced Grant of the necessity for reinforcements. On January 21, Grant informed Sherman that the 20,000-man XXIII Corps was on its way to North Carolina.[11]

After Fort Fisher's capture, the Union military directed its efforts to supporting Sherman's occupation of Goldsboro. To develop this final strategy, Grant traveled to the North Carolina coast accompanied by Assistant Navy Secretary Gustavus V. Fox and General Schofield. Grant and his party arrived at Cape Fear, where they met with General Terry, commander of army forces, and Admiral Porter, commander of the North Atlantic Blockading Squadron. Terry and Porter, under Schofield's command, were assigned the task of capturing Wilmington.[12]

Grant used this meeting to further define the final phases of his strategy to "open communication between the seacoast and Goldsboro by rail, so as to meet Sherman with supplies for his army and to put at his disposal an available force." During the meeting, the senior leaders decided upon Wilmington as the primary port of entry for supplies and personnel intended for Sherman's Goldsboro objective. Several factors drove the leaders to select Wilmington rather than the Union-occupied port cities of Beaufort, Morehead City, and New Bern. First, they assumed the Wilmington & Weldon Railroad was operational to Goldsboro based on its current use by the enemy. This was not case with the Atlantic & North Carolina Railroad, where the Confederates had removed a large section of the rail west of New Bern. Second, Wilmington's capture also provided a contingency in the event Sherman required a safe haven

11 OR 47, pt. 2, 101-102. Grant believed the relocation of the XXIII Corps to the coast a better use of idle troops since Maj. Gen. George H. Thomas in Nashville displayed no eagerness to resume operations.

12 OR 46, pt. 1, 45; ORN 27, 710.

Goldsboro Railroad Station, circa 1870.
State Archives of North Carolina

or resupply from the coast. In addition to the Wilmington & Weldon, two other railroads served Wilmington. The Wilmington, Charlotte & Rutherford, then under construction, would link the coast to Charlotte, North Carolina, and the Wilmington & Manchester provided access to Charleston, South Carolina, and other points south of the port city. Finally, the Cape Fear River provided a water route all the way to Fayetteville in the event Sherman required re-supply. However, Confederate forces still held Wilmington, so it was a risky choice. To mitigate the risk, Union troops would have to seize Wilmington quickly to save as much rolling stock as possible.[13]

Pleased with the meeting, Grant departed the Cape Fear River and sailed north up the coast to Morehead City, where he met with Brig. Gen. Innis N. Palmer, the commander of the District of North Carolina. Caught off guard by Grant's sudden arrival at Morehead, Palmer hastily traveled down the railroad from New Bern to meet with the general-in-chief. As planned during the Cape Fear strategy session, Palmer was to assume a supporting role from New Bern and Morehead. Grant used his short visit to ensure that Palmer fully understood the plan and his duties. Grant and his party walked the streets, and after a short

13 Fonvielle, *The Wilmington Campaign*, 331-332.

boat ride across the harbor, visited Union forces occupying the port of Beaufort.[14]

For Palmer, Grant's visit confirmed the reasoning behind Sherman's earlier correspondence. Prior to Grant's strategy session, Sherman had requested from Palmer specific details about his forces and how far his line extended toward Kinston. He had also ordered Palmer to secure "at once" the railroad crossing over the Neuse River near Kinston. Sherman's message surely awakened Palmer to the reality that his once-quiet command was now at the center of a major operation.[15]

On January 21, Sherman provided Palmer with specific instructions on his supporting role in seizing Goldsboro. More importantly, Sherman countermanded his order of January 16 to secure the Neuse River crossing "at once." Sherman hoped to prevent the Confederates from guessing his intended destination. He instructed Palmer: "don't attract attention, but hold New Bern and Morehead City (Fort Macon) secure as points for me to depend on. As I approach you may aim for the railroad, near where it crosses the Neuse [River] near Kinston."[16]

Sherman's January 21 correspondence with Palmer demonstrated his concern for preserving secrecy at all costs. Sherman was notorious for his distrust of the press, for he believed that it often leaked vital information that helped the Confederates. As events unfolded throughout February, Palmer displayed a sense of paralysis in setting his forces in motion to secure Kinston. Sherman may have inadvertently contributed to Palmer's lack of immediate action.

In his after-action campaign report, Sherman explained that he had initiated all of these efforts "to prepare the way for my coming." The officer that Grant and Sherman selected to carry out the task was General John Schofield, a veteran of both the Atlanta and Tennessee campaigns. On January

---

14 Thomas Kirwan, *Memorial History of the Seventeenth Regiment Massachusetts Volunteer Infantry (Old and New Organizations) In the Civil War From 1861-1865* (Salem, MA, 1911), 256-258; Browning and Smith, eds., *Letters from a North Carolina Unionist*, 250. Grant's surprise visit added suspense to an already confusing command structure in eastern North Carolina. Hedrick wrote, "We can't find out who commands us. Some say Foster and others Palmer." Hedrick is referring to Bvt. Maj. Gen. John G. Foster, commander of the Department of the South, with headquarters in Beaufort, South Carolina.

15 *OR* 47, pt. 2, 49, 67, 78-79.

16 Ibid., pt. 2, 111-112.

Brig. Gen. Innis N. Palmer
Library of Congress

31, the capable Schofield assumed command of the newly established Department of North Carolina, which would be subject to General Sherman's orders.[17]

Major Gen. John M. Schofield was born in Gerry, New York, and raised in Freeport, Illinois. He attended the U.S. Military Academy, graduating seventh in the class of 1846. He then served nine years in South Carolina and Florida before transferring to West Point as an instructor. In the summer of 1860, disillusioned by the peacetime army's slow promotion rate, Schofield resigned his commission and moved west with his wife and two sons to St. Louis, Missouri.[18]

At the outbreak of the Civil War, Schofield's military experience proved invaluable in the recruitment and training of the 1st Missouri Infantry. The soldiers expressed their gratitude by electing him major. In June 1861, Brig. Gen. Nathaniel Lyon appointed Schofield as his adjutant general. He later served under Lyon in the battle of Wilson's Creek, Missouri. A promising officer in the Western Theater, Schofield rose to lead the Army of the Ohio under Sherman's command during the Atlanta campaign. Following Atlanta's capture, Schofield's XXIII Corps took part in the defeat of Hood's Army of Tennessee in the battles of Franklin and Nashville, Tennessee, in late 1864. A proven field commander, Schofield developed a reputation for moderation and restraint. He more than compensated for his shortcomings as a battlefield commander by demonstrating shrewdness in the politics of high command,

17 *OR* 47, pt. 1, 18; ibid., pt. 2, 179.

18 For biographical information on General Schofield, the authors consulted Connelly, *John M. Schofield & the Politics of Generalship* (Chapel Hill, NC, 2006); Fonvielle, *The Wilmington Campaign*; and Warner, *Generals in Blue*, 425-426.

which proved invaluable in his new role as department commander in North Carolina.[19]

Shortly after returning to Virginia from his meetings with Generals Terry and Palmer, Grant instructed Schofield to assume overall command of operations in North Carolina—a move based on Sherman's recommendation, but one initiated by Schofield weeks earlier. Following the Union victories at Franklin and Nashville, Schofield sought to convince Grant and Sherman to transfer his XXIII Corps east. Schofield did so because he was keenly aware that the only substantial Confederate forces were in the Eastern Theater. His efforts soon paid off, for on January 15, 1865, Grant ordered the transfer of the XXIII Corps to the Atlantic Coast.[20]

Not surprisingly, the victors of Fort Fisher, Porter and Terry, did not welcome the news of Schofield's transfer to North Carolina. If Grant was aware of their disappointment, he chose to ignore it. Sherman had also requested Schofield for the position, and whenever possible, the Union general-in-chief granted the wishes of his most trusted subordinate.[21]

As the Union strategy for the Carolinas unfolded in the beginning months of 1865, the harsh reality of the situation became all too apparent to the Confederate high command. The forces defending that region were hopelessly scattered and lacked a guiding hand to direct them. Historian Thomas L. Connelly observed, "for almost two critical months in 1865, the Confederacy confronted Sherman in the Carolinas with nothing but chaos." Gen. Braxton Bragg commanded the Department of North Carolina and reported directly to General Lee, the

Maj. Gen. John M. Schofield
Library of Congress

19 Connelly, *John M. Schofield*, 12-16.

20 Connelly, *John M. Schofield*, 1, 147-148.

21 Fonvielle, *The Wilmington Campaign*, 234-235.

Confederate army's newly appointed commander-in-chief. General P. G. T. Beauregard, commander of the Military Division of the West, was responsible for organizing an effective Confederate response to Sherman's drive north. Beauregard oversaw the disparate forces of Lt. Gen. William J. Hardee, commander of the Department of South Carolina, Georgia and Florida, elements of the Army of Tennessee, Maj. Gen. Joseph Wheeler's cavalry corps, and the Georgia state militia, commanded by Maj. Gen. Gustavus W. Smith. Beauregard's motley force of about 16,000 of all arms faced the very daunting task of stopping Sherman's powerful and victorious army of more than 60,000 men.[22]

The tangled lines of authority violated a proven principle of war: unity of command. In the Carolinas, the Confederate army lacked an overall commander who ensured that all subordinates worked together. In February 1865, the Confederates faced numerically superior Union forces under one commander—Sherman. Unlike the Confederates, Sherman's forces had one clear objective: to capture Goldsboro.

On February 1, 1865, with most of his grand army across the Savannah River, Sherman ordered his commanders to begin the campaign. As he had during the March to the Sea, Sherman divided his army into two wings, the movements of which deceived the Confederates as to his real objective. The pair of wings moved along a front about 40 miles wide, creating the illusion that Sherman was simultaneously threatening Augusta, Georgia, on the left, and Charleston, South Carolina, on the right—all while aiming more directly toward Columbia, the capital of the Palmetto State.[23]

On February 2, General Beauregard convened a council of war near Augusta, Georgia, to evaluate his limited options. The council discussed the possibility of concentrating forces at Branchville, South Carolina, to improve the odds of stopping Sherman's approaching army. Beauregard, however, had high hopes for an upcoming peace conference in Virginia, and therefore believed it was in the South's interests to attempt to defend both Augusta and Charleston. His decision to divide his forces to do so, instead of concentrating them, observed historian Mark L. Bradley, "played directly into Sherman's

---

22 Thomas L. Connelly, *Autumn of Glory* (Baton Rouge, LA, 1971), 518; Bradley, *Last Stand*, 21-22.

23 Smith and Sokolosky, *No Such Army*, 9; Sherman, *Memoirs*, vol. 2, 272-274; Bradley, *Last Stand*, 3-4.

hands, and the Federal advance through South Carolina was virtually unopposed."[24]

As a result, Union foragers, or "bummers," enjoyed the fruits of the countryside, stripping away all resources in their path. As they rampaged across South Carolina, Sherman's men gleefully implemented his idea of taking the war to the demoralized Southern public. The bummers helped themselves to anything they wanted, partly as punishment for what they believed was South Carolina's status as "the cradle of secession."[25]

On February 17, Sherman's army occupied Columbia. Implementing Sherman's policy of destroying anything of value to the Confederate war effort, the bluecoats razed the arsenal and many government warehouses containing military supplies. The Federals also replenished their supply wagons with captured bags of corn meal and other commissary supplies. Columbia suffered a fate far worse than any other city occupied by Sherman's men, with more than a third of it burning to the ground. The retreating Confederates' burning of cotton bales started a fire that rapidly spread throughout the city, stoked by high winds and drunken Union soldiers. Afterward, Sherman and Confederate cavalry chief Wade Hampton blamed each other for the inferno. Regardless of who caused the fire, the conflagration left many Columbians homeless, hungry, and unemployed. With his destructive work in Columbia finished, Sherman began moving toward his next objective: Fayetteville, North Carolina.[26]

While Sherman marched virtually unimpeded through South Carolina, the lead elements of Schofield's XXIII Corps arrived off the North Carolina coast. After the arrival of additional forces at Cape Fear, Schofield and Terry began offensive operations against Bragg's forces below Wilmington. The Union plan called for two separate forces to approach the city from the south along both banks of the Cape Fear River. The attack along the west bank succeeded, forcing the Confederates to abandon two strong positions at Fort Anderson

---

24 Smith and Sokolosky, *No Such Army*, 10; Bradley, *Last Stand*, 23. The peace negotiations were called the "Hampton Roads Conference," and were held aboard President Lincoln's steamer *River Queen* on February 3, 1865.

25 Smith and Sokolosky, *No Such Army*, 10.

26 Smith and Sokolosky, *No Such Army*, 14; Sokolosky, "The Role of Union Logistics," 68; Sherman, *Memoirs*, vol. 2, 280-288; John G. Barrett, *Sherman's March Through the Carolinas* (Chapel Hill, NC, 1956), 89-91; For a more detailed account of the burning of Columbia, see Marion Brunson Lucas, *Sherman and the Burning of Columbia* (College Station, TX: Texas A&M University Press, 1976).

and Town Creek, opening the door to seize Wilmington. Early on February 22, Bragg ordered his command to evacuate and marched north toward Goldsboro as Union soldiers prepared to enter Wilmington from the south.[27]

Throughout the day, Bragg's rear guard skirmished with the pursuing Federals, who by dusk had finally caught up with the Confederate main column at Northeast Station, nine miles north of Wilmington. The Rebels' lone pontoon bridge over the Northeast Cape Fear River prevented a rapid crossing and dangerously exposed the rear of Bragg's formation. Because of the bottleneck, Brig. Gen. William W. Kirkland's brigade and elements of the 8th North Carolina deployed to halt the Federal advance and allow time for the others to safely cross the bridge.[28]

After the remaining troops had crossed, the Confederates burned the Wilmington & Weldon Railroad bridge over the river and hastily cut the lines to the pontoon bridge, allowing the strong river current to do the rest of their work. For the time being, at least, Maj. Gen. Robert F. Hoke's division had denied the Federals a foothold on the far bank of the Northeast Cape Fear River.[29]

Sporadic gunfire continued during the remainder of the day and finally faded around 9:00 p.m., with both sides exhausted from the day's constant fighting. For the moment, the Federals were content to celebrate Wilmington's capture and allowed Bragg to continue his retreat unmolested. In the pre-dawn hours of February 23, Kirkland's rear guard formed on the Duplin Road to begin its journey north with the other units.[30]

Wilmington's evacuation was the final event in a series of February disasters that had befallen Confederate president Jefferson Davis. In South Carolina, Beauregard's vain attempts to halt Sherman's advance had resulted in the capture of Columbia, the evacuation of Charleston, and the destruction of the Confederates' vital infrastructure. Facing increased pressure for a change, President Davis—against his own wishes—acceded to Lee's suggestion of reinstating Gen. Joseph E. Johnston to command. Lee, the Confederate army's newly appointed commander-in-chief, restored Johnston to field command

---

27 Fonvielle, *The Wilmington Campaign*, 424.

28 Ibid., 432.

29 Fonvielle, *The Wilmington Campaign*, 432.

30 Ibid., 433.

with authority over the Department of South Carolina, Georgia and Florida, and the remnants of the Army of Tennessee.[31]

In abiding with Lee's order to "concentrate all available forces and drive back Sherman," Johnston began combining the widely scattered Confederate units already in the Carolinas with the remnants of the Army of Tennessee. Johnston instructed Beauregard to coordinate the necessary troop movements for those entering North Carolina. This relieved Johnston of burdensome staff work and freed him to focus his efforts on developing a plan for attacking Sherman's approaching army.[32]

Although Sherman remained the primary threat, Schofield's forces along the coast were growing stronger. The ports at Morehead City and New Bern bustled with vessels of all types discharging both men and materiel. All signs indicated a military operation in North Carolina unlike any seen in the previous four years of war in the Tar Heel State.

31 OR 47, pt. 2, 1,247. Johnston's return to command is beyond the scope of this study. For a more detailed discussion, see Connelly, *Autumn of Glory*, 517-525.

32 OR 47, pt. 2, 1,247, 1,257, 1,274; Bradley, *Last Stand*, 73.

Chapter 2

"[W]e're from Sherman's Army"

— *Mary Phinney Von Olnhausen*

The Union Buildup

According to the nineteenth century military theorist Carl von Clausewitz, "The provisioning of troops is a necessary condition of warfare and thus has great influence on the operations." Supporting General Sherman required an operational railroad between the coast and Goldsboro capable of transporting essential supplies in a timely manner. The Federal occupation of Wilmington, North Carolina, and the subsequent discovery of the Wilmington & Weldon Railroad's poor condition, put the Union strategy of provisioning troops at risk. The Confederates had withdrawn all operable locomotives and rolling stock from Wilmington. Moreover, the Rebels destroyed key rail trestles and other infrastructure, all of which was necessary for rail operations, which further hindered Schofield's ability to move north toward Goldsboro.[1]

Fortunately, the port at Morehead City, about 80 miles north of Wilmington provided Union forces a secondary point of entry with an existing rail link via the Atlantic & North Carolina Railroad. The Federals controlled the railroad from the port to Batchelder's Creek, roughly 19 miles beyond New Bern. The serviceability of the rail line west of Batchelder's Creek toward

---

1   Hans W. Gatze, ed., *Principles of War, 1812* (1942; reprint, Mineola, NY, 2003), 51; Fonvielle, *The Wilmington Campaign*, 434.

Kinston required the laying of new track to support military operations. During the past few years, the portion of the railroad between Union-occupied New Bern and Confederate-occupied Kinston had become a "no man's land." The roadbed still existed, but between 1863 and 1864 the Atlantic & North Carolina Railroad Company had reluctantly removed 17 miles of track for the Confederate navy's use in rolling iron plates for naval vessels. West of Kinston, the Confederates used the railroad to move personnel and supplies to and from Goldsboro.[2]

Following the Union's successful campaign and subsequent occupation of the region in 1862, the railroad had continued operating between Morehead City and New Bern under control of the U.S. Army Quartermaster Department. By 1865, however, military maintenance of the line had proven to be woefully inadequate. Rail crossties were rotting and not replaced, there were too few water tanks in existence, and bridges had deteriorated to the point of being unsafe. The ongoing neglect of the railroad cost the Union time, labor, and resources in restoring it to handle transport of large quantities of men and materiel.[3]

The responsibility of putting into operation a rail link from Morehead City to Goldsboro fell upon Brig. Gen. Innis N. Palmer, commander of the District of Beaufort, headquartered in New Bern. Palmer, a career army officer, graduated from the U.S. Military Academy at West Point in 1846. His first assignment as a lieutenant was with the 2nd U.S. Mounted Rifles, where he served with distinction in the Mexican War and earned a brevet promotion to captain. Later, Palmer received an appointment as captain in the Regular Army, and was assigned to the 2nd U.S. Cavalry. At the outbreak of the Civil War, Palmer was commissioned a major in the 5th U.S. Cavalry, and once again received a promotion for battlefield bravery. By January 1865, Palmer was a

---

2 OR 47, pt. 2, 79; *Proceedings of the Annual Meeting of the Stockholders of the Atlantic & North Carolina R. R. Company, 1865* (Goldsboro, NC, 1865), 15. The order to remove the iron rails stemmed from an arrangement made between the governor of North Carolina, Zebulon Vance, and the Stephen Mallory, the Confederate Secretary of the Navy. The governor felt as though he was compelled to comply with the request to prevent the Confederate government from simply taking the rail iron without permission.

3 *Old North State* (Beaufort, NC), February 18, 1865; Charles L. Price, "The United States Military Railroads in North Carolina, 1862-1865," in *North Carolina Historical Review*, vol. 53, no. 3 (July 1976), 244, 249-250. For reasons that remain unclear, the U.S. Military Railroads did not assume control of the captured North Carolina line as it had in other theaters of the war. OR 47, pt. 2, 79.

Port of Morehead City. *U.S. Army Military History Institute*

brevet major general of volunteers serving as the commander of the District of Beaufort.[4]

The shifting of logistics effort from Wilmington to Morehead City came as no surprise to Palmer, given his earlier correspondence with Sherman about the possibility of using Morehead City as the primary port of entry for supplies. The two commanders had corresponded throughout January and early February, even as Grant and Schofield designated Wilmington as the primary port.[5]

The common theme of Palmer's response to Sherman's inquiries focused on transportation problems, and above all else, the poor condition of the railroad. Moreover, Palmer expressed concern about relying upon the railroad as the only means of transporting supplies to Goldsboro. The possibility of the Confederates destroying the Kinston-Goldsboro portion of the rail line, which was currently not under U.S. control, remained a distinct possibility. Palmer recommended the use of small steamers operating between New Bern and Kinston on the Neuse River as a possible alternative to transporting supplies

---

4   Warner, *Generals in Blue*, 357-358; Palmer's duty in North Carolina was not without personal tragedy. In August 1864, his two-year-old daughter, Fedrica, died of illness in the military hospital at Morehead City. *North Carolina Times* (New Bern), August 9, 1864.

5   *OR* 47, pt. 2, 49, 78-79, 111-112, 415-416.

overland. Ironically, Palmer did not disclose to Sherman the issue of wagon shortages until his last message in mid-February, by which time Sherman was at Columbia, South Carolina, out of reach of official military correspondence.[6]

Palmer also addressed the issue of his district's limited transportation assets with Grant, Quartermaster General Montgomery Meigs, and Maj. Gen. John G. Foster, the commander of the Department of the South, ensuring that his superiors were fully aware of the situation. As for the wagons, Palmer reported, "we will have barely sufficient to supply the troops now here." In explaining the shortage he wrote that in May 1864, "every wagon, horse, and mule that could be spared was sent to Virginia, and none of them have ever been returned." Palmer's concern with wagons increased as the weeks passed and the flow of additional troops into the district further exacerbated the problem.[7]

Two key events beginning in early January coincided with the lack of wagons. The first centered on the movement of Brig. Gen. Thomas F. Meagher's Provisional Division of the Army of the Tennessee from Decatur, Alabama, to its assembly point at Annapolis, Maryland, and then to eastern North Carolina. Meagher's command consisted of about 5,000 convalescents, new recruits, and returning veterans destined for Sherman's army. Because of the command's temporary structure, it contained no wagons—a point Palmer stressed to Grant. "The troops of Meagher's division are just arriving at Morehead," wrote Palmer. "They have no transportation."[8]

In addition to Meagher's command, the XXIII Corps traveled from Tennessee to North Carolina without its wagons. Unlike Meagher's hastily assembled command, the XXIII Corps had its assigned complement of wagons. However, to facilitate the rapid movement east via rail and water, the desire for speed overshadowed the need for capability, and the Quartermaster Department retained the wagons in Kentucky. Correspondence at the time revealed a lack of understanding by Meigs and his quartermaster officers regarding the current wagon shortage in North Carolina. Retaining the corps' wagons in Kentucky only made the issue worse. Palmer wrote to Sherman explaining that Meigs presumed "that General Schofield sent transportation

6   Ibid., pt. 1, 212-213, 415-416.

7   OR 47, pt. 2, 212-213, 341-342, 356-357. In May 1864, Grant initiated his Overland campaign against Lee's Army of Northern Virginia.

8   Ibid., pt. 2, 316-317, 383.

with the troops lately arrived. This is not the case, and if it becomes necessary to move very soon we would be badly off."[9]

By mid-February Meigs issued orders to his subordinate quartermaster officers in other departments to collect and forward all available wagons to the depot in Washington, D.C., for further redistribution to Schofield at Morehead City and Wilmington. Comically, the quartermaster officers in Kentucky executed Meigs's order, much to Schofield's annoyance. Dumbfounded, Schofield wrote to chief of staff Henry W. Halleck, complaining that his experienced supply train left in Kentucky was ordered to Washington for turn-in to the central depot, requiring his quartermaster "to draw from the general supply."[10]

The lack of wagon transportation significantly retarded the Union advance toward Goldsboro. A Civil War army in the field required supply trains for sustainment of its units. The arrival of the XXIII Corps without its normal complement of wagons exacerbated an already critical lack of essential logistical function.[11]

Based on Palmer's thorough assessment, Sherman recognized that the limited capacity of rail and other infrastructure in Morehead City and New Bern would hinder any large-scale logistical buildup at Goldsboro. The magnitude of the buildup required experience and expertise in planning support for a force that numbered almost 85,000 men by March 1865. With this in mind, Sherman dispatched his trusted chief quartermaster, Bvt. Brig. Gen. Langdon Easton, and his chief commissary, Col. Amos Beckwith, to supervise logistical operations. In addition to his senior logisticians, Sherman directed Col. William W. Wright, chief engineer of U.S. Military Railroads, to report to the North Carolina coast to supervise repairs on the railroads between Wilmington, Morehead City, and Goldsboro."[12]

---

9   *OR* 47, pt. 1, 415-416, 593-594.

10 Ibid., pt. 2, 593-594.

11 Ibid., pt. 1, 974.

12 Smith and Sokolosky, *No Such Army*, 8-9; *OR* 47, pt. 1, 18; Wright's solid reputation for civil engineering continued into the late 1800s, most notably for his work on the Panama Canal. He died in a Philadelphia prison cell in March 1882, having been found lying drunk in the street the night before. The last two years of his life proved sad for such an accomplished man. Upon his return from Panama, Wright failed to fulfill his duties as the keynote speaker for a banquet in honor of the canal project due to intoxication. Wright never married and was buried in the city of Philadelphia, Pennsylvania. *New York Times*, March 11, 1882.

Brig. Gen. Langdon C. Easton
U.S. Army Military History Institute

The detailed level of planning and execution required for the logistics buildup in eastern North Carolina exceeded the capability of even Sherman's experienced staff. The repositioning of forces from Tennessee to North Carolina and the sheer volume of materiel needed to support Sherman at Goldsboro required an extensive effort throughout the War Department and its supply and service bureaus: Quartermaster, Ordnance, Subsistence, and Medical. At the forefront, the Quartermaster Department played a prominent role because of its responsibility for supporting the other bureaus with transportation.

Responsibility for repair and reconstruction of the railroad fell to the U.S. Military Railroads Department (USMRR). Created in 1862, and staffed with experienced railroad men, the civilian-run USMRR was established for the purpose of reconstruction and operation of railroads captured by Federal forces. A key component of the USMRR, the Railroad Construction Corps, had developed a solid reputation for efficiency. In the Western Theater a close working relationship existed between Sherman and Colonel Wright. Sherman's respect for Wright grew from the engineer's superb effort in maintaining a tenuous rail supply line to Chattanooga during the Atlanta campaign in 1864.[13]

In December 1864, the USMRR tasked Wright and one division from his Construction Corps with supporting Sherman's army during the pending Carolinas campaign. On January 4, Wright's organization departed Nashville, Tennessee, "fully equipped for any kind of railroad work." After a brief delay awaiting transport in Baltimore, Maryland, Wright and his division traveled by sea to Hilton Head, South Carolina, arriving on January 28. At Hilton Head,

13 Price, "The United States Military Rail Roads in North Carolina, 1862-1865," 244; *OR* Series III, vol. 5, 29-30.

Sherman immediately ordered Wright to relocate up the coast to Wilmington and Morehead City and "to make the railroad connection to Goldsboro by the middle of March."[14]

Arriving at Morehead on February 5, Wright relieved a small detachment of railroad construction engineers commanded by Charles L. McAlpine, which had deployed from Virginia several weeks earlier under orders from Grant. Palmer had requested assistance from Grant in putting the affairs of the railroad in order. Unfortunately, McAlpine's rapid arrival from Virginia caught Palmer ill-prepared to receive his force. Palmer advised McAlpine that he could not proceed with repairs until reinforced with additional troops, leaving the civilian engineer frustrated.[15]

Until Wright's arrival, McAlpine's crew accomplished limited repairs, focusing its labor on cutting new rail ties. Wright confirmed McAlpine's initial assessment of the rail line's need for major engineering work. The track's poor condition rendered it inadequate to support increased rail traffic. Although lacking the required stock, Wright reported that he had three locomotives and 62 cars in running order.[16]

To support Wright's efforts, the USMRR shipped south from Virginia additional iron, locomotives, and other rolling stock. To keep Wright's construction crews focused on repair, workers in Virginia cut more than 15,000 crossties and shipped them from Portsmouth for use along the line from Morehead City. In the upcoming weeks a total of 13 locomotives and 96 types of rolling stock flowed into Morehead aboard ocean-going steamers, a large portion of which was shipped from the Union Army of the Potomac's forward supply depot at City Point, Virginia.[17]

Simultaneous with Wright's effort to increase freight capacity, the Quartermaster Department orchestrated the flow of shipments to Morehead from major points along the eastern seaboard. Vessels laden with commissary, uniforms, ammunition, and animal forage arrived from points as far north as Boston, Massachusetts, and as far south as Port Royal, South Carolina.[18]

---

14 Ibid., 30.

15 Price, "The United States Military Rail Roads in North Carolina, 1862-1865," 249-250.

16 *OR* Series III, vol. 5, 30.

17 Ibid., 35, 76;

18 Ibid., 225.

U.S. Army Quartermaster Depot, New Bern. The Union buildup overwhelmed existing supply facilities. *U.S. Army Military History Institute*

The shallow inland waters along North Carolina's coast hindered the Quartermaster Department's efforts, impeding the efficient and timely discharge of men and materiel at Morehead City. At the beginning of the Union buildup on the coast, the Quartermaster Department lacked sufficient numbers of ocean-going vessels with the minimum draft to navigate the shallow channels. Coastal operations taxed the transportation abilities of the Quartermaster Department, forcing it to contract suitable commercial vessels to mitigate the shortage. Meigs's department "was much embarrassed at this time" by the difficulty of procuring ocean steamers that could enter into Morehead. Vessels drawing more than twelve feet were deemed unsafe. The shortage of suitable ships required improvisation, transferring cargo to smaller ships off the coast. This method proved susceptible to changing weather and sea conditions and delayed the timely discharge of materiel.[19]

19 *OR* Series III, vol. 5, 288.

To meet requirements, the Quartermaster Department operated or contracted more than 73 ocean steamers and 15 sailing ships, plus varying numbers of support vessels such as tugs and pilot boats. As the number of vessels laden with men and materiel increased, Morehead's railroad wharf lacked the capacity for quickly unloading them. The wharf supported the discharge of only two vessels at a time. To improve efficiency, Wright's experienced crew, aided by two steam-powered pile drivers, increased the wharf's size, allowing it to handle as many as eight ships at once. Wright's crew also laid new sidetracks to facilitate offloading and staging of rolling stock near the wharf.[20]

The surge of materiel into Morehead City required the construction of overhead storage and warehousing facilities. To aid in this process, the Quartermaster Department dispatched a force of carpenters from its Washington, D.C., depot to construct new buildings to support the receipt of stores until transported to the front lines. As an interim solution, Easton and Beckwith confiscated the few suitable existing structures in Morehead and converted them into temporary storage facilities, much to the chagrin of local citizens.[21]

As the Quartermaster Department expanded its capability, so too did the Medical Department in anticipation of increased military personnel requiring treatment. At the beginning of the Union surge into the area, the U.S. Army operated three medical facilities: Foster General Hospital in New Bern, Mansfield General Hospital in Morehead City, and the Hammond General Hospital in Beaufort. The Medical Department's plan called for the temporary establishment of hospitals near Goldsboro to provide care to men who did not require immediate evacuation. The soldiers who required more serious treatment were evacuated to the army's Foster General Hospital in New Bern. Foster General's close proximity to the Atlantic & North Carolina Railroad was ideal for evacuation of sick and wounded from Goldsboro. Established in 1862 following the Union occupation of New Bern, Foster General's capacity

---

20 *OR* Series III, vol. 5, 293; ibid., 33. The wharf measured more than 53,000 square feet, requiring more than 700,000 feet of board measure in construction; *Proceedings of the Annual Meeting of the Stockholders of the Atlantic & North Carolina R. R. Company, 1865*, 13. In constructing the wharf, Wright sacrificed quality for speed, and his use of wooden piles proved temporary. In less than two years, the destructive nature of naval shipworms rendered the new pilings worthless.

21 *OR* Series III, vol. 5, 390.

U.S. Army Foster General Hospital, New Bern.
North Carolina Collection, University of North Carolina Library at Chapel Hill

increased during the war by combining existing structures with newly constructed wards. Medical authorities expanded Foster's pre-1865 capacity of 442 beds to 1,500 beds at the start of the campaign, and ultimately to 3,000 beds. In the coming weeks, Foster General would treat both wounded Union and Confederate soldiers in the aftermath of the battles at Wise's Forks, Averasboro, and Bentonville.[22]

Along with the expansion of Foster General in New Bern, authorities established an additional hospital in Beaufort—the 600-bed Mansfield Hospital—to facilitate patient overflow. Ironically, Sherman's chief quartermaster, General Easton, had shut down the former Mansfield Hospital in Morehead City to use the buildings for storage of off-loaded supplies from the port.[23]

Easton's decision drew immediate and sharp criticism from army nurse Mary Phinney Von Olnhausen, who had served at the recently confiscated Morehead Hospital. Her daily and invaluable journaling captured the entire

22 Surgeon General's Office, United States Army, *The Medical and Surgical History of the Civil War*, vol. 2 (formerly *The Medical and Surgical History of the War of the Rebellion*) (Wilmington, NC, 1990), 240.

23 Ibid., 240.

U.S. Army Nurse Mary Phinney
Baroness Von Olnhausen
Sketch by Col. Darrell L. Combs, USMC (Ret.)
from Adventures of an Army Nurse in Two Wars

buildup from early February through March 1865. Von Olnhausen's troubles began with the arrival of Wright's Construction Corps and subsequent encampment adjacent to the hospital. She wrote of "twelve hundred men, wagons, and 400 mules that roar all the time." Von Olnhausen kept a constant guard surrounding the hospital "to prevent the rascals from stealing everything."[24]

General Easton and Colonel Beckwith did not escape Von Olnhausen's wrath. She noted that the "Quartermaster and the Commissary saw with envious eyes the front row of [hospital] buildings, all houses built before the war, and claimed them as quarters for themselves. If they are remonstrated with, they fall back on we're from Sherman's Army, as if that could cover all the enormities. I am getting about sick of Sherman's army, if this is the way we are to be treated by them."[25]

The eviction of her patients and the subsequent occupation by Beckwith and his commissary staff fostered resentment over what Von Olnhausen perceived as an uncaring attitude toward fellow Union soldiers. Beckwith first took possession of the outbuildings surrounding the hospital, but later demanded control of the main structure. The Union army's use of one of her wards as storage for oxbows, tent poles, wagon tires, and old tarps was the last straw. Von Olnhausen wrote, "I am utterly disgusted with the selfishness of these men. Was ever such an outrage on our soldiers?"[26]

---

24 James P. Munroe, ed., *Adventures of an Army Nurse in the Two Wars: Edited from the Diary and Correspondence of Mary Phinney Baroness von Olnhausen* (Boston, MA, 1903), 175-181.

25 Munroe, *Adventures of an Army Nurse*, 175-181.

26 Ibid., 179-180; Mrs. Charles Tolson (Eva Mae Hardesty), "History of Morehead City," in *The Researcher*, Carteret County Historical & Genealogical Society, Inc. (Spring 2001), vol. 17,

In conjunction with the ongoing supply and medical efforts, the War Department executed the eastward movement of Federal forces as part of Grant's reinforcement along the North Carolina coast. The journey was an exhilarating experience for these predominantly Western men, especially for some who voyaged for the first time on the Atlantic Ocean.

Throughout the transfer from Tennessee to North Carolina, the soldiers experienced freezing temperatures, frozen rivers, and rough seas. Despite some of Mother Nature's worst behavior, the Union Army demonstrated its administrative efficiency, executing a more than one-thousand-mile transfer via rail, riverboats, and ocean-going vessels in less than 30 days.

For Meagher's command and the XXIII Corps, the journey east occurred in two geographical phases. The first entailed transport from Tennessee to Annapolis, Maryland, Washington, D.C., or Alexandria, Virginia. From these destination points the men awaited ocean transports for the final phase of their voyage to North Carolina.

The XXIII Corps received official notification to begin its movement on January 14, 1865, from Clifton, Tennessee. The units embarked on transports traveling on the Tennessee and Ohio Rivers to Cincinnati, Ohio, where they boarded railcars bound for northern Virginia. The movement from Cincinnati required the use of three separate railroads: the Little Miami, the Central Ohio, and the Baltimore & Ohio. Severe weather plagued the mid-winter journey but it occurred without delay, accident, or extreme suffering on the part of the troops—a remarkable operation considering the 1,400-mile movement took only 11 days to complete. At Alexandria, Virginia, the unexpected freezing of the Potomac River limited navigation for almost two weeks, causing unavoidable delay.[27]

Private William C. Benson of the 120th Indiana recorded in his diary the unit's transfer east from Tennessee. Although the regiment traveled in railcars in the worst of winter, the War Department's planning and preparation, in conjunction with civilian railroad companies, helped mitigate the discomfort of freezing temperatures. During the regiment's 10-day river and rail movement from Clifton to Washington, D.C., it drew rations multiple times and received

---

no. 1, 19. The Mansfield Hospital complex encompassed an entire city block. Within the enclosed area stood the hospital, storehouses, a pest house, and other outbuildings.

27 OR 47, pt. 1, 909; James A. Huston, *The Sinews of War: Army Logistics 1775-1953* (Washington, DC, 1988), 210.

bales of hay and hot coffee at designated rail stops. Upon arriving in Alexandria, the men received a hot meal, coffee, and warm barracks.[28]

To facilitate the final leg of the journey to North Carolina, the Quartermaster Department used two of the largest ocean-going steamers of the era, the *Atlantic* and the *New York City*, each capable of transporting two regiments. Despite their immense size, the vessels had some eventful moments in the treacherous waters off North Carolina's Outer Banks—the Graveyard of the Atlantic.[29]

Considering the majority of these Western men had never seen the ocean, their experience initially seemed tranquil and beautiful, and they were overjoyed to witness whales spurting water. However, their tranquility vanished when the ocean suddenly turned violent from a gale off the coast. In describing their journey, the majority of soldiers highlighted one topic—seasickness. Although most of the men experienced seasickness and were able to manage it, some were not so lucky and spent the entire voyage never finding their "sea legs." Edwin Williams from Illinois wrote that "The vessel would at times be tossed on the waves almost like a feather in the wind." He recalled that many of his fellow soldiers vomited, creating a foul stench throughout the ship. In describing his own fate, Williams wrote, "I vomited for two days. I just more than heaved up Jonah." Forty years after the war, Pvt. Daniel Fish spoke at his regiment's reunion and vowed "I have never asked for a pension, but if I ever do so, the memory of that stormy voyage around Cape Hatteras will be my sufficient excuse."[30]

Upon reaching the coast off Morehead City, soldiers traveling on the larger vessels, such as the *Atlantic* or *New York City*, required transfer to lighter steam transports, which ferried the troops to the wharf. The process, conducted in the open ocean, proved dangerous and susceptible to rough seas and currents.[31]

---

28 William C. Benson, "Civil War Diary of William C. Benson," in *Indiana Magazine of History*, 23, no. 3 (September 1927), 352; *OR*, Ser. III, vol. 5, 241, 246, 248.

29 Both vessels measured more than 360 feet in length, quite impressive for the era.

30 Edwin L. Williams to wife, February 12, 1865, in Civil War Miscellaneous Collection, U.S. Army Heritage and Education Center, Carlisle, PA; Daniel Fish, *The Forty-Fifth Illinois: A Souvenir of the Re-union Held at Rockford On the Fortieth Anniversary of the its March in the Grand Review* (Minneapolis, MN, 1905), 9; Animals suffered from ocean travel as well. In one recorded incident, a steamer loaded with 360 mules lost 90 of the animals during the voyage. *New York Times*, March 29, 1865.

31 *OR* Series III, vol. 5, 288.

Upon disembarking from the ships, the men proceeded by rail to New Bern. For Sgt. Joseph J. Brown of the 180th Ohio, the journey by rail afforded little comfort and no protection from the weather. The Ohioans traveled "crowded like hogs" on flat cars and were exposed to rainy weather, which commenced shortly after their departure from Morehead. In a letter sent home to his girlfriend, Sergeant Brown wrote, "we just had to sit and take it, but had plenty of fun about it though."[32]

The heavy flow of ships carrying men and materiel created a backlog at the port while awaiting rail transport to New Bern. For enlisted men, this meant work details unloading supplies while their officers took advantage of the privileges afforded by rank to visit the local area. A topic that captured the curiosity of a few soldiers focused on the ramifications of abolition and the social implications for several thousand former slaves who now inhabited the Union-occupied coastal regions of North Carolina—especially for those dwelling in camps near New Bern and Beaufort.[33]

Dr. Alonzo Garwood, Chief Surgeon, First Division, XXIII Corps, spent a day visiting Morehead City and Beaufort before traveling on to New Bern. His walk around Beaufort afforded him the opportunity to visit a colored school under the supervision of a Massachusetts woman. Dr. Garwood and other surgeons arriving from the Western Theater were inquisitive about the education of Negro children and, as opportunities arose, took time to visit the special schools established for their study.[34]

Dr. S. C. Rogers, Asst. Surgeon of the 30th Iowa, in charge of Meagher's Provisional Division Hospital, satisfied his curiosity by visiting both colored schools and those established for white refugees who had taken residence in the coastal communities. Comparing the two types of schools, Dr. Rogers discovered "the colored schools excelled them in enthusiasm and application to their studies, and particularly in singing." He resigned himself to the belief that

32 OR 47, pt. 1, 155-157; Joseph J. Brown to Rosa, March 1, 1865, *Civil War Times,* Illustrated Collection, U.S. Army Heritage and Education Center, Carlisle, Pennsylvania.

33 In addition to detailing soldiers to assist in offload operations, the Quartermaster Department posted want ads in the local papers for African American laborers. The army promised $20 per month and rations for the workforce. *Old North State* (Beaufort, N.C.), March 11, 1865.

34 Alonzo Garwood, diary, February 28, 1865, http//www.michiganinthecivilwar.org/infantry/diary.htm; Seven separate schools for African Americans operated in New Bern, and three operated in Beaufort.

"there is then a competition between the freed men and . . . the poor white trash. And they who are most industrious, most virtuous, and most intelligent will win."[35]

For the Western men, coastal North Carolina was very different from their farms back home. These newly arrived soldiers formed a rather poor opinion of the region and its inhabitants. One Indiana soldier, Pvt. William Fifer, wrote to his sister, "I wouldn't give one good farm in the north for all that I have seen in the south." He viewed "rebeldom" as "a destitute wilderness settled with heathens of all colors and grades. The whites here are the [most] ignorant people that I have ever [seen]." Such feelings permeated the officer ranks as well. Captain Dwight Fraser of Company G, 128th Indiana wrote home expressing his true feelings about his new surroundings. "I cannot say much concerning the country, only that it is good for darkies, cotton, and turpentine."[36]

Others took a less harsh view of the coastal region. Capt. Thomas J. Davis of the 18th Wisconsin found New Bern to be "larger and prettier than expected, however the poor land and ignorance of the population ruled out the possibility of ever living here."[37]

In contrast to their earlier reception at Alexandria, Virginia, the Western soldiers found no warm shelters awaiting them in New Bern. They marched several miles from the train station and discovered their new quarters consisted of open fields surrounded by tall pine trees. Over time, the veteran soldiers improved their living conditions by constructing "shebangs," or temporary shelters, out of existing materials such as shelter-tent halves or rubber ponchos. Officers, however, in accordance with privileges of rank, occupied new wooden huts that sprang up throughout the regimental camps. As the days passed the men fell into a daily routine of drill, camp maintenance, and other military duties reflecting a more peaceful time. For many, February's remaining days provided the opportunity to catch up on mail to loved ones and receive their first pay in two months.

35 *Old North State* (Beaufort, N.C.), March 7, 1865.

36 William Fifer to Angeline Fifer, February 26, 1865, in William Fifer Papers, Bentley Historical Library, University of Michigan, Ann Arbor; Dwight Fraser to W. H. Parker, March 2, 1865, in Dwight and Joshua Fraser Letters, Indiana Historical Society, Manuscripts and Archives, Indianapolis, Indiana.

37 Thomas P. Nanzig, ed., *The Badax Tigers: From Shiloh to the Surrender with the 18th Wisconsin Volunteers* (Lanham, MD, 2002), 306, 308.

The overall mood of the men, especially the veterans of the XXIII Corps, conveyed a "this is it" mentality. Most regarded the war as almost over, and the approaching campaign in North Carolina would provide the one big push to end it. With this sense that the end was at hand, the idea that a fight loomed in the near future still existed. Despite the possibility of an impending battle, these veterans of Sherman's army displayed confidence in "Uncle Billy" to finish the job. For the new recruits destined for Sherman's army, the pending campaign would result in their first combat experience, or in the parlance of the Civil War soldier, their first time "seeing the elephant."

Unlike their fellow combatants from the XXIII Corps, Meagher's Provisional troops lacked traditional command structure and suffered from the lack of leadership necessary to ensure their health and welfare. An Illinois private noted that upon arrival to New Bern via rail, he and other soldiers marched three miles out from the town and received instructions to camp. They found themselves in the middle of an open field, exposed to freezing temperatures and strong winds—a situation worsened by the fact that replacement troops lacked the standard issued tent-half to construct proper cover.[38]

As men and materiel flowed into Morehead City, the increased military activity did not go unnoticed by the local citizens, especially a few who took a keen interest in the Federal buildup. Consequently, in early February military authorities arrested one of North Carolina's most notable female spies, Emeline Pigott, and her brother-in-law, Rufus Bell. Active for several years in crossing through Union lines, Ms. Pigott's capture coincided with increased diligence in denying the Confederates information regarding Union military operations. Following Ms. Pigott's arrest, Union authorities required all women from Beaufort and Morehead City "who have arrived at the age of discretion to the oldest, whether decrepit from age, lame, halt or blind" to swear their oath of allegiance to the Union—a requirement not well received by those with Confederate loyalties.[39]

---

38 Edwin L. Williams to wife, February 12, 1865.

39 *Old North State* (Beaufort, N.C.), Feb 18, 1865. A search by authorities of Ms. Pigott led to the discovery of an assortment of items hidden under her clothing, which consisted of a pair of fine boots, two pairs of pants, a shirt, numerous other sundries, an estimated five pounds of candy, and letters to Confederate soldiers; Judkin Browning, ed., *The Southern Mind under Union Rule: The Diary of James Rumley, Beaufort, North Carolina 1862-1865* (Gainesville, FL, 2009), 166-167.

Confederate Spy Emeline Pigott
Courtesy of the State Archives of North Carolina

Since Grant's visit in late January, the once quiet port of Morehead had acquired a role of great significance, a major logistics hub essential to Union operations in North Carolina. Private James O'Connell of the 130th Indiana provided an excellent account of the soldiers' viewpoint. On March 2, detailed along with others from his command to assist in the offload of supplies, O'Connell recorded in his journal the bustle of activity:

> One of the ships had a complete locomotive. . . . [D]uring the night the engine was unloaded, set on the tracks and fired up. It is now hooked up to about 30 railroad cars, and we are going to ride the cars to Newbern. There are several acres of supplies, rations, ammunition, etc., stacking up around here, all of which are waiting to be transported by railroad as soon as we get the tracks repaired. There are also over 1,000 head of horses in the corrals here that are going to Uncle Billy's Cavalry. Everywhere I look there is some sort of activity going on in preparation of our movement west.[40]

Private O'Connell's description of operations during the first week of March 1865 is a testament to the tremendous energy expended in preparation for Sherman's arrival. Much had been accomplished in the month since Easton, Beckwith, and Wright had arrived at Morehead from Savannah. Union forces in New Bern, however, had yet to move one mile closer to Goldsboro. Sherman, on the other hand, had blazed through South Carolina and was within days of entering North Carolina.

For Schofield, the logistics success at Morehead did little to relieve his anxiety. Now, it was time to focus his attention on seizing Goldsboro.

---

40 Thomas L. Lawrence, *Grandfather's Civil War Diary: A Biography* (Buffalo, NY, 1994), 268-270.

Chapter 3

"[Sherman] will meet a lion in his path."

— *Lt. Col. Rufus A. Barrier, 8th North Carolina*

Johnston Forges an Army

From his headquarters in Charlotte, North Carolina, General Joseph Johnston suddenly found himself "thrust back into the maelstrom," tasked with the daunting mission of forging an army to contend with Sherman's and Schofield's. Johnston knew the difficulties involved in such a task, but faced a greater leadership challenge from within the ranks of the army he was trying to create.[1]

As the scattered forces of various commands and departments came together under Johnston's direction in North Carolina, so too did the personalities and reputations of their generals, jeopardizing the harmonious working relationship needed to overcome the odds that confronted them. Throughout the war, Confederate President Jefferson Davis had reassigned general officers of questionable ability to various department commands to appease egos and ensure harmony with their political connections in Richmond. This was true for none other than Johnston himself.

General Braxton Bragg's Department of North Carolina provided Johnston an immediate source of strength within the Tar Heel State. Unfortunately, the two generals were not on the best of terms, ever since Johnston had replaced Bragg as commander of the Army of Tennessee in late

---

1 Bradley, *Last Stand*, 27; Smith and Sokolosky, *No Such Army*, 18, 25; OR 47, pt. 2, 1,256-1,257.

Gen. Joseph E. Johnston
Library of Congress

1863. Their relationship continued to sour upon Johnston's subsequent relief from command during the 1864 Atlanta campaign due to what he perceived as Bragg's influence upon President Davis while serving as his military advisor.

At first the two men carried on a cooperative partnership, considering Johnston's command authority did not include Bragg's Department of North Carolina. However, once Robert E. Lee, as Confederate commander-in-chief, approved Johnston's request for authority over all available forces in his area of operations, General Bragg requested that President Davis relieve him "from this embarrassing position." Unfortunately for Bragg, his request fell on deaf ears.[2]

A native of North Carolina, Braxton Bragg was born in Warrenton on March 22, 1817, and later graduated fifth in the West Point class of 1837. Bragg's combat service included the Second Seminole War in Florida and the war with Mexico. During the latter, Bragg served with distinction, receiving three brevets for valor under fire. Unfortunately, Bragg's "naturally disputatious" personality and legendary bad temper characterized his service in the prewar army. Bragg had an infamous reputation for feuding with others, and on at least one occasion, he reportedly feuded with himself. Weary of army life, Bragg resigned his commission in 1856 and settled in Louisiana, where he married the wealthy Eliza Brooks Ellis. The former soldier found success in civilian life as a planter and a public servant for the state.[3]

2   OR 47, pt. 2, 1,320, 1,328.

3   For biographical information on Bragg, the authors consulted Ezra J. Warner, *Generals in Gray: Lives of the Confederate Commanders* (Baton Rouge, LA, 1987), 30-31; and Fonvielle, *The Wilmington Campaign*, 84-86.

Gen. Braxton Bragg
Library of Congress

In 1861, as Louisiana followed other Deep South states in seceding from the Union, Bragg volunteered to serve as commander of the state's militia. His years of experience in the prewar army proved invaluable to the growing Confederate army, where his efficiency as an organizer and administrator was essential to success. In March 1861, Bragg received an appointment as brigadier general in the Confederate army, and within thirteen months had risen to the rank of full general. In June 1862, Bragg assumed command of the Army of the Mississippi (later renamed Army of Tennessee), and commanded it in the battles of Perryville, Stones River, Chickamauga, and Chattanooga. Throughout his tenure, success proved elusive for the unfortunate Bragg. When victory appeared at hand, his army fell short of expectations and decisive victory. As early as the fall of 1862, Bragg's subordinates were criticizing his conduct of the Kentucky campaign and calling for his removal. This poor command climate continued into the spring of 1863, raising further doubts about Bragg's competence as a senior commander, both from leaders in Richmond and from within the ranks of his generals. Following the army's disastrous defeat at Missionary Ridge, Tennessee, in November 1863, Bragg resigned from command.

After Bragg's resignation, President Davis reassigned the general to duty in Richmond as his military adviser. In October 1864, Davis, in a controversial move, placed Bragg in command of the Cape Fear District with the responsibility of defending Wilmington, North Carolina—the South's last major port of entry for critical war materiel. Bragg's poor reputation caused a stir, especially from North Carolinians who questioned the president's decision. Davis remained steadfast about his faith in Bragg's leadership. In November 1864, the president elevated Bragg's duties to commander of the newly formed

Maj. Gen. Robert F. Hoke
State Archives of North Carolina

Department of North Carolina, responsible for the entire geographic region of the state east of the Blue Ridge Mountains.[4]

Over the next several months, Bragg focused his attention primarily on the defense of the Cape Fear region. However, the increased Union military activity along the North Carolina coast concerned Bragg, a worry he conveyed to Governor Zebulon B. Vance. Bragg foresaw a simultaneous coastal advance from the Cape Fear region and New Bern that would threaten the interior of the state. He urged the governor's support by advocating for the consolidation of available forces from within the department. Although well-intentioned, Bragg's recommendations appeared self-serving, for they focused on the situation at Wilmington.[5]

The strength within Bragg's command came from Maj. Gen. Robert F. Hoke's division, a veteran unit on loan from the Army of Northern Virginia. Lee had transferred the division to North Carolina in December 1864 to reinforce Wilmington's defenses. Hoke, a native North Carolinian, carried a solid reputation as a combat commander. His lack of formal military training did not prevent him from gaining the respect and confidence of his men and superiors. Hoke's army service began as a second lieutenant in the 1st North Carolina, but within 15 months he attained the rank of colonel, commanding the 21st North Carolina. His standing rose in Lee's army, and in recognition for his superior performance at Fredericksburg in December 1862, Hoke earned a promotion to brigadier general. Unfortunately, during the Chancellorsville

---

4   *OR* 42, pt. 3, 1,209-1,210; ibid., 778-779; Fonvielle, *The Wilmington Campaign*, 88-89; Louis H. Manarin, Weymouth T. Jordan, Jr., Matthew M. Brown, and Michael W. Coffey, comps., *North Carolina Troops 1861-1865 A Roster*, 19 vols. to date (Raleigh, NC, 1966-), vol. 17, 60.

5   Fonvielle, *The Wilmington Campaign*, 340.

campaign in May 1863, he suffered a serious wound that required a long convalescence at his home in Lincolnton, North Carolina.[6]

In early 1864, Hoke returned to his brigade, where he served under Maj. Gen. George E. Pickett in eastern North Carolina. After Pickett's dismal performance in the campaign to retake New Bern and his subsequent return to Virginia, Hoke remained in North Carolina. In April, he assumed command of a renewed operation against the Federal presence in his native state. Hoke's initial target, the Union-occupied town of Plymouth, was his "crowning glory." In a brilliant display of tactical genius, Hoke captured Plymouth along with its garrison of 3,000 Union soldiers. He followed Plymouth's defeat with the occupation of Washington, and stood at the fringes of New Bern when Lee summoned him to Virginia to help confront Gen. Ulysses S. Grant's spring offensive. For his actions at Plymouth, Hoke received a promotion to major general and division command, and went on to lead his men in operations against Union advances on Richmond and Petersburg in Virginia.

In December 1864, Hoke and his division transferred south to assist in Wilmington's defense. Over the next two months, Hoke's infantry participated in Confederate efforts to deny the Federals a foothold on the Cape Fear coastline. During an ill-timed trip by Bragg to Richmond, Hoke executed a brilliant tactical withdrawal in the face of overwhelming odds. Notably, his removal of critical war materiel from Wilmington on the eve of its evacuation was crucial to sustaining future Confederate operations. Historian Chris Fonvielle noted that Hoke's "actions, while prolonging the inevitable, allowed Joe Johnston and the Confederacy to fight on in North Carolina."[7]

Following Bragg's evacuation of Wilmington, Hoke withdrew his division north to Rockfish Creek along the Wilmington & Weldon Railroad in Duplin County. Temporarily relieved of any Union threat of pursuit, Hoke's division gained a respite from the fighting. The lull was beneficial for Hoke as he used the time to reorganize his depleted ranks and incorporate other displaced units from the Wilmington area into his command.[8]

6 For biographical information on Hoke, the authors consulted Daniel W. Barefoot, *General Robert F. Hoke: Lee's Modest Warrior* (Winston Salem, NC, 1996); Warner, *Generals in Gray*, 140-141; and Fonvielle, *The Wilmington Campaign*, 115-116.

7 Fonvielle, *The Wilmington Campaign*, 437.

8 Rockfish Creek is south of the modern town of Wallace, NC. In 1865, Wallace was known as Duplin Roads.

By early March 1865, Hoke's division fielded an estimated 4,00 soldiers, organized into four separate brigades. The strength of Hoke's division centered on Brig. Gen. William W. Kirkland's North Carolina brigade and Alfred Colquitt's Georgia brigade, commanded by Col. Charles T. Zachry. Kirkland's and Colquitt's commands fielded more than 1,000 men each. The division's two remaining brigades, Brig. Gen. Johnson Hagood's South Carolina brigade and Thomas Clingman's Tar Heel brigade, commanded by Col. William S. Devane, fielded about 500 men each.[9]

The recent fighting in Virginia and North Carolina had exacted a serious toll on Hoke's troops, especially Hagood's South Carolinians. From August 1864 to February 1865, Hagood's South Carolina regiments lost more than 1,300 soldiers. When the brigade reached Duplin County by the last week of February, it fielded only 500 men. Captain Thomas Y. Simmons, the ranking officer left in the 27th South Carolina, reported "about 40 men" present for duty.[10]

Hagood's effort to reorganize his units was met with dissatisfaction from his soldiers, who did not welcome consolidation. Confederate units throughout the war preserved their regimental identity, even after suffering tremendous losses, by filling depleted ranks with new replacements. Unfortunately, by 1865, the required replacements did not exist. Nineteen-year-old Lt. Henry M. Cannon of the 21st South Carolina expressed to his parents the displeasure in

9 See Appendix B, Table B for Hoke's estimated effective strength during the battle of Wise's Forks. On February 10, 1865, Hoke listed a total of 4,826 men as "Effective Total Present." *OR* 47, pt. 2, 1,154; This number was calculated before the disaster that befell Hagood's brigade immediately prior to Wilmington's evacuation, where the outfit suffered 350 casualties in killed, wounded, and missing. Barefoot, *General Robert F. Hoke*, 276; Historian Timothy W. Auten lists the division's strength based on the February 10, 1865 report. See Timothy W. Auten, *The Battle of Wyse Fork: North Carolina's Neglected Civil War Engagement* (Wilmington, NC, 2008), 200; Brigadier Gen. Thomas L. Clingman was severely wounded in August 1864 and because of his injuries remained absent throughout the subsequent battles in North Carolina. Clingman would not be able to return to his command until just prior to the surrender at Durham Station in April 1865.

10 Johnson Hagood, *Memoirs of the War of Secession* (Columbia, SC, 1910), 351; File of Capt. Thomas Y. Simmons, Records of Confederate Soldiers Who Served During the Civil War, Compiled Service Records of Confederate Soldiers Who Served in Organizations from the State of South Carolina, M267, roll 360, Records Group 109, National Archives. Simmons' resignation letter dated March 14, 1865, stated "my regiment has been reduced to about 40 men by the casualties of war, present for duty." Based on available historical material, the 27th South Carolina suffered no losses during the battle of Wise's Forks so his "about 40" is a fair representation of the regiment during the battle.

Brig. Gen. Johnson Hagood
U.S. Army Military History Institute

consolidation and eroding morale among Hagood's troops: "I never saw a body of men so demoralized in my life as this Brigade. All of my men swear that if they are consolidated they are going straight home." The young South Carolinian remained committed to the cause, but with limitations. Cannon wrote, "If I am retained in office I must be put under officers I respect if not I will not serve. I never intend to bootlick for a position that will avoid the musket. The position of a private soldier is the most honorable in the army."[11]

Hoke strengthened Hagood's brigade by assigning 650 former artillerymen to his command. These men constituted the remnants of several North Carolina heavy artillery units that escaped capture when the Confederate defenses below Wilmington collapsed. Hagood organized these Tar Heels into two separate battalions, where they served the remaining months of the war as "Red Infantry."[12]

Despite the dissent within Hagood's brigade, opinions from other soldiers in the division varied as to the prospect of victory. Lieutenant Col. Rufus A. Barrier of the 8th North Carolina expressed to his father, "I am pretty well at this time although we have had quite a severe time on our retreat." Barrier maintained confidence in the Confederacy's ability to defeat the Union advances into North Carolina. Writing of General Sherman, Barrier predicted, "I think he will meet a lion in his path that will send him howling into the wilderness in the direction of the coast." However, a private in the same brigade explained to his sister a fact that would make defeating Sherman all the more

11 Henry M. Cannon to parents, February 9, 1865, in Private Collection, Ms. Linda W. Meadows.

12 Hagood, *Memoirs*, 351.

Lt. Henry M. Cannon,
21st South Carolina Infantry
Linda Matthews

difficult: "The men are leaving the army at a sad rate but I hope that they will see the earor and not go any more."[13]

Written accounts of the movement north from Wilmington describe the weather as cold and wet. Lieutenant William Calder of the 1st North Carolina Heavy Artillery recorded in his diary, "During this week my life has been altogether miserable. Rain has fallen almost without intermission, and our camp has been a low wet place surrounded on all sides by marshes." For the individual soldier in the ranks, the simple task of finding a suitable location to make his bed became difficult. The persistent rain had turned the surrounding fields and roads into mud, hindering the movement of men and wagons.[14]

Traveling north with Hoke's division out of Wilmington, Capt. Nicholas W. Schenck, Asst. Commissary of Subsistence for the Department of North Carolina, had the tremendous responsibility of moving the army's rations in what he described as "a long line of mules, wagons and servants." He recalled one morning during the retreat that when General Bragg and his staff approached along the road, "It was proposed to ask the general to indulge in a glass of good sherry. He readily accepted and gave me thanks and rode on." Later that evening, after battling the elements, mud-swollen roads, and the always-stubborn mules, darkness found Captain Schenck at an old school house where he eagerly sought shelter. He shared the one-room structure that

---

13 Billy D. B. Auciello and Beverly B. Troxler, eds., *Dear Father: Confederate Letters Never Before Published* (1989), 78; John D. McGeachy to sister, March 2, 1865, in Catherine Jane Buie Papers, Perkins Library, Duke University, Durham, North Carolina.

14 William Calder, Diary, February 26-March 5, 1865, Calder Family Papers, Southern Historical Collection, University of North Carolina at Chapel Hill.

night with 40 other individuals, both white and black. According to Schenck, after a "good supper . . . all hands were stretched on the floor, all had blankets [and a] negro servant to keep up fire." Captain Schenck's recollections of fine drinks and "good suppers" stood in sharp contrast to what the individual soldiers in the ranks subsisted upon during the retreat. For the men in the 51st North Carolina, rations consisted of "one pound of cornbread and the same of beef."[15]

While encamped, mail resumed for Hoke's men and provided them with an opportunity to update family back home. A recurring topic found in the soldiers' letters at the time dealt with the issue of clothing. Throughout the war, Confederate soldiers relied on items sent from home to compensate for the army's failure to properly provide for them. Private John D. McGeachy of the 51st North Carolina requested that his sister make him two more shirts, because his others were "getting thin and will be worn out." Colonel Barrier of the 8th North Carolina described to his father the misfortune that had befallen him in evacuating Wilmington: "My boy Henderson was captured in Wilmington and with him I lost part of my under clothing. I am now minus my boy and a shirt, pair of drawers and several pairs of socks." Several days later when Henderson had still not returned, Barrier requested his father replace the missing clothing as well as the servant.[16]

As Hoke held his position in Duplin County along the Wilmington & Weldon Railroad, Bragg shifted his headquarters 30 miles north to Goldsboro, a suitable location considering the increased enemy activity at New Bern. In early February, Bragg had initiated efforts to consolidate forces in the Goldsboro and Kinston areas, which were part of Brig. Gen. Laurence S. Baker's Second Military District, Department of North Carolina. Aware of the Federals' intention to move west along the railroad toward Kinston, Bragg ordered Baker to keep his cavalry near New Bern to monitor and report Union activity.[17]

Kinston was the headquarters of Col. John N. Whitford's Second Sub-District of Baker's command, consisting of the 67th North Carolina, the

15 Nicholas W. Schenck, journal, East Carolina Manuscript Collection, J. Y. Joyner Library, East Carolina University, Greenville, NC, 30-41; John D. McGeachy to sister, March 2, 1865.

16 John D. McGeachy to sister, March 2, 1865; Auciello and Troxler, eds., *Dear Father*, 77.

17 *OR* 47, pt. 2, 1,114-1,115, 1,120, 1,164.

13th Battalion North Carolina Light Artillery, the 6th North Carolina Cavalry, the 8th Georgia Cavalry (Company G), and a local defense force.[18]

The 6th North Carolina Cavalry, commanded by Maj. John J. Spann, monitored the Gum Swamp region between Kinston and New Bern, keeping watch along the two primary wagon roads and railroad leading west out of the city. Captain Patrick Gray's Company G, 8th Georgia Cavalry maintained a presence north of the Neuse River in Pitt County.[19]

Unfortunately, problems with desertion and lack of discipline throughout 1864 had cast doubt on the effectiveness of the Georgia and Tar Heel horse soldiers. The beginning months of 1865 showed no change in their character. New Bern's local newspaper, the *North Carolina Times*, reported multiple occurrences of troopers from the two units deserting into Union lines. On February 2, one incident caused quite a stir in New Bern when Lt. Hilton H. Ray and 11 soldiers from Company B, 6th North Carolina Cavalry deserted. Around the same time mounted infantry of Capt. George W. Graham's Company L, 1st North Carolina (Union) surprised Captain Gray's Georgia horsemen in camp, capturing 18 men, including two officers.[20]

Fortunately for Bragg, his department contained another cavalry regiment that had proven itself reliable—the 2nd South Carolina Cavalry, commanded by Col. Thomas J. Lipscomb. Following the Confederate evacuation of Wilmington, Bragg had posted Lipscomb's regiment north of the city to monitor possible movement by Union forces.

As the Confederate cavalry kept watch of the Federals along the coast, additional units arrived at Kinston to strengthen Whitford's command. The colonel's 67th North Carolina relocated from Goldsboro to Kinston, along with the 68th North Carolina. Unlike other Tar Heel regiments serving in

18 Manarin et al., *North Carolina Troops*, vol. 18, 96-97.

19 Ibid., *North Carolina Troops*, vol. 2, 456. Companies A and F of the 6th North Carolina Cavalry were detached and still operating along the Roanoke River at the time of the battle. John W. Moore, "Sixty-Fifth Regiment," in Clark, ed., *Histories of the Several Regiments and Battalions from North Carolina in the Great War 1861-'65*. 5 vols. (Goldsboro, NC, 1901), vol. 3, 681.

20 *North Carolina Times* (New Bern), January 15, 1865; Manarin et al., *North Carolina Troops*, vol. 2, 463-470; See Aldo S. Perry's *Civil War Court Martial of North Carolina Troops* (Jefferson, NC, 2012). Desertion reached a high in May 1864, with 116 soldiers; *OR* 47, pt. 2, 1406; File of Company G, 8th Georgia Cavalry, Records of Confederate Soldiers Who Served During the Civil War, Compiled Service Records of Confederate Soldiers Who Served in Organizations from the State of Georgia, M266, rolls 40 through 41, Records Group 109, National Archives.

Confederate field armies, the state raised the 67th and 68th for service only in North Carolina. These units were theoretically controlled by the governor. In the last year, both regiments had seen active field service defending against Federal raids in eastern North Carolina. What the units lacked in combat experience, they made up for in strength of numbers, which benefited the concentration of forces at Kinston. With an approximate strength of 700 men in March 1865, the 67th North Carolina was one of the largest regiments in Bragg's department.[21]

The North Carolina Junior Reserves represented another sizeable element within General Bragg's department. Formed out of necessity due to diminishing manpower available for the army, the reserves were created by the Confederate Congress in February 1864 with passage of the Third Conscription Act. The Act specified that white males between the ages of 17 and 18 were eligible for service in the Junior Reserves. Moreover, men between the ages of 45 and 50 were eligible for service in the Senior Reserves. The reserves relieved regular line units from mundane missions such as guarding railroad bridges, thus enabling the latter to return to their respective field armies and battle the Yankees more directly. However, during the closing months of the war these young boys found themselves primarily serving on the front lines, a policy that President Davis referred to as "grinding up the seed corn of the Confederacy."[22]

Prior to the battle of Wise's Forks, the Junior Reserves' combat experience ranged from a few small skirmishes to witnessing the massive Federal naval bombardment and capture of Fort Fisher. Disease, illness, and poor logistical support proved to be the young men's greatest adversary. A New York soldier who took part in the capture of 200 Junior Reserves at Fort Fisher in December of 1864 observed the poor physical health of the young soldiers. According to him, he had never seen "such a lot of spindle shanks as they were." The cumulative effect of these factors weighed heavily as the root cause of the Junior Reserves' high attrition rate. An analysis of individual service records indicates that a significant number of youngsters were absent because of desertion, the need for hospitalization, or furlough during the months of February and March 1865. For example, the February 28 muster roll for one

21 Manarin et al., *North Carolina Troops*, vol. 15, 409, 510, 519, 521-523.

22 Manarin et al., *North Carolina Troops*, vol. 17, 1; Bradley, *Last Stand*, 139.

company in the 1st Regiment Junior Reserves reported only 35 men present for duty.[23]

At Bragg's insistence, North Carolina created the Junior Reserves brigade in January 1865 to alleviate issues of poor administration and discipline. However, because of the regiments' dispersal throughout the state, the brigade did not take the field in its entirety until at Kinston, a week prior to the battle of Wise's Forks.[24]

Simultaneous with Bragg's operations, the Confederate Army of Tennessee began a long and difficult journey toward the Carolinas, and ultimately the battles of Wise's Forks and Bentonville. Sherman's recent successful Savannah campaign weighed heavily in President Davis's decision to transfer the Army of Tennessee to the Carolinas. Sherman's March to the Sea convinced the Confederate president of the necessity to transfer reinforcements east in an effort to bolster forces confronting Sherman and to boost the public's morale. Davis wrote, "Sherman's campaign has produced [a] bad effect on our people. Success against his future operations is needful to reanimate public confidence."[25]

Unfortunately, by January 1865, attrition had reduced the once-proud army of 70,000 troops to a mere skeleton of its former grand self, poorly clad and equipped and barely numbering 20,000. Constant combat through most of 1864 had culminated in Gen. John B. Hood's failed campaign into Middle Tennessee and the bloody defeats of Franklin and Nashville.[26]

Following the army's defeat at Nashville, Tennessee, in December 1864, it endured a painful winter retreat to Tupelo, Mississippi, where the shattered units occupied winter camps. Captain Samuel C. Kelly of the 30th Alabama wrote his wife, "some of the men are entirely barefooted, all are hungry and tired." A Mississippi officer who had escaped Hood's Tennessee campaign because of previous wounds, returned to his old regiment at Tupelo. In a letter

---

23 Manarin et al., *North Carolina Troops*, vol. 17, 96-98; Fonvielle, *The Wilmington Campaign*, 169.

24 Manarin et al., *North Carolina Troops*, vol. 17, 93-96, 100, 254n.

25 *OR* 45, pt. 2, 778-779.

26 William R. Scaife, *The Campaign for Atlanta* (Cartersville, GA, 1993), 156. On June 30, 1864, the Army of Tennessee reported present for duty 69,946 men; OR 45, pt. 2, 780; Horn, *The Army of Tennessee* (Norman, OK, 1953), 422; Connelly, *Autumn of Glory*, 514; See Stephen E. Hood's *John Bell Hood: The Rise, Fall, and Resurrection of a Confederate General* (El Dorado Hills, CA, 2013). Stephen Hood's award-winning book is a superb study on the myths surrounding General Hood, how they developed, and the sources upon which his detractors rely.

home, he described the wretched scene that welcomed his return: "I found them in a bad condition, and can't tell when I felt so sad just to behold men barefooted and so nearly naked and the weather so cold." Throughout the army, the mood of the soldiers turned to frustration and anger due to prolonged hunger and miserable conditions.[27]

The severe winter conditions and bloody combat that characterized Hood's Tennessee campaign had exacted a heavy toll on the army, in both materiel and men, with the most notable losses at senior command levels. The battles of Franklin and Nashville cost the Army of Tennessee 16 of its general officers and numerous senior field grade officers. The impact of these losses was felt throughout the coming weeks, as leaders struggled to maintain order and discipline while confronting a proven adversary in Sherman's army.

The Army of Tennessee that wintered in Tupelo in January 1865 was a ghost of its former self. Some regiments no longer fielded enough men to form one company, forcing consolidation. The depleted Alabama regiments of Brig. Gen. Thomas M. Scott's brigade were an example of the serious situation. The 27th Alabama reported only 17 men present at Tupelo, with one captain remaining out of ten authorized in the regiment. Colonel James Jackson, the regiment's surviving field grade officer, had to assume command of the brigade as the ranking officer remaining. Two sister regiments, the 37th and 49th Alabama, experienced similar shortages. The three regiments were consolidated, with Capt. W. B. Beeson of the 49th Alabama taking command due to seniority. Less than two months later, Beeson's consolidated regiment took 60 soldiers into the battle of Wise's Forks.[28]

The army suffered from shortages in uniforms, shoes, blankets, and tents for adequate shelter from winter temperatures. Some units lacked weapons and the accoutrements required to properly equip the men.[29]

---

27 Samuel C. Kelly to His Wife, January 17, 1865, in Alabama Department of Archives and History; H. Grady Howell, Jr., *To Live and Die in Dixie: A History of the Third Regiment Mississippi Volunteer Infantry, C.S.A.* (Jackson, MS, 1991), 410-411.

28 *OR* 45 pt.1, p. 664; John V. Brogden and Noel Crowson, eds., *Bloody Banners and Barefoot Boys: A History of the 27th Regiment Alabama Infantry, C.S.A.: The Civil War Memoirs and Diary Entries of J. P. Cannon, M. D.* (Shippensburg, PA, 1997), 135.

29 Robert P. Bender, ed., *Worthy of the Cause for Which They Fight: The Civil War Diary of Brigadier General Daniel Harris Reynolds, 1861-1865* (Fayetteville, AR, 2011), 170-171; R. Hugh Simmons, "The 12th Louisiana Infantry in North Carolina, January-April, 1865," *Louisiana History: The Journal of the Louisiana Historical Association*, vol. 36, no. 1 (Winter 1995), 82, 84.

Despite the senior leaders' contention that if the army "moved in its present condition, it will prove utterly worthless," President Davis stood firm in his decision to send forces east, ignoring their pleas to allow time for "rest, consolidation, and reorganization." In a move that further fragmented the army, Davis chose to send only a portion of the Army of Tennessee to confront Sherman. Concerned about the continued threat from Union forces in the Western Theater, Lt. Gen. Richard Taylor, commander of the Department of Alabama, Mississippi, and East Louisiana, retained control of approximately ten thousand infantry and cavalry. General P. G. T. Beauregard, commander of the Military Division of the West, would oversee the elements sent east to the Carolinas. Davis had approved Hood's request for relief from command, and the general departed Tupelo with dreams of raising another army west of the Mississippi River.[30]

Prior to departing, Hood recommended 100-day furloughs for the Trans-Mississippi units. Richmond denied his request. Despite Hood's failed attempt, Beauregard instituted what he described as "a judicious system of furloughs" to prevent disorder and desertion within the army. Unfortunately, Beauregard's judicious system included only units from Alabama, Mississippi, and Tennessee, leaving soldiers from other states disgruntled.[31]

For those units granted furloughs, Beauregard set parameters to maintain a semblance of order. Captain Kelly of the 30th Alabama described to his wife how the new stipulations ruled out any chance for a furlough: "One [furlough] for every fifteen men and one officer to be retained for every fifteen men. That lets me out, and nearly all the rest, too, as we have only thirty one men in the company."[32]

In planning the eastward movement, Beauregard selected Augusta, Georgia, as the location to assemble the Army of Tennessee units as they arrived from Mississippi. Augusta was a suitable location to refit and rearm the men as they moved into the Carolinas, as the city possessed an arsenal and various quartermaster and commissary supply warehouses.[33]

---

30 OR 45, pt. 2, 772, 789; Connelly, *Autumn of Glory*, 513-514; OR 45, pt. 2, 781, 792. Taylor briefly assumed command of the army following Hood's relief.

31 OR 45, pt. 2, 778-779; ibid., 1,285-1,286; ibid., 786.

32 Samuel C. Kelly to wife, January 17, 1865.

33 OR 45, pt. 2, 792-793.

Maj. Gen. Daniel Harvey Hill
Library of Congress

The commanding officer in Augusta was a controversial North Carolinian, Maj. Gen. Daniel Harvey Hill. Commonly known as D. H. Hill, the general possessed a reputation as a fighter, but his caustic mannerisms on more than one occasion put him at odds with superiors and peers alike. Hill graduated from West Point in 1842 and received his baptism of fire during the war with Mexico, earning two brevets for bravery. Hill resigned his commission in 1849 and went on to serve in various capacities at several academic institutions in North Carolina and Virginia.[34]

At the outbreak of the Civil War, Hill commanded the 1st North Carolina. He led the green volunteers at Big Bethel, the war's first battle. He quickly rose to the rank of major general and assumed command of a division in General Lee's Army of Northern Virginia. The mysteries surrounding "Lee's lost order" during the Maryland campaign overshadowed Hill's gallant stand on South Mountain in September 1862, but what likely ended his service in the Army of Northern Virginia was his outspoken criticism of Lee and other officers. Confederate military authorities reassigned Hill to positions of lesser importance until August 1863, when he assumed command of a corps in Bragg's Army of Tennessee. He played an active, if often obstreperous, role the Confederate victory at Chickamauga, Georgia, in September 1863, where his poor performance and outspoken criticism of Bragg led to his removal from the army.

34 For biographical information on Hill, the authors consulted Hal Bridges, *Lee's Maverick General: Daniel Harvey Hill* (Lincoln, NE, 1961); and Warner, *Generals in Gray*, 136-137; See Hal Bridges for a detailed account and circumstances surrounding "Lee's lost order."

Forced to the sidelines, Hill performed ancillary duties in Virginia until authorities in Richmond restored him to command in January 1865, primarily because of Beauregard's assistance in the matter, and the help of the governor and other North Carolina politicians. Richmond initially assigned Hill to Gen. William J. Hardee in the Department of South Carolina, Georgia, and Florida, as commander of the District of Georgia, located in Augusta. However, on January 27, with Beauregard sick in Montgomery, Alabama, and unable to carry out his duties, he ordered Hill to assume command of the Army of Tennessee troops arriving at Augusta.[35]

Hill accepted the Augusta assignment with his characteristically vigorous attitude and worked diligently to achieve the timely arrival of reinforcements from Mississippi. His arrival at Augusta coincided with the beginning of Sherman's Carolinas campaign, which caused Hill serious concern. By design, Sherman had feinted toward Augusta, creating the illusion that the city and all its valuable war resources were in danger. Hill urgently attempted to coordinate Confederate forces available in his district, along with units arriving from the Army of Tennessee, in an attempt to defend Augusta.[36]

Regardless of the energy Hill displayed, nothing could bring about the rapid arrival of reinforcements. The Confederacy faced a major logistical hurdle in deploying the army east from Mississippi. By 1865, the rail infrastructure throughout the south showed the effects of limited capital reinvestment in upgrading or maintaining the rail network, including locomotives and rolling stock. Simply put, the Southern railroads had died of neglect—a death facilitated by the Confederate government's unwillingness to invest in future infrastructure or aid railroad companies whose lines sustained damages during the war. Historian Chris Gable describes the decline of Confederate railroads as an example of the "states rights philosophy of limited government, whose inaction is inconsistent with the government's willingness to conscript railroad workers and confiscate rails." The Confederate government took a "willing to take, but not give" attitude with the rail companies.[37]

---

35 OR 47, pt. 2 p. 1,023, 1,049-1,051.

36 *OR* 47, pt. 2, 1,051. Sherman's cavalry feinted toward Augusta, and on February 11, 1865, Confederate cavalry under command of Maj. Gen. Joseph Wheeler engaged the Federal horsemen at Aiken, South Carolina.

37 Christopher R. Gabel, *Rails to Oblivion: The Decline of Confederate Railroads in the Civil War* (Fort Leavenworth, KS, 2002), 24-26.

The movement toward the Carolinas required the use of nine different railroads that often failed to link with one another, resulting in units marching overland to the next railhead. Varying sizes of rail gauge were another major source of frustration. Due to incompatibility, lengthy delays developed while troops unloaded and reloaded onto different trains. To maximize the use of railcars for infantry, the army's supply wagons traveled overland in separate formations and artillery was loaded onto riverboats for transport as far as Columbus, Georgia, before boarding railcars.[38]

The staggered movement of units and untimely delays broke down the typical corps and division command structure, resulting in the piecemeal arrival of brigades into areas threatened by Union forces. During the ensuing battles in the Carolinas, it was common to find Confederate brigades from one division or corps temporarily attached to other commands. During the battle of Wise's Forks, 10 Army of Tennessee brigades participated in the battle, comprising elements from two infantry corps and five different divisions.

The army began moving on the morning of January 19 as three divisions of Lt. Gen. Stephen D. Lee's corps, under the command of Maj. Gen. Carter L. Stevenson, departed Tupelo by rail. The combination of poor rail management and lack of railcars resulted in Lee's Corps taking five days to complete the nearly 200-mile journey to Montgomery, Alabama. A week later, the units of Lt. Gen. Frank Cheatham's corps departed on January 25, and finally Lt. Gen. Alexander P. Stewart's corps on January 30.[39]

The journey of Brig. Gen. Edmund W. Pettus's brigade highlighted the hardships the soldiers faced as they traversed the Deep South toward the Carolinas. On January 19, the men departed by rail en route to Augusta, Georgia. Throughout the 500-mile trek, Pettus's brigade rode nine different rail lines, crossed the Tombigbee River by ferry, traveled up the Alabama River via steamboats, and marched 35 miles overland from Milledgeville, Georgia, to the railhead at Mayfield where they continued to their final destination. Reaching Augusta on the night of January 27, the brigade had completed the arduous journey remarkably fast, requiring only nine days of travel. As Captain Kelly of

38 Robert C. Black, III, *The Railroads of the Confederacy* (1952; reprinted, Wilmington, NC, 1987), 272-274; Only the cannons traveled by river boat. The artillerymen and horses traveled cross country to Macon, Georgia, to link up with their artillery pieces. See Larry J. Daniel, *Cannoneers in Gray: The Field Artillery of the Army of Tennessee, 1861-1865* (Tuscaloosa, AL, 1984), 183.

39 R. H. Simmons, "The 12th Louisiana Infantry in North Carolina, January-April, 1865," 84.

the 30th Alabama described it, "we have had a wet bad time, but it is better than walking."[40]

For soldiers traveling on the trains, the officers established a system where one group rode on top of the boxcars while another group crowded inside. To reduce exposure, as the trains halted, the soldiers rotated positions, which allowed the exposed men an opportunity for cover. Unfortunately, the limited number of boxcars forced some soldiers to travel on open flatcars exposed to the elements with no option for dry transport. The *Augusta Constitutionalist* helped reveal the extreme conditions the men experienced while traveling, reporting that five Arkansas soldiers had frozen to death while aboard train.[41]

The soldiers faced other hazards in addition to suffering from exposure. Several incidents of train derailments occurred. One accident on a troop train en route to Milledgeville resulted in the death and injury of several men.[42]

The terrible conditions and hardships endured along the way induced many of the soldiers to desert at the first opportunity. As the Army of Tennessee moved across the Deep South and into the Carolinas, units passed near their homes, tempting soldiers to slip away. In reporting the arrival of two brigades at Augusta, General Hill noted that "more than half of the two advanced brigades have deserted . . . nine hundred arrived out of 1,600 started."[43]

The psychological impact of Sherman's operations on Southern civilians and military targets induced many Confederate soldiers to take "unauthorized leave of absences," most notably those from Georgia and South Carolina. The 10th South Carolina, a battle hardened, well-disciplined unit, witnessed firsthand the devastation caused by Sherman's execution of "hard war" as they moved through the Palmetto State. Lieutenant Col. Cornelius Irvine Walker, commander of the 10th South Carolina, recorded that "everything seemed now to be lost, our backs turned on our homes, our State given up to the foe, our families exposed to their outrages." In the immediate days following Columbia's evacuation, Walker received a very grim report one morning—only 83 "noble fellows" remained of the 233 present the day before. Losses

---

40 Samuel Kelly to wife, January 21, 1865.

41 Ibid.; *Augusta Constitutionalist*, February 16, 1865.

42 *Augusta Constitutionalist*, February 10, 1865. The five soldiers killed were members of the 8th Arkansas. OR 47, pt.1, 1,080.

43 OR 47 pt. 2, 1,061-1,062.

continued during the next several weeks, and when the 10th South Carolina took the field at the battle at Wise's Forks, Walker commanded only 45 men.[44]

Along with the issue of desertion, Hill observed the poor logistical state of the men as they reached Augusta. "The troops arriving are destitute of everything—arms, clothing, etc." Historian R. Hugh Simmons noted that when the 12th Louisiana departed Tupelo, many of the soldiers lacked weapons. Approximately 235 Louisiana soldiers reached North Carolina and participated in the battle of Wise's Forks, of which 47 lacked weapons. In President Davis's haste to send the army east, the consequences of not allowing for time to refit the troops became all too apparent.[45]

Aside from desertion and poor supply conditions, the sporadic arrival of troops at Augusta convinced the sharp-tongued Hill that the enemy controlled the movement of trains. In Hill's typical style, he penned a sarcastic note to General Hardee on January 30 informing him, "the troops are coming in very slowly. How happens it that whenever there is an emergency for the movement of troops there is something wrong with railroads? Is it because superintendents and employe[e]s are nearly all Yankees? So I think." In a matter-of-fact tone, Hill notified the acting commander of Lee's Corps, General Stevenson, of the tardy arrival of his brigades: "The railroad is entirely in the hands of Yankees and they delay every movement."[46]

Southern newspapers like Raleigh's *Daily Confederate* echoed similar hostilities toward the railroad companies when it reported that "The officers of railroad corporations . . . are no better friends to the Confederacy than Grant or Sherman. . . . God save the country, if its destiny in any wise depends on proper and conscientious performance of duty by railroad corporations."[47]

---

44 See Mark Grimsley *The Hard Hand of War: Union Military Policy Toward Southern Civilians 1861-1865* (New York, 1995), for an analysis of Sherman's execution of "hard war" and its impact on the civilian populace; Cornelius I. Walker, *Rolls and Historical Sketch of the Tenth Regiment, So. Ca. Volunteers, in the Army of the Confederate States* (1881; reprinted, Alexandria, VA, 1985), 131; Charles D. Runion and William L. White, eds., *Great Things Are Expected of Us: The Letters of Colonel C. Irvine Walker, 10th South Carolina Infantry, C.S.A.* (Knoxville, TN, 2009), 169-170, 173.

45 *OR* 47, pt. 2, 1,061; Email correspondence between the authors and R. Hugh Simmons, July 12, 2005; Johnston struggled throughout the months of March and April to properly equip his soldiers. Shortages of weapons, leather accouterments, and shoes continually plagued the commander.

46 *OR* 47, pt. 2, 1,061-1,062.

47 *Daily Confederate* (Raleigh), February 7, 1865.

Arriving first to Augusta, Lee's Corps found little opportunity for recovery. The city bustled with activity because of its logistical importance to the Confederacy and close proximity to Sherman's advancing army. As troop trains arrived, others departed loaded with critical war materiel, seeking refuge from the reach of Sherman's grasp. Lee's Corps moved across the Savannah River into South Carolina to reinforce Confederate troops confronting Sherman.[48]

Upon arriving at Augusta, Brig. Gen. W. S. Featherston's Mississippi brigade from Stewart's Corps crossed the river and moved 17 miles east to Graniteville, South Carolina. Graniteville's value to the Confederacy came from the town's large textile mill. For Featherston's Mississippians, however, mills and cotton mattered little. The mill employed more than 400 female workers, offering a more pleasing picture and escape from war.[49]

Captain John F. Saucier of the 3rd Mississippi described how the women "completely besieged our encampment and captured every rebel soldier of Featherston's brigade. . . . I received yesterday from a fair and kind one, two and half dozen fine light biscuits in a good new haversack. Today they are all busy cooking for our troops five days rations." The kindness was typical of the reception the army received moving across the South. Captain Saucier and his men's respite ended when they received orders to march toward Columbia.[50]

Sherman's skillful advance through South Carolina and Beauregard's refusal to consolidate his available forces resulted in no large battle, only small skirmishes and delaying actions. The Union army also laid waste to the state's central railroads. Cooperating with other Confederate forces in the Palmetto State, the lead elements of the Army of Tennessee defended crossing sites along the Edisto and the Congaree Rivers. Despite gallant efforts, they stood no chance against the full weight of Sherman's advance, but provided Beauregard time to coordinate an evacuation of Columbia. Though necessary, these delaying actions were costly. Brigadier Gen. Joseph B. Palmer reported the loss of 75 men from his brigade in one skirmish alone—a significant loss considering his effective strength was only 553 soldiers.[51]

---

48 OR 47, pt. 2, 1,083, 1,088.

49 Ibid., pt. 2, 1,146.

50 Howell, To Live and Die in Dixie: A History of the Third Regiment Mississippi Volunteer Infantry, C.S.A., 415-416.

51 OR 47, pt. 2, 1,176, 1,262.

Major Robert N. Hull of the 66th Georgia, part of Colonel Jackson's brigade, penned a letter to his brother-in-law just hours before being mortally wounded along the South Edisto River. "My men are completely demoralized," he admitted, "and I fear when the crisis comes they will be found wanting." When he wrote these last words, Jackson's brigade fielded less than 100 men, and in less than a month at the battle of Wise's Forks, the brigade consisted of only 76 men.[52]

In the chaos of Columbia's evacuation, confusion existed amongst military authorities about who or what had priority on the trains: civilians, troops, or supplies. Prior to General Sherman's arrival the system collapsed, resulting in the Confederate military abandoning critical provisions. Union ordnance officers later accounted for 1,900 Enfield rifled muskets left behind in the city's arsenal—a costly error considering that many hundreds of soldiers in the Army of Tennessee still lacked weapons and proper accouterments.[53]

With the loss of Columbia, Beauregard selected Chesterville, north of the capital along the South Carolina & Charlotte Railroad, as an assembly point for the army's units in South Carolina and for those still en route. From Chesterville, they moved north to Charlotte, North Carolina, by rail or by foot. Captain Kelly of the 30th Alabama remembered that Pettus's brigade marched northward to Charlotte with no opportunity for rail. Foot marches upward of 20 miles a day, miserable rain, and muddy roads characterized the infantry's movement. Complaining that his horse had not caught up with him from the earlier train ride, Captain Kelly wrote, "He would be worth fifty dollars a day to me during this campaign."[54]

More fortunate units secured passage by rail. Lieutenant M. M. Peyton of the 3rd Mississippi wrote that the soldiers "weakly hoisted one another aboard the decrepit cars and after a jerking start the regiment was soon gliding through the rugged, scenic country to Charlotte." Luck had shined upon the Mississippi regiment in securing transportation in the face of fierce competition for use of the railroad.[55]

---

52 Ibid., 1,262; ibid., pt. 1, 1,088.

53 Ibid., 181-182.

54 William M. Kelly, "A History of the Thirtieth Alabama Volunteers (Infantry) Confederate States Army," in *Alabama Historical Quarterly*, vol. 9, no. 1, 164.

55 Howell, *To Live and Die in Dixie, C.S.A.*, 417.

By February 23, 2,000 men of Lee's Corps, comprising six brigades, were camped in the Charlotte vicinity. On February 27, General Johnston conducted a review of the corps, where he witnessed the pitiful remains of the Army of Tennessee. The majority of men greeted the news of Johnston's return with joy, for they had a profound respect for their former commander. One Alabama officer wrote home, "I have no war news only that 'Old Ma's Joe' as he is called has taken command of this army. He lives in the heart of the Tennessee army and is worth more than a reinforcement of ten thousand armed each with a twelve pounder [artillery piece]." Considering the visibly poor state and reduced numbers of Lee's Corps, Johnston would have welcomed an additional 10,000 men.[56]

As Johnston entered his second week in command, "a confused state of affairs" existed as he tried to direct a concentration. Hardee's Corps and Hampton's cavalry were withdrawing from South Carolina in a race with Sherman's advancing columns. For Johnston, the situation became more desperate with each passing day. Reports indicated Sherman's cavalry had crossed the state line with infantry following only days behind. And from along the North Carolina coast, earlier signs of a pending advance from New Bern had become reality—General Schofield's forces were on the move.

Recognizing the need for immediate concentration, Johnston designated Smithfield, North Carolina, as the assembly point for units of the Army of Tennessee arriving in the Tar Heel State. Smithfield was an ideal location because of its close proximity to Raleigh and adjacency to the North Carolina Railroad.[57]

Wise to his old antagonist's game of maneuver, Johnston sought to attack a vulnerable portion of Sherman's army, thereby mitigating the risk to his outmanned forces. Johnston identified the Cape Fear River at Fayetteville as an ideal location to engage Sherman's army as it crossed the river. Upon Hardee's arrival at Fayetteville, Johnston would reinforce "Old Reliable" with elements of the Army of Tennessee assembled at Smithfield, about 40 miles away.[58]

Unfortunately for Johnston, the fluid situation in eastern North Carolina required him to deal with the more immediate threat out of New Bern.

56 *OR* 47, pt. 2, 1,264; Francis H. Nash, diary, n.d., 20, Dolph Briscoe Center of American History, University of Texas at Austin, Texas; Samuel C. Kelly to wife, March 2, 1865.

57 *OR* 47, pt. 2, 1,298.

58 Bradley, *Last Stand*, 73.

Throughout February, spies from within Federal lines had reported large numbers of reinforcements arriving at New Bern and repair work on the railroad—both indicators of a pending advance.[59]

On March 3, Johnston wrote to Bragg about the probability of Sherman and Schofield's forces uniting, and suggested that Bragg engage the latter to deny this junction. To deal with the threat out of New Bern, Bragg relocated Hoke's division from Duplin County to Kinston to strengthen Col. John N. Whitford's small command.[60]

Johnston, in a risky decision, chose to support Bragg's efforts to contest Schofield's advance from the coast. By reinforcing Bragg's forces with elements of the Army of Tennessee, Johnston deviated from his original concentration plan. He turned his focus away from Sherman, leaving Hardee and Hampton to their own accord. Bragg's offensive action against Schofield might result in wasting precious manpower, or at worst, total destruction.

Johnston recognized Schofield as the more immediate threat and chose to accept the risk. He could not avoid the Union threat from the coast. Thus, the die was cast for the battle of Wise's Forks, the first of four major battles fought in North Carolina in March 1865—the bloodiest month of fighting on her soil throughout the entire Civil War.

59 OR 47, pt. 2, 1,110.

60 Ibid., 1,318.

Chapter 4

"Let nothing detain you."

— *Maj. Gen. John M. Schofield*

Cox Advances

I n late February 1865, Union forces appeared paralyzed at New Bern. A month had passed since Grant had met Palmer at Morehead City, and the general remained idle. Even Schofield's February 11 correspondence with Palmer to "advance as soon as you can get ready" accomplished little. As Gen. William T. Sherman's Union army neared Goldsboro, Schofield lost all patience with Palmer and informed Grant of his dissatisfaction with the lack of progress. Grant, equally displeased, authorized Schofield to make any "changes in commanders you may think necessary."[1]

Schofield summoned Palmer to Wilmington for an update on his progress. Palmer boarded the steamer *Escort* on February 25 accompanied by his wife and staff, as if attending a social event. The meeting did not go well. Palmer's update confirmed that he had not moved as ordered and Schofield relieved him of command. Maj. Gen. Jacob D. Cox, a trusted subordinate from the XXIII Corps, received orders to replace Palmer as commander of the District of Beaufort at New Bern.[2]

The 36-year-old Cox was born in Montreal, Canada, and graduated from Oberlin College in Ohio in 1851. Soon afterward, he became superintendent of

---

1 *OR* 47, pt. 1, 911; pt. 2, 394, 578-579.

2 Ibid., pt. 1, 911; pt. 2, 722; pt. 1, 903-931.

Maj. Gen. Jacob D. Cox
Library of Congress

schools in Warren, Ohio, and practiced law there. Cox was politically active and helped organize the Republican Party in Warren. In 1859, he served in the Ohio Senate and became good friends with Governor William Dennison, who appointed him brigadier general of the Ohio militia in 1860. Though Cox had no military training, he took the appointment seriously, reading every military tactics and theory book available to him at the time.[3]

When the Civil War began, Governor Dennison commissioned Cox as brigadier general of Ohio State Volunteers. Cox's early military successes in West Virginia established him as a competent leader. He commanded a division in the IX Corps during the Maryland campaign. At the battle of South Mountain Cox assumed temporary command of the IX Corps after the death of Maj. Gen. Jesse L. Reno. At Antietam, Cox's men successfully stormed across Burnside Bridge after several failed attempts by other Union troops. Upon the conclusion of the Maryland campaign Gens. Ambrose E. Burnside and George B. McClellan recommended Cox for promotion to major general "for gallant and meritorious service in the battles of South Mountain and Antietam." However, the army later withdrew Cox's promotion, as the number of major generals exceeded the maximum authorized by Congress.

Cox served as a division commander in Schofield's XXIII Corps during the Atlanta campaign in 1864. Once again, Cox's performance was exemplary, prompting another request for promotion by his superiors. Schofield wrote, "I have no hesitation in saying I have never seen a more able and efficient division commander." Sherman concurred and forwarded Cox's recommendation for promotion to army chief of staff Henry W. Halleck.

---

3 For biographical information on Cox, the authors consulted William C. Cochran, *General Jacob Dolson Cox, Early Life and Military Service* (Oberlin, OH, 1901), and Warner, *Generals in Blue*, 97-98.

As Sherman prepared to launch his March to the Sea, he sent Schofield with the IV Corps and the XXIII Corps into Tennessee. Cox accompanied Schofield as commander of the XXIII Corps. Cox's presence helped compensate for Schofield's weakness as a field commander. Schofield relied heavily on the Ohioan throughout the Tennessee campaign, where Cox distinguished himself yet again. At Spring Hill, Tennessee, advance elements of Gen. John B. Hood's Army of Tennessee had managed to get in front of and to the east of Schofield's army. During the night, Cox slipped past Hood's encamped army, avoiding potential disaster for the Federals.

At the battle of Franklin, Cox achieved his greatest moment in command while leading the Union force tasked with protecting the wagon train crossing of the Harpeth River. Cox's well entrenched troops waited for Hood's army to attack. Schofield chose to observe the battle at Fort Granger across the river. On the afternoon of November 30, 1864, Hood attacked Cox's strongly fortified position with his entire army. The fierce battle raged for hours, and when it was over Cox's line had held. The Confederates suffered staggering losses, more than one-fourth of the men engaged. The victory induced Schofield to recommend Cox once more for promotion. On December 7, 1864, Cox received a major general's commission. Soon after his promotion, Cox and the XXIII Corps were transferred to North Carolina where they took part in the successful capture of Wilmington.

In late February 1865, Schofield stressed to Cox the urgency for immediate action: "Time is very important. . . . I rely upon you to regain what has been lost. Let nothing detain you." He assigned Cox three key tasks:

1. Gain possession of the railroad from New Bern to Goldsboro for the use of the army.

2. Secure the crossing of the Neuse River and the occupation of Kinston and Goldsboro.

3. Begin operations at once and push forward rapidly to avoid delay in reconstructing the railroad.[4]

Before Schofield's meeting with his generals had concluded, severe weather set in, delaying for several days Cox and Palmer's return to New Bern. Finally,

4   *OR* 47, pt. 2, 580, 620.

Brig. Gen. Samuel P. Carter
U.S. Army Military History Institute

on the morning of February 28, the winds diminished enough for the *Escort* to put to sea. Following a rough voyage, the two generals arrived at Morehead City late in the day and took the train to New Bern. Cox established temporary headquarters in the Gaston Hotel. The journey from Wilmington had cost Cox several days, but the clarity and attention to detail exhibited in his March 1 orders indicate that he used the time while stranded aboard the *Escort* to evaluate the situation at New Bern. To Palmer's credit, he harbored no ill feelings toward Cox, and at least outwardly exhibited courtesy and cooperation.[5]

On March 1, Cox issued three orders that established his command authority, organized a Provisional Corps, and initiated the Union army's movement toward Kinston. General Order No. 1 was the customary order announcing the assumption of command. However, the last sentence demonstrated an immediate change in focus: "Headquarters of the district will be in the field." Cox would not remain safely behind at New Bern, and accordingly moved his headquarters to Camp Claassen at Batchelder's Creek, on the western extremity of New Bern's defenses.[6]

Cox's Provisional Corps was comprised of three infantry divisions. Two divisions were temporary and created by reducing or relocating units within the District of Beaufort, supplemented by Brig. Gen. Thomas F. Meagher's disbanded command. Cox appointed Palmer commander of the First Division, District of Beaufort. Brig. Gen. Samuel P. Carter, of Meagher's former organization, led the Second Division, District of Beaufort.[7]

---

5 Ibid., pt. 2, 930-931.

6 Ibid., 637-638; pt. 1, 931.

7 *OR* 47, pt. 2, 654.

Carter was a career military officer, having served the majority of his time in the navy. The 45-year-old East Tennessee native graduated from the U.S. Naval Academy at Annapolis in 1846. In the years prior to the Civil War, he served in various shore and shipboard assignments. When the war came, the navy transferred Carter to the War Department. He participated in the seizure of Cumberland Gap and the siege of Knoxville, Tennessee, where he briefly commanded a cavalry division in the XXIII Corps. After his transfer to eastern North Carolina, Carter assumed command of Meagher's Provisional Division. Meanwhile, the 4,000 men of Bvt. Maj. Gen. Thomas H. Ruger's XXIII Corps division had yet to arrive at New Bern. Altogether, Cox's Provisional Corps would field about 13,000 men.[8]

The District of Beaufort consisted of regiments from New England and the Mid-Atlantic States. Regiments such as the 17th Massachusetts and the 12th New York Cavalry had seen little combat, while the 27th Massachusetts and other veteran frontline units had recently arrived from Virginia, where they had served in Grant's bloody Overland and Petersburg campaigns. Most of the regiments experienced severe personnel shortages prior to Cox's arrival. In addition to normal attrition, enlistment expirations during the latter half of 1864 caused several regiments' numbers to decline significantly. Losses reduced the 17th Massachusetts from ten companies to four, requiring the transfer of several hundred artillerymen from the 2nd Massachusetts Heavy Artillery. By February 1865, losses had so reduced the 99th New York that it no longer constituted a regiment, and its two remaining companies transferred to the 132nd New York.[9]

The assembling of the Provisional Corps at New Bern required the transfer of units from Morehead City, Fort Macon, Newport, and Roanoke Island. Despite transportation delays, all but two—the 9th New Jersey and 85th New York—arrived in time to deploy in accordance with Cox's timetable. The 85th New York, located on Roanoke Island, arrived late because of the time required to travel across Pamlico Sound.[10]

---

8 Warner, *Generals in Blue*, 74; OR 47, pt. 2, 654.

9 Kirwan, *Memorial History of the Seventeenth Regiment Massachusetts*, 225-229; During August and September 1864, a large number of recruits swelled the ranks of the 2nd Massachusetts Heavy Artillery to nearly 2,000 men. The War Department issued orders that winter to redistribute about 400 of them to the 17th Massachusetts.

10 OR 47, pt. 2, 674.

Palmer reduced the units stationed in outlying garrisons but still maintained a military presence for security and civil order. To fill the void, he relied on North Carolina Union volunteers and African American regiments. At Beaufort, Morehead City, and Fort Macon, departure of the 9th New Jersey and 17th Massachusetts required the soldiers of the 1st North Carolina (Union) and the 1st North Carolina Colored Heavy Artillery to assume garrison responsibilities. Palmer doubted the reliability of the Unionists based on previous incidents. Throughout 1864, the Union volunteers showed a tendency to desert when faced with the possibility of capture, a fear manifested by the Confederates' hanging of 22 soldiers from the 2nd North Carolina (Union) at Kinston in February 1864.[11]

In New Bern, Palmer reduced the strength of the city's fortifications to maximize the number of men available for field service. He relieved the 15th Connecticut of provost duties and ordered five companies of the 2nd Massachusetts Heavy Artillery, along with Battery A, 3rd New York Light Artillery to trade their cannons for rifles. To replace the departing artillerymen, Palmer ordered the 5th Rhode Island Heavy Artillery and the 23rd New York Independent Battery to garrison the vacated forts. Colonel Charles H. Stewart of the 3rd New York Light Artillery assumed responsibility for New Bern's defenses.[12]

Troops from Meagher's disbanded Provisional Division served to further strengthen Carter and Palmer's divisions. Cox's decision to disband Meagher's command was not surprising given Grant and Halleck's dissatisfaction with his earlier deployment to North Carolina. When Meagher's command departed Tennessee, the Irishman went ahead to New York City with the understanding that his men would travel from there to North Carolina. However, the Quartermaster Department had changed the embarkation point to Annapolis,

---

11 Ibid., 621. Palmer also directed the 2nd Massachusetts Heavy Artillery to leave Company G to garrison Fort Macon. Paul Branch, *Fort Macon: A History* (Charleston, SC, 1999), 239; On February 27, 1865, the depleted units of the 2nd North Carolina (Union) consolidated with 1st North Carolina (Union) at Morehead City; The 1st North Carolina Colored Heavy Artillery garrisoned Fort Macon. On March 17, 1865, its designation changed to the 14th U.S. Colored Heavy Artillery; Paul Branch, "Shelter for Buffaloes," http://friendsoffortmacon.org/archives/shelter-for-buffaloes/.

12 Company K of the 15th Connecticut performed provost duties in New Bern through March 8. The company arrived at the battlefield at Wise's Forks on the afternoon of March 9; *OR* 47, pt. 2, 655, 684-685. Stewart was a commander with no units. His five field batteries were attached to Palmer's and Carter's divisions.

Maryland. With the commander absent, confusion reigned among the officers and men. Although Meagher rejoined his command at New Bern, he had long since lost the confidence of his superiors.[13]

An irate Grant wrote to Halleck, "If he has lost his men it will afford a favorable pretext for doing what the service would have lost nothing by having done long ago—dismissing him." When Meagher caught up with his command at New Bern, he settled in as if nothing had happened. On the day Cox arrived at New Bern, Meagher hosted a party at Camp Chattanooga. A local newspaper described the gathering as "quite animated" with a "bountiful supply of eatables and drinkables." Meagher's guests included Carter, Palmer, and other senior officers.[14]

Meagher's casual leadership style proved to be his undoing. On February 24, Schofield relieved him of command. Meagher did not receive official notification until March 1, possibly due to Palmer's absence from New Bern until February 28.[15]

With Meagher's departure, Cox reassigned his three brigades to Palmer's and Carter's divisions. These brigades lacked sufficient officers, and the men either formed battalions or filled out under-strength regiments. Despite the challenges, Cox had achieved much in a matter of days, demonstrating the initiative and leadership that Schofield expected. A surgeon from the 23rd Massachusetts described Cox's hastily assembled Provisional Corps as a "queerish medley," a mixture of veteran Eastern and Western troops combined with raw recruits and bounty jumpers.[16]

Cox, however, faced a greater challenge with logistics, which hampered his effort to capture Goldsboro. Lack of transportation was his "chief embarrassment," limiting his ability to advance without outdistancing his supply points. A meager 50 supply wagons and mule teams were available to resupply his 13,000-man corps. Because of the importance of repairing the

13 OR 47, pt. 2, 501, 509. On February 20, 1865, Grant ordered Schofield to relieve Meagher. The army published an official order on February 24, 1865, which directed Meagher to report to Washington, D.C. for further orders.

14 Ibid., 318; *North Carolina Times* (New Bern), March 3, 1865. Camp Chattanooga was located on the Trent River across from New Bern to accommodate several thousand men of Meagher's command.

15 OR 47, pt. 2, 561; pt. 1, 931.

16 James A. Emmerton, *A Record of the Twenty-Third Regiment Mass. Vol. Infantry in the War of the Rebellion 1861-1865* (Boston, MA, 1886), 243.

Brig. Gen. Thomas F. Meagher
Library of Congress

railroad, Cox further reduced the supply wagon allotment to 10 per division, allocating the balance to Col. W. W. Wright's railroad construction teams. To mitigate the shortage of wagons, Cox planned for his infantry to remain close to the railroad, which sacrificed speed and maneuverability. He estimated that his forces could advance no farther than six miles from the repaired rail line.

Faced with the limitations of the railroad and wagons, Cox directed his staff to plan for using the Neuse River as an alternate mode of forwarding supplies. Cox's previous service in the Western Theater had taught him a valuable lesson in using rivers as a supply route. He ordered the Quartermaster Department to made available shallow-draft steamers and barges that could transport supplies upriver or ferry troops across.[17]

In December 1862, Union Maj. Gen. John G. Foster had demonstrated the feasibility of using the river as a supply line to Kinston during his Goldsboro expedition. To open the Neuse as far as Kinston, the Federals had to remove channel obstructions above New Bern designed to block the Confederate ironclad gunboat CSS *Neuse*. They had considerable difficulty removing the obstacles and were unable to open the river until March 6.

Union river transport was risky as long as the CSS *Neuse* maintained a presence near Kinston. However, Cox wanted river transportation at New Bern ready to move at a moment's notice. The shortage of pontoon bridge equipment also hampered Cox's plans, for it compelled him to use known bridge and ferry sites the Confederates had already destroyed before withdrawing. The War Department's decision to withhold the XXIII Corps'

17 *OR* 47, pt. 2, 683-684; pt. 1, 975-975; pt. 2, 707; On March 5, 1865, Cox notified the naval element at New Bern of his plan to utilize the Neuse River. See, *OR* 47, pt. 2, 696.

wagons and bridging equipment during the transfer to North Carolina forced Cox to improvise.[18]

The Provisional Corps would move along the Atlantic & North Carolina Railroad, thereby providing security to Colonel Wright's construction teams and facilitating resupply of Cox's advancing forces. The area between New Bern and Kinston was difficult to operate in because it consisted of low-lying areas, large impassable swamps, and but few roads. The Dover Swamp alone extended nearly from New Bern to Kinston. Two main roads ran along the fringes of the Dover Swamp: the Neuse Road to the north and the Trent Road to the south. The Neuse Road followed the Neuse River, while the Trent Road coursed along the Trent River, with the Dover Swamp resting in between. The railroad ran along a causeway through the middle of the swamp. Cox discovered the Neuse Road was closer to the railroad than was the Trent Road, which dipped farther to the south.[19]

Cox selected the rail crossing at Core Creek, nine miles west of Batchelder's Creek, as the assembly point for units clearing out of New Bern and for those still en route. He placed a higher priority on commencing the operation than on allowing time to organize the recently formed brigades in Carter's and Palmer's divisions. Time was no friend to Cox. He recognized that the longer he delayed the start of the campaign, the more time the Confederates would have to concentrate against him.

Late on March 1, Cox issued detailed orders to initiate the march to Core Creek the following day. In order to enable Wright to begin repairing the railroad, Palmer's division marched west along the railroad bed to clear it of Confederate mounted forces. Simultaneously, Carter's division used the Neuse Road to travel to the Dover Road fork, leaving one brigade there before continuing its march along the Dover Road to the Core Creek crossing. The Dover Road cut through the swamp, crossing the railroad at Gum Swamp and Tracey Swamp on a course that led through Wise's Forks toward Kinston. In order to minimize wheeled traffic on the railroad bed, the supply trains and

18 Tyndall, *Threshold of Freedom: Lenoir County During the Civil War* (Goldsboro, NC, 1984), 60, 105-106. Tyndall observed that the Neuse was a highly unpredictable river, characterized by shifting sand bars, underwater obstacles, and constant depth changes. *OR* 47, pt. 2, 683-684, 707.

19 J. Waldo Denny, *Wearing the Blue of the Twenty-Fifth Mass. Volunteer Infantry, with Burnside's Coast Division, 18th Army Corps, and the Army of the James* (Worcester, MA, 1879), 209; John G. Barrett, *The Civil War in North Carolina* (Chapel Hill, NC, 1963), 286.

Col. Peter J. Claassen
U.S. Army Military History Institute

artillery of both Union divisions followed Carter's route along the Neuse Road.[20]

Colonel Peter J. Claassen's 132nd New York, stationed at Batchelder's Creek, spearheaded the advance. Claassen, a 34-year-old Dutch immigrant, had commanded the regiment since its formation in July 1862, the majority of the unit's service having been in eastern North Carolina. The regiment suffered its worst combat loss in February 1864 during Gen. George Pickett's Confederate advance on New Bern. Three of Claassen's companies had fought a desperate delaying action at the Neuse Road Bridge, resulting in 91 killed, wounded or captured.[21]

Palmer ordered Claassen to occupy the rail crossing at Core Creek, leaving behind a small force to maintain the picket line. Based on the 132nd New York's duty location, Palmer's decision to employ Claassen's New Yorkers was an obvious choice. However, the 132nd also possessed considerable knowledge of the routes, terrain, and Confederate defenses near Kinston. The 132nd New York was composed of white and Native American soldiers from the Empire State's Six Iroquois Nations. In June 1864, the unit participated in a raid toward Kinston in which Lt. Cornelius C. Cusick and his fellow Iroquois assisted in the capture of Col. George N. Faulk, commander of the 6th North Carolina Cavalry, and 44 other men at Southwest Creek.[22]

---

20 *OR* 47, pt. 1, 974-975.

21 *New York Times*, January 1, 1897.

22 Laurence M. Hauptman, *A Seneca Indian in the Union Army: The Civil War Letters of Sergeant Isaac Newton Parker, 1861-1865* (Shippensburg, PA, 1995), 40; During the June 1864 raid toward Kinston, Claassen commanded a force of approximately 800 infantry and cavalry.

A previously unpublished image of
Lt. Cornelius C. Cusick, Co. D,
132nd New York Infantry
Wade Sokolosky Collection

Claassen assigned Capt. Thomas B. Green and four companies the mission of securing the rail crossing at Core Creek. Captain Green was a proven officer and highly respected by his regimental commander. The speed with which Green carried out his orders is a testament not only to his abilities as a leader, but also to the regiment. Claassen received the order at 11:00 p.m. on March 1, and by 2:00 a.m., Green had already departed. Aided by darkness, Green's detachment proceeded without incident, reaching Core Creek by sunrise. They secured the crossing and awaited the arrival of follow-on units.[23]

At 4:00 a.m., the remaining companies of the regiment, along with Battery D, 3rd New York Light Artillery departed under the command of Lt. Col. George H. Hitchcock. Hitchcock's column marched west along the Neuse and Dover Roads toward Green's position. Claassen departed at sunrise with Company B of the 12th New York Cavalry and reached Green by noon. Claassen's command had completed the move within 12 hours of receiving orders.[24]

With his first objective secured, Cox began moving his remaining units toward Kinston. Another regiment with knowledge of the area, Col. James W. Savage's 12th New York Cavalry, departed its campsite at Rocky Run Creek along the Trent Road, moving west to a point opposite Core Creek Station. Its

23 *OR* 47, pt. 1, 988; Edwin L. Williams to father, February 20, 1865. Private Williams was one of several hundred Provisional soldiers from Illinois regiments assigned to the 132nd New York as temporary replacements. Williams served in Captain Green's company and wrote very fondly of the officer's caring leadership.

24 *OR* 47, pt. 1, 988-989. Claassen reported that he departed Batchelder's Creek with the outposts intact; Sergeant Patrick Ryan of Company B recorded that his unit and one other (possibly Company F) remained at the guard posts along Batchelder's Creek through March 8. Ryan's company departed for the front on the morning of March 9. Patrick Ryan, diary, Manuscripts Division, Library of Congress, Washington, D.C.

task was to screen the corps' southern flank. Savage's orders were to open communication between Gum Swamp and the assembly area at Core Creek. Cox also ordered Savage's troopers to reconnoiter as far west as possible along the Trent Road to confirm the presence of Confederate forces. According to the most recent credible intelligence, Cox believed that enemy troops operating between New Bern and Kinston were "not of the most reliable character."[25]

Most of Cox's corps began the march on March 3, contending with with foul weather and muddy roads. Some units required an entire day to march the nine miles from New Bern to Batchelder's Creek. As the columns continued past the creek, they encountered additional obstacles in the form of felled trees across the roads, which delayed progress until axe-wielding pioneer troops could clear a path.

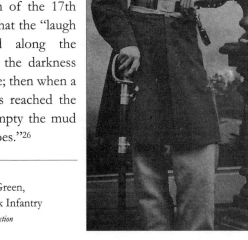

The long columns of soldiers, horses, and artillery batteries churned and thus worsened the already horrendous state of the roads. It was not uncommon for men to sometimes sink up to their knees in the muck. Private Thomas Kirwan of the 17th Massachusetts recalled that the "laugh of hundreds sounded along the column as someone in the darkness would walk into the mire; then when a dry spot of ground was reached the victims proceeded to empty the mud and water from their shoes."[26]

Capt. Thomas B. Green,
Co. D, 132nd New York Infantry
Wade Sokolosky Collection

25 OR 47, pt. 1, 974; pt. 2, 684; Companies A and B of the 23rd New York Cavalry were attached to the 12th New York Cavalry. *Supplement to the Official Records of the Union and Confederate Armies*, 100 vols. (Wilmington, NC, 1994-1999), pt. 2, vol. 53, 697. Company A and men not dismounted from Company B departed New Bern with the 12th New York on March 3, 1865.

26 Kirwan, *Memorial History of the Seventeenth Regiment Massachusetts*, 322.

Bvt. Maj. Gen. Thomas H. Ruger
Library of Congress

By the evening of March 5, General Ruger had arrived with his division. The 31-year-old Ruger was a native of Wisconsin and the son of an Episcopal minister. A graduate of the West Point class of 1854, Ruger served briefly in the Army Corps of Engineers before resigning to practice law in his hometown. Ruger began the Civil War as lieutenant colonel of the 3rd Wisconsin and within two months had been promoted to colonel of the regiment. In August 1862, Ruger had the misfortune of serving under Maj. Gen. Nathaniel P. Banks in the Shenandoah Valley and at Cedar Mountain, where Maj. Gen. Thomas J. "Stonewall" Jackson routed the Federals. In September 1862, Ruger commanded a brigade in the XII Corps during the Maryland campaign. Wounded in the battle of Antietam, he later returned to command his brigade at Chancellorsville and temporarily led a XII Corps division at Gettysburg.[27]

When the XI and XII corps transferred to the Western Theater, Ruger remained a brigade commander and continued in that capacity when the two consolidated to form the XX Corps. After the Atlanta campaign, Ruger accompanied Maj. Gen. George H. Thomas's command into Tennessee. During the battle of Franklin, Ruger commanded a division of the XXIII Corps, where his heroism earned him a major general's brevet.[28]

With the arrival of Ruger's division, all of Cox's Provisional Corps had settled into camps around Core Creek. Cox halted briefly to establish the brigade organizations as specified in General Order No. 2, as not all the brigades had completely formed before departing New Bern.

27 *OR* 47, pt. 1, 939; Warner, *Generals in Blue*, 415-416.

28 Ibid.

Brigadier Gen. Edward Harland's brigade of Palmer's division departed New Bern without the 9th New Jersey and 85th New York. Both units were still en route from their previous garrisons. In the case of Lt. Col. Henry Splaine's brigade of Carter's division, the 25th Massachusetts and Battery A, 3rd New York Light Artillery arrived at Core Creek before their brigade commander. Lack of transportation had delayed Splaine and his regiment, the 17th Massachusetts, at Newport until the morning of March 4.[29]

During the movement from New Bern, Cox deemed the District of Beaufort units poorly prepared for such a campaign. He described the troops as "slow getting in motion . . . a movement which our old troops would have made in a day, it will take these two or three to make." Cox thought his Western soldiers far superior to their Eastern counterparts. General Schofield agreed, later describing Palmer's command as "little better than militia."[30]

Harland's brigade, consisting of the 23rd Massachusetts and the 2nd Massachusetts Heavy Artillery—both augmented with Provisional soldiers—endured a grueling, 17-mile march over two days, reaching Core Creek on the night of March 4. For the former heavy artillerymen, the tiresome march contrasted sharply with their less demanding garrison duties at New Bern.[31]

Palmer's Third Brigade, commanded by Col. Horace Boughton, departed New Bern at mid-morning on March 4 and completed the same 17 miles in nine hours. Boughton led the only brigade in the two District divisions composed entirely of soldiers en route to Sherman's army. The 18th Wisconsin consisted of veterans from the Western Theater returning from furlough. The brigade's remaining two Provisional battalions contained hundreds of new recruits led by experienced officers, such as Prussian-born Maj. Theodore Stimming of the 31st Iowa, who had briefly led his regiment during the Atlanta campaign and was now returning from leave.[32]

Assistant Surgeon James A. Emmerton of the 23rd Massachusetts described the Western men as "a new type" of soldier compared to the veterans

29 OR 47, pt. 1, 984; Kirwan, *Memorial History to the Seventeenth Regiment Massachusetts*, 258-259.

30 OR 47, pt. 1, 931; pt. 2, 743.

31 Ibid., pt. 1, 984; Only two of the four regiments that constituted Harland's brigade were at New Bern at the time of departure. The 9th New Jersey and 85th New York were still en route.

32 OR 47, pt. 1, 931.

from eastern North Carolina. He wrote that the Westerners were "undisciplined and seemed never to have so much as heard of any deference to rank . . . [with a] long, slim, swarthy appearance capable of getting over much ground and pushing forward with every appearance of cheerful alacrity."[33]

Inexperience in the District units led to supply shortages. Cox had directed that each soldier have three days' rations in his haversack, enough to last until resupplied at Core Creek. In the veteran divisions, Cox's order was routine. Because of their haste in departing New Bern, however, several new brigades failed to comply with Cox's General Order No. 2. As a result, when Battery A, 3rd New York Light Artillery arrived at Core Creek on the evening of March 3, the soldiers were already short of rations. Private Charles A. Tournier wrote, "March 4, we remained in camp all day and had very little to eat as we were to be assigned to a brigade which has not taken place yet and our rations have run out and we can't draw from the brigade supply train on account of not belonging to any." For Cox, this was just the beginning of his supply problems.[34]

Nevertheless, Colonel Wright's railroad engineers had managed to keep pace with Cox's troops, repairing the railroad to within a mile of Core Creek. To facilitate Cox's supply effort, Wright rushed forward railcars loaded with ammunition and rations. In turn, details from Ruger's division aided Wright's railroad construction effort by cutting new rail ties. To the Western soldiers, the longleaf pine trees of North Carolina presented a novel sight. "These are the strangest looking pine trees," wrote one soldier, "60 feet tall, straight as a new nail and the only branches were at the very top."[35]

A wide, water-filled ditch next to the railroad prevented the use of mule teams, so the soldiers carried the rough-cut wood from the forest up to the rail bed. Private James O'Connell of the 130th Indiana noted the irony of their labors: "Someone thought we should be doing something, so we went to work repairing the railroad. I should have kept track of how many times we've had to work on railroad tracks, but I suppose it doesn't matter much difference as we've probably torn up as much as we've repaired."[36]

33 Ibid., 991; Emmerton, *A Record of the Twenty-Third Regiment Mass.*, 243.

34 *OR* 47, pt. 2, 638; Charles A. Tournier, diary, March 4, 1865, East Carolina Manuscripts Collection, East Carolina University, Greenville, North Carolina.

35 *OR*, Series 3, vol. 5, 30-33. Wright had prepositioned stocks of pre-cut rail ties for use at Batchelder's Creek; Lawrence, *Grandfather's Civil War Diary*, 271.

36 Lawrence, *Grandfather's Civil War Diary*, 271-272.

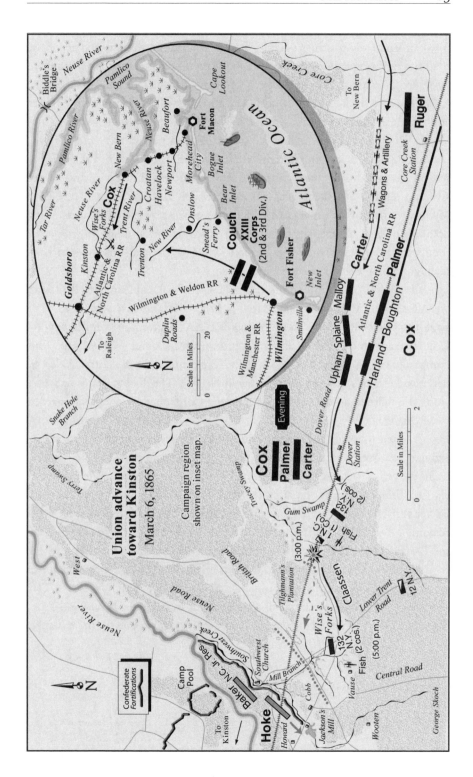

Union advance
toward Kinston
March 6, 1865

Campaign region
shown on inset map.

Unfortunately for the Federals, the Confederates had damaged all of the road and rail bridges along their route, and Wright's engineers had to rebuild the structures. To assist Wright, Ruger's soldiers provided the bulk of the hard labor. For one bridge, an Indiana soldier noted they had to cut down 60 trees and then roll them up to the roadbed. To operate the railroad west of Core Creek, Wright's engineers had to reconstruct the entire 100-foot bridge.[37]

In addition to assisting Wright, Ruger's veterans corduroyed the existing wagon roads to make them passable. The work was difficult owing to the swampy terrain. Seventeen-year-old Pvt. Charles L. Cummings of the 28th Michigan wrote of his experience, "I fell off a cypress log into the water, nearly up to my neck. A regiment of cavalry was passing on the corduroy, when one of them called out, 'Hey web foot, get on to your bureau and float over.' I have been gunning for that man ever since."[38]

With his corps assembled and resupplied, Cox ordered Palmer to deploy an advance guard. At 7:00 p.m. on March 5, Colonel Claassen received orders to seize the Dover Road railroad crossing at Gum Swamp, seven miles beyond Core Creek. Once again, Claassen sent forward Captain Green and four companies of the 132nd New York as the lead element for the corps. Aided by darkness, Green's column marched unmolested. The Federals headed west along the railroad and seized the abandoned Confederate works that guarded the crossing site.[39]

Claassen followed the next morning with the remainder of the regiment, arriving at Green's location before noon. The brigade's artillery and wagon trains moved west along the Dover Road, while the Provisional regiment under Lt. Col. Frank S. Curtiss repaired the road toward Gum Swamp. Palmer and Carter's divisions followed Claassen's advance. Palmer moved west with his remaining brigades along the railroad, while Carter's brigades marched along the Dover Road. The two divisions reached Gum Swamp by evening where they established camp and awaited further orders. Ruger's division remained at Core Station, providing security and work details for Wright's crews. Cox ordered the 12th New York Cavalry to place squadrons on the Neuse and Trent Roads to provide surveillance along the corps' northern and southern flanks.

37 Ibid.; OR, Series 3, vol. 5, 33.

38 Charles L. Cummings, *The Great War Relic: Valuable as a Curiosity of the Rebellion* (Harrisonburg, PA, n.d.), 4.

39 OR 47, pt. 1, 989; 981. Companies, C, D, E, and K comprised Captain Green's detachment.

Capt. George W. Graham,
Co. L., 1st NC Union Volunteers
U.S. Army Frontier Museum, Fort Leavenworth, KS

The mounted infantry of Capt. George
W. Graham's Company L, 1st North
Carolina (Union) and two 12-pound
mountain howitzers, commanded by
Capt. Joseph M. Fish, augmented the
squadron operating on the Neuse
Road.[40]

The 23-year-old Graham boasted a
reputation as a hard fighter, but was
also a notorious "bad man" given to
gambling, drinking, and chasing
women. Though "a scourge to the poor
people inhabiting" the state's coastal region, Graham's heroic deeds had earned
him praise from superiors. Because of his fearlessness, Graham's mounted
infantry company was the only unit from the 1st North Carolina (Union) to
participate in Cox's operation to capture Goldsboro.[41]

Palmer reached Claassen's forward position shortly after noon and ordered
the colonel to advance three miles farther west to Wise's Forks. Anticipating
strong enemy resistance, Claassen deployed his entire regiment, supported by
Graham's mounted company and Captain Fish's artillery. Claassen's force had
traveled only a short distance when they encountered stiff Confederate
resistance at Tracey Swamp. Aided by Fish's guns, Graham's mounted infantry
and two companies of Green's New Yorkers quickly forced the Confederates to
abandon their forward position. Pressing on, Claassen encountered no further
opposition, and by 4:30 p.m. had reached Wise's Forks.[42]

Able to observe Confederate activity farther west on the Dover Road,
Claassen positioned a strong skirmish line well forward toward Southwest

40 Ibid., 932, 981, 989. Captain Fish commanded Company A, 12th New York Cavalry.

41 Kirwan, *Memorial History of the Seventeenth Regiment Massachusetts*, 133; W. L. Pohoresky, *The Notorious George W. Graham During the Civil War* (Havelock, NC, 1982), 204-205.

42 *OR* 47, pt. 1, 981, 989.

Creek. Because of his vulnerable advanced position, Claassen also deployed skirmishers along the British and Lower Trent Roads to provide warning in case of an enemy advance. Having successfully accomplished his task, Claassen reported his progress to Palmer.

To date, Cox had enjoyed a relatively uneventful campaign. The Confederates had offered minimal resistance to his advance, and aside from the struggles with logistics, Cox's deployment had proceeded well. By the evening of March 6, the Union army was a hard day's march from Kinston. In support of Cox's advance, Schofield had ordered Maj. Gen. Darius N. Couch and the Second and Third Divisions of the XXIII Corps to advance north from Wilmington. Couch's column departed the port city on March 6, moving north toward Kinston.[43]

Located on the banks of the Neuse River, the town of Kinston had thus far remained relatively untouched by the ravages of the war. In December 1862, it had endured a brief Union occupation by forces under Gen. John G. Foster, who withdrew to New Bern several days later. With his departure, the Confederates regained the town and had since maintained control. As a counter to future Union threats, Confederate forces garrisoned Kinston and strengthened their position with a series of fixed artillery emplacements and infantry entrenchments along the approaches to New Bern.[44]

The Confederate defense of Kinston in March 1865 exploited existing earthworks three miles east of town along the western bank of Southwest Creek. At the time, all of the wagon roads from New Bern and Wilmington to Kinston traversed Southwest Creek, as did the Atlantic & North Carolina Railroad. Combined with the surrounding swampy terrain, Southwest Creek—with its considerable width, troublesome depth, and steep banks—presented a formidable obstacle to any attacking force. The Confederates further strengthened the line with substantial earthworks and artillery emplacements. Spanning about five miles, the defensive line along the

---

43 Ibid., 932; pt. 2, 694-695. Schofield issued the order to Couch on March 5; Couch was a relatively new division commander in the XXIII Corps, having reported for duty in early December 1864—prior to the battle of Nashville. Couch's reassignment to the corps irritated Schofield, as the new general replaced Ruger as division commander. Couch's seniority also displaced Cox as the senior division commander within the corps. To appease Schofield, Maj. Gen. George Thomas agreed to reconstitute the badly depleted First Division of the XXIII Corps and assigned Ruger as its commander. Connelly, *John M. Schofield*, 140.

44 Tyndall, *Threshold of Freedom*, 63-66.

creek ran from the Neuse Road on the north end to the Upper Trent Road on the south end. Any Federal movement from New Bern along the railroad would have to confront these works. Beyond the Southwest Creek line, Col. John Whitford, the commander at Kinston, had established outposts at Wise's Forks, Gum Swamp, and the crossing at Moseley's Creek on the Neuse Road to give warning of a Union advance from New Bern.[45]

Not surprisingly, Cox's advance provoked an immediate Confederate response. General Bragg acted on General Joseph Johnston's March 3 suggestion of moving against the Federal advance by relocating Hoke's division from Rockfish Creek to Kinston. On March 5, General Hoke and two of his brigades—Kirkland's Tar Heels and Colquitt's Georgians under Colonel Charles Zachry—departed by train. After a cold and windy overnight trip, Hoke and his lead brigades arrived at the Kinston rail station at sunrise. A railroad accident delayed the arrival of his Hoke's remaining brigades, Clingman's Tar Heels under Col. William Devane, and Gen. Johnson Hagood's South Carolinians. Hagood's brigade was the last to depart Rockfish Creek and would not arrive at Kinston until early on March 8.[46]

From his headquarters at Goldsboro, Bragg directed Hoke to prepare to fight. "Push all to the front and be ready for a blow," Bragg instructed. "All arrivals will report to you. Move them to position immediately that no time may be lost after I join." Upon reaching Kinston, Hoke assumed command from Colonel Whitford and established his headquarters at the Sam Howard house near the intersection of the Neuse and Dover Roads. To further strengthen the Southwest Creek defensive line, Hoke positioned Kirkland's and Colquitt's brigades in the trenches along the west bank from Jackson's Mill northward to the Neuse Road. Above of the road, Brig. Gen. Laurence Baker's Junior Reserves brigade defended the bridge.[47]

Early on March 6, Hoke presented Bragg with a bold plan to combine Hoke's command at Kinston with the Army of Tennessee contingent at Smithfield and crush the oncoming Federals. Bragg forwarded Hoke's proposal to General Johnston with the assurance that the concentration "would suffice to insure victory." He informed Johnston that "the enemy's advance was this

45 Barrett, *The Civil War in North Carolina*, 284-285; Tyndall, *Threshold of Freedom*, 93-95; OR 47, pt. 1, 974-975.

46 OR 47, pt. 2, 1,318; Calder, diary, March 5, 1865; Hagood, *Memoirs*, 349-351.

47 OR 47, pt. 2, 1,341, 1,334-1,335.

morning nine miles from Kinston . . . and moving in confidence," indicating that Cox was unaware of the strong Confederate force gathering in his front. Johnston approved committing the Army of Tennessee troops against Cox, but warned Bragg that "these troops are required against Sherman also" and could be spared for a few days only.[48]

Johnston's decision to reinforce Bragg was risky, for Sherman was fast approaching Fayetteville. A narrow window of opportunity existed, however, because the railroad between Smithfield and Kinston allowed the rapid transfer of troops from one front to another. While limiting the time Bragg could use the Army of Tennessee, Johnston nevertheless gave him the chance he sought to defeat Cox.[49]

To confront the Federal advance on the morning of March 7, Hoke mustered about 5,200 infantry along the Southwest Creek defensive line, with an additional 500 en route from Hagood's brigade. With guns from Starr's artillery battalion deployed at each bridge site supporting the infantry, the Confederates posed a considerable threat to the enemy.[50]

Cox recognized the importance of gaining control of Southwest Creek, as it commanded the approaches to Kinston. With two divisions at Gum Swamp, Cox had at his disposal six brigades of infantry and four batteries of artillery along with supporting cavalry. The Union army fielded an estimated 9,000 men, a force seemingly more than sufficient to seize Southwest Creek.[51]

However, instead of pushing forward to seize the critical terrain and bridges on March 7, Cox cautiously advanced only Palmer's division while retaining Carter in reserve at Gum Swamp. Ruger's division—Cox's strongest—would advance only as far as Gum Swamp and remain in reserve. On the Provisional Corps' left flank, Cox ordered Colonel Savage's New York horsemen to seize the bridges over Southwest Creek on the Upper Trent Road and the Wilmington Road.[52]

48 Ibid., 1,334-1,335.

49 Ibid.

50 See Appendix B, Table E for Confederate infantry strength on March 7. Hagood's South Carolina contingent was still en route from Rockfish Creek on March 7. Colonel Starr's artillery battalion fielded 18 guns. See, *OR* 43, pt. 3, 1,321-1,322 for a listing by individual battery.

51 *OR* 47, pt. 1, 975; The 9,000 soldiers comprised the forces deployed from the District of Beaufort. See Cox's official report. *OR* 47, pt. 1, 973, 975.

52 Ibid., 975.

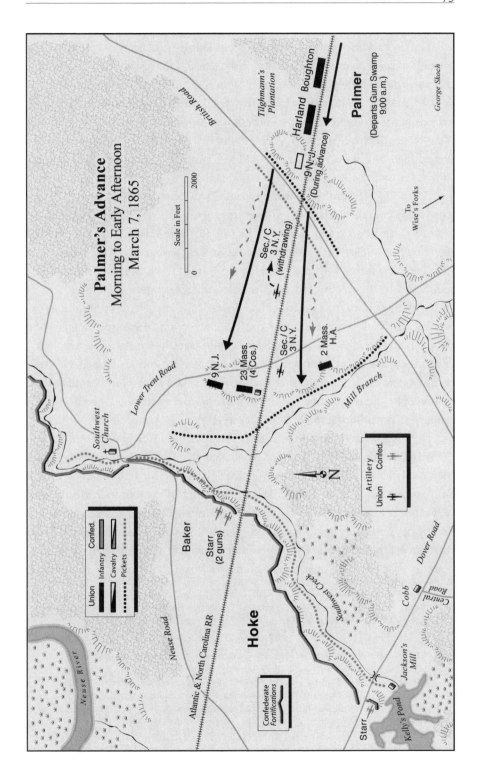

Palmer's Advance
Morning to Early Afternoon
March 7, 1865

Scale in Feet

0   2000

Palmer
(Departs Gum Swamp
9:00 a.m.)

George Skoch

Tilghmann's
Plantation

Harland   Boughton

9 N.J.
(During advance)

To
Wise's Forks

British Road

Sec./C
3 N.Y.
(withdrawing)

9 N.J.   23 Mass.   Sec./C   2 Mass.
(4 Cos.)   3 N.Y.   H.A.

Mill Branch

Lower Trent Road

Southwest Church

N

Artillery
Union   Confed.

Baker

Starr
(2 guns)

Union   Confed.

Infantry

Cavalry

Pickets

Hoke

Neuse River

Neuse Road

Atlantic & North Carolina RR

Southwest Creek

Confederate
Fortifications

Cobb

Dover Road

Central
Road

Jackson's
Mill

Starr

Kelly's Pond

Harland and Boughton's brigades from Palmer's division moved to secure the railroad and Neuse Road bridges to the north. On the morning of March 7, the late arrival of the division supply wagons delayed their departure from first light to 9:00 a.m. The two brigades marched up the railroad, with Harland's brigade in the lead, preceded by four companies of Lt. Col. James Stewarts 9th New Jersey deployed as skirmishers. Palmer cautioned Harland "not to leave the railroad and go down the Trent Road" until Boughton had secured the bridge across the creek.[53]

Although Harland's column met with no Confederate resistance, "there were everywhere abundant signs" that the enemy was nearby. As the 9th New Jersey's skirmishers approached the British Road, the Southerners welcomed them with a volley of musketry that soon led to a heated exchange. The Confederates stubbornly held their ground, but the New Jersey skirmishers, reinforced by the regiment's remaining companies, pressed the Southerners back. By 2:00 p.m., the Federals had forced the enemy to withdraw across Southwest Creek but came under fire from a section of Confederate artillery posted behind the creek. "The Johnnies, who were in strong force, admirably entrenched, not only refused to vacate, but promptly sent back their compliments in the shape of shot and shell," recalled a New Jersey soldier. The Confederate guns belonged to Starr's battalion, which had positioned its artillery at key points along Southwest Creek.[54]

Harland ordered forward a section from Capt. William E. Mercer's Battery C, 3rd New York Light Artillery to silence the Confederate guns. Captain Mercer deployed his two 3-inch ordnance rifles along the railroad between the British and Lower Trent Roads. The accurate fire of the Confederate artillery, however, soon forced him to withdraw. Undaunted, Harland ordered Mercer to deploy his remaining two sections farther up the railroad at the Lower Trent Road crossing. Supported by a battalion of infantry, Mercer deployed his four guns in an open field just south of the railroad. This time, the combined

53 OR 47, pt. 1, 981, 984; James M. Drake, *The History of the Ninth New Jersey Veteran Vols.: A Record of Its Service from Sept. 13th, 1861, to July 12th 1865, With a Complete Official Roster and Sketches of Prominent Member* (Elizabeth, NJ, 1889), 275.

54 Drake, *History of the Ninth New Jersey*, 275; There are no historical records that confirm which battery from Starr's battalion occupied the gun emplacement along the railroad. However, one possible clue lies in Harland's official report of the action, in which he states that they encountered two guns, one rifled and one smoothbore. Only Dickson's Battery (Company E) of Starr's battalion fielded rifled guns, the rest being smoothbores. See, OR 43, pt. 3, 1,321-1,322.

Brig. Gen. Edward Harland
U.S. Army Military History Institute

firepower of Mercer's artillery and the Federal infantry succeeded in silencing the Confederate guns.[55]

The New Jersey skirmishers halted their advance at a fence line approximately 150 yards from the Rebel works along the creek. From their advanced position, the Federals had a clear view across an open field toward the Confederate defenses. Captain Charles Hufty, commander of Company I, came forward to the fence and fell victim to an enemy sharpshooter. A Rebel bullet shattered the young officer's pocket watch into two pieces, carrying one piece directly through his body and mortally wounding him.[56]

To lengthen the Federal line along the Lower Trent Road, Harland deployed Lt. Col. John W. Raymond's 23rd Massachusetts to the right of the 9th New Jersey, up the road up to its junction with the Neuse Road. Surprisingly, Harland failed to seize the railroad bridge or the Neuse Road Bridge when he had the chance. Assuming that the Confederates had destroyed the two bridges, he merely exchanged fire with the enemy for the rest of the afternoon, while Boughton's brigade and Battery D, 3rd New York Light Artillery remained back at the railroad. During Harland's engagement, Palmer remained at Claassen's headquarters near Wise's Forks, leaving the brigade commander to fight the action alone. Palmer's passivity must have been contagious, for the normally aggressive Claassen had allowed almost eight hours of daylight to pass before he began to move toward Southwest Creek. Unaware of Claassen's inaction, Cox erroneously reported to General Schofield

55 *OR* 47, pt. 1, 984-985.

56 *Trenton Evening Times* (Trenton, NJ), August 30, 1883. Captain Hufty died on March 14, 1865, at Foster General Hospital in New Bern.

Capt. Charles Hufty,
Co. I, 9th New Jersey Infantry
U.S. Army Military History Institute

that "Palmer moved early this morning to occupy the various road crossings of Southwest Creek." This, of course, suggested that Cox's orders had been carried out.[57]

Claassen failed to comply with the corps commander's intent. At 2:30 p.m., Palmer wrote Cox from Wise's Forks, notifying him of Harland's engagement to the north but saying nothing about Claassen, presumably because the latter had not yet moved out. Instead, Palmer reported the presence of an estimated 15,000 Confederate troops under Maj. Gen. Robert Hoke in the area. Hoke's name no doubt evoked disturbing memories for Palmer. In April 1864, the Rebel general had captured Plymouth and Washington, North Carolina, and was threatening New Bern when Gen. Robert E. Lee summoned him back to Virginia.[58]

Palmer seemed reluctant to seize the bridge over Southwest Creek at Jackson's Mill, opting instead for a reconnaissance with a mixed force consisting of 300 infantry, a section of artillery, and a company of cavalry. Around 2:00 p.m., Captain Green led the reconnaissance west along the Dover Road, supported by Lt. John Stevenson's section of Battery D, 3rd New York Light Artillery. Upon reaching the intersection at the British Road, Green's force encountered a Confederate skirmish line. A hot exchange quickly developed, during which Sgt. Foster J. Hudson, a Seneca Indian from the 132nd New York, received a severe wound in the knee. The Confederates captured the injured sergeant and relieved him of his watch. When Green's force

---

57 Harland's official report did not indicate Palmer's presence during the afternoon fight of March 7. OR 47, pt. 1, 984-985.

58 Ibid., pt. 2, 723-725. According to Claassen's after-action report, he received the order "about 2:00 p.m." OR 47, pt. 1, 989.

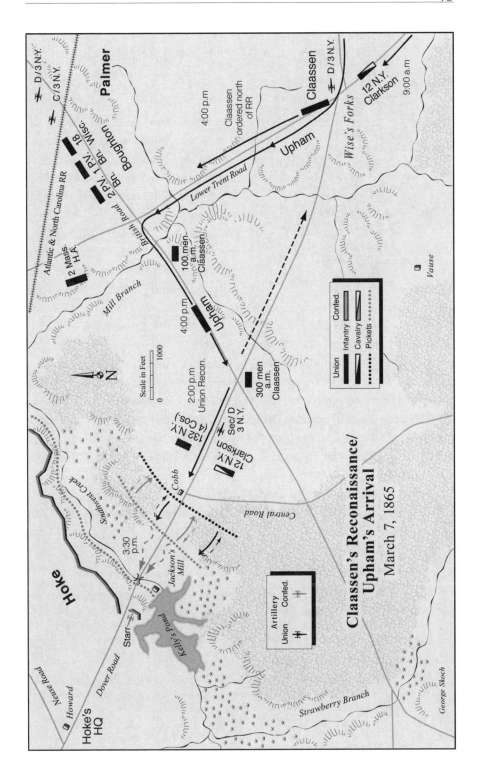

Claassen's Reconaissance/
Upham's Arrival
March 7, 1865

Col. Charles L. Upham
U.S. Army Military History Institute

counterattacked a second time, the Southern troops withdrew, leaving Hudson behind and allowing the New Yorkers to rescue their comrade.[59]

As the Rebel skirmishers fell back to the safety of the creek, Confederate artillery behind Jackson's Mill opened fire on Green's position, preventing any farther advance. For the first time since departing New Bern, the aggressive Green failed to brush aside the enemy. Claassen determined that the Confederate line at Southwest Creek was too strong for Green's detachment and ordered him to withdraw to Wise's Forks.[60]

In response to Palmer's repulse, Cox ordered General Carter to advance his division to Wise's Forks. For most of the day, Carter's division had remained at Gum Swamp awaiting orders. At 2:00 p.m., Col. Charles L. Upham's brigade from Carter's division marched to relieve Claassen, with orders to guard the British Road and the area between the road and Southwest Creek. Near Wise's Forks, Carter placed Col. Adam G. Malloy and Lt. Col. Henry Splaine's brigades across the Dover Road.[61]

Colonel Upham's Second Brigade comprised two veteran regiments: the 15th Connecticut, consisting of 700 officers and men, and the 27th

59 OR 47, pt. 2, 725. Claassen wrote in his official report that Palmer ordered the reconnaissance at 2:00 p.m., and that Major Clarkson led the reconnaissance accompanied by his entire squadron of cavalry, along with Captain Green's infantry and artillery. The 2:00 p.m. reconnaissance was the first action on March 7 in Claassen's report; ibid; Henry Hall and James Hall, *Cayuga in the Field, A Record of the 19th Volunteers, all the Batteries of the 3d New York Artillery and 75th New York Volunteers* (Auburn, NY, 1873), 270; Hauptman, *A Seneca Indian in the Union Army*, 41. Sergeant Hudson died on March 23, 1865, at the military hospital in New Bern.

60 OR 47, pt. 1, 989.

61 Sheldon B. Thorpe, *The History of the Fifteenth Connecticut Volunteers in the War for the Defense of the Union, 1861-1865* (New Haven, CT, 1893), 89. Thorpe recounts that the regiment's pickets were assembled at noon, and by 2:00 p.m. had begun moving toward Claassen; OR 47, pt. 1, 998.

Massachusetts, numbering 217. Due to attrition, both units had been under-strength and received a large number of men from Meagher's old command prior to departing New Bern. The 15th Connecticut was now so large that Upham, serving as brigade commander, divided the regiment into two battalions commanded by Lt. Col. Samuel Tolles and Maj. Eli W. Osborn.[62]

Lieutenant Col. Walter Bartholomew, a colorful and experienced commander, led the 27th Massachusetts. On March 6, before Bartholomew dismissed the regiment for the evening, he addressed the assembled men on what lay ahead the next day: "Boys, we are going into another fight, and I expect you will maintain the honor of the old Twenty-Seventh. Don't run until you see me run, and be sure you mistake no other man for me. When you see *me* going, run like hell."[63]

Around 4:00 p.m., Upham relieved Claassen's brigade, and instructed Colonel Tolles to deploy skirmishers along Southwest Creek to connect with Palmer's division to the north. Captain Minott A. Butricks's Company I deployed south of the Dover Road, while Capt. Julius Bassett's Company A covered the ground north of the road. Both captains pressed their skirmish lines as close to the creek as possible. As the companies moved forward, they drove "the few remaining Confederate skirmishers back across the creek." Bassett's skirmishers had to feel their way along the creek until they connected with Palmer's troops on the right, all while drawing small arms and artillery fire from across the stream. Once established, the dangerously thin 15th Connecticut skirmish line stretched approximately three-quarters of a mile.[64]

The remainder of Tolles's battalion deployed a few hundred yards to the rear, with Company C to the left of the road and Company D to the right. Tolles established his headquarters at the home of Confederate doctor John Cobb, as it provided an excellent view of the Confederate position at Jackson's Mill.[65]

As Tolles deployed his battalion along Southwest Creek, Upham oversaw the deployment of the remaining units. The ground Upham selected for his

---

62 Thorpe, *History of the Fifteenth Connecticut*, 87.

63 Ibid., 459.

64 Ibid., 91-92.

65 Tom J. Edwards and William H. Rowland, *Through the Eyes of Soldiers: The Battle of Wyse Fork, Kinston, North Carolina March 7-10, 1865* (Kinston, NC, 2006), 36. The Cobb house is one of several historic structures from the battle that remain standing. The house is not open to the public.

defensive position consisted of swampland and marshy thickets. Private William P. Derby of the 27th Massachusetts recalled, "The ground was nearly dead level and sloped gently from the British Road to Southwest Creek, only dropping 10 feet in terrain." The ground along the British Road, with its slightly higher elevation, may have been more suitable as a defensive position. Upham selected a point just east of the Cobb house for his brigade headquarters.[66]

Upham deployed Major Osborn's 2nd Battalion, 15th Connecticut on the left side of the Dover Road about 200 yards southeast of the Cobb house. The 27th Massachusetts posted on the right side of the road parallel to Osborn's battalion. Around sundown, Lt. Edgar W. Seymour's two-gun section of 12-pound Napoleon smoothbores from Battery I, 3rd New York Light Artillery replaced Stevenson's section of Battery D. Seymour unlimbered his guns along the road in rear of the main line.[67]

While Upham deployed his brigade, almost a mile to the rear the two remaining brigades of Carter's division established a defensive line across the Dover Road, 200 yards west of Wise's Forks. Malloy's brigade formed a line north of the road, while Splaine deployed his brigade on the south side. The day proved uneventful, enabling the men to build strong defensive works. Carter's decision to post the two brigades at Wise's Forks left Upham's position dangerously isolated.[68]

Meanwhile, Cox refused to relinquish the initiative to the Confederates. Late that afternoon, he ordered Palmer "to test the condition of the Neuse Road crossing and [the] presence of the enemy there" by sending one regiment north to the intersection. However, neither Palmer nor his subordinates acknowledged carrying out the corps commander's order.[69]

By nightfall, only one company from Harland's 2nd Massachusetts Heavy Artillery had deployed troops at the junction of the British and Neuse Roads. The remainder of the division assumed a defensive posture south of the Neuse Road on the Lower Trent and British Roads. Harland's 23rd Massachusetts and

66 William P. Derby, *Bearing Arms in the Twenty-Seventh Massachusetts Regiment of Volunteer Infantry During the Civil War 1861-1865* (Boston, MA, 1883), 461.

67 Hall and Hall, *Cayuga in the Field*, 270. Stevenson's section returned to Battery D's location north of the railroad.

68 OR 47, pt. 1, 994.

69 Cox, *Military Reminiscences of the Civil War*, 2 vols. (New York, NY, 1900), vol. 2, 432; OR 47, pt. 1, 976.

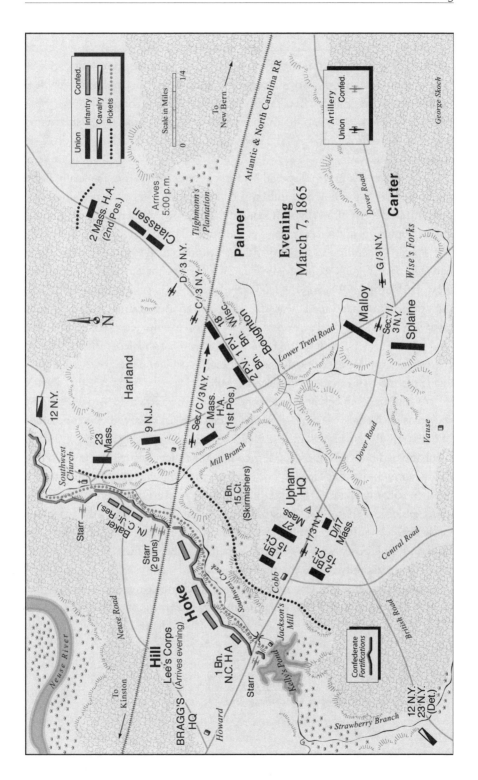

Evening
March 7, 1865

9th New Jersey occupied positions along the Lower Trent Road, with skirmishers positioned in front of the Confederate defenses along the creek. A mile to the rear along the British Road, the 2nd Massachusetts Heavy Artillery established a picket line, while Palmer placed Boughton's brigade south of the railroad. Claassen, who had finally moved from Wise's Forks, established a line north of the railroad, posting Batteries C and D of the 3rd New York Light Artillery in the center.[70]

Like Carter, Palmer had spread his forces dangerously thin, especially along the Lower Trent Road, where only two regiments were in position. Palmer had concentrated most of his division along the British Road, thereby protecting his line of communication to the rear via the railroad.

Toward evening, an artillery duel commenced along the Dover Road between Starr's guns at Jackson's Mill and Lieutenant Seymour's section of New York artillery. During the exchange, neither side gained the upper hand, but the infantry stationed near the guns found the errant artillery rounds terrifying. Starr observed a strong force of Union infantry east of the creek and strengthened his position during the night. Lieutenant Halcott Pride Jones of Battery B, 13th Battalion North Carolina Light Artillery placed one of his guns inside the works to the left of Jackson's Mill.[71]

As night fell, an eerie calm descended upon the battlefield, broken only by the occasional crack of small arms fire. Aided by darkness, the two companies of Connecticut skirmishers moved closer to the creek and dug rifle pits. As each company had only one shovel, the men used bayonets, plates, and cups to dig. Oddly enough, neither Upham nor his men thought to entrench, indicating a lapse in judgment and discipline on the part of everyone from the brigade commander down to the enlisted men, all of whom knew the value of fieldworks from their combat experience in Virginia. The only diligence displayed by Upham was requiring the men to sleep on their weapons due to their close proximity to the enemy.[72]

The hollow thud of axes striking wood soon broke the stillness along the creek. Captain Reuben Waterman of Company F, 15th Connecticut later wrote, "Major Osborn and myself were watching the Confederate line in our front. My

---

70 *OR* 47, pt. 1, 981-982, 985-987.

71 Halcott Pride Jones, diary, March 7, 1865, Museum of the Confederacy. Stevenson's section fired an estimated 100 rounds before withdrawing.

72 Thorpe, *The History of the Fifteenth Connecticut*, 81.

Capt. Reuben Waterman,
Co. F, 15th Connecticut Infantry
Wade Sokolosky Collection

company was on picket on the extreme right; at intervals we heard the sound of axes opposite us, across the creek and knew works of some kind were being constructed there." Veteran officers such as Osborn and Waterman assumed the enemy was building strong fortifications, and that tough work lay ahead for the attacking force. Unknown to the officers, however, the noise indicated that the Confederates were preparing to attack.[73]

Worse yet for the Federals, Palmer's and Carter's tactical dispositions invited disaster. A mile-long gap along the Lower Trent Road separated the two divisions. Only their picket lines connected along the banks of Southwest Creek and Mill Branch. Moreover, Carter's placement of Upham a mile beyond his main line showed a reckless disregard for the enemy lurking nearby. If the Confederates were to reach the Lower Trent Road, they could drive a wedge between the two Federal divisions and possibly fight them one at a time and defeat them in detail.[74]

* * *

As the opposing forces under Cox and Hoke concentrated at Southwest Creek, elements of the Army of Tennessee boarded railcars at Smithfield and headed for Kinston. Major Gen. Daniel H. Hill, the newly assigned commander of Ed Johnson's division of Stephen D. Lee's Corps, received orders from General Johnston to proceed to Kinston and cooperate with Bragg. Aware that

73 Ibid., 231.

74 Due to Schofield's anticipated arrival on the morning of March 8, Cox's headquarters remained at Gum Swamp along with Ruger's. Cox, *Military Reminiscences*, vol. 2, 434. Mill Branch is sometimes referred to as Cabin Branch Creek.

Hill despised Bragg, Johnston appealed to his patriotism: "I beg you to forget the past for this emergency."[75]

By all accounts, Hill was welcomed back into the Army of Tennessee by its soldiers—even by one of Bragg's few admirers, Lt. Col. C. Irvine Walker of the 10th South Carolina. Walker, who had traveled with Hill on the train from Charlotte to Smithfield, became quite acquainted with the controversial North Carolinian. Obviously struck by their discussions, Walker wrote his wife, "I think he [Hill] will make a most magnificent division commander." He described Hill as "a very modest unassuming gentlemen, and hope that he may prove (and I believe that he will) as good a general as he is a gentlemen." Captain James A. Hall, a company commander in the 24th Alabama, wrote to his father about Hill: "I like him very much."[76]

As the senior officer at Smithfield, Hill assumed temporary command of Lee's Corps. On March 7, about 1,300 of Hill's men were camped at Smithfield. Hill departed for Kinston with his division and Brig. Gen. Edmund W. Pettus's brigade from Stevenson's division, arriving at dusk.

Colonel John G. Coltart, the commander of Brig. Gen. Zachariah C. Deas's brigade, assumed leadership of D. H. Hill's division. The 39-year-old Coltart was a Huntsville, Alabama native, and had been a bookseller, druggist, and insurance agent prior to the Civil War. As colonel of the 26th Alabama (later redesignated as the 50th Alabama), Coltart led the regiment at Shiloh, where he was seriously wounded. Upon his return, he was wounded a second time during the Atlanta campaign at the battle of Ezra Church. After General Deas was wounded at the battle of Franklin in November 1864, Coltart assumed command of the brigade.[77]

Hill's division consisted of Manigault's brigade (commanded by Lt. Col. John C. Carter) and Deas's brigade (led by Col. Harry T. Toulmin). The remaining division under Maj. Gen. Henry D. Clayton, comprising Stovall's brigade (Col. Henry C. Kellogg) and Jackson's brigade (Lt. Col. James C.

---

75 *OR* 47, pt. 2, 1,317-1,318.

76 White and Runion, eds., *Great Things Are Expected of Us*, 172; James A. Hall to father, March 14, 1865, Bolling Hall Family Papers, Alabama Department Archives and History, Montgomery, Alabama.

77 For biographical information on Coltart, the authors consulted Allardice, *Confederate Colonels*, 108. Colonel Coltart would survive the war, only to died in 1868 in a lunatic asylum in Tuscaloosa.

Maj. Gen. Henry De Lamar Clayton
Alabama Department of Archives and History,
Montgomery, Alabama

Gordon) departed later that night and arrived at Kinston the following morning.[78]

Henry De Lamar Clayton was 38 years old in March 1865. A lawyer by profession, he had been a member of the Alabama legislature when the Civil War broke out. In 1862, Clayton led the 39th Alabama during Bragg's failed Kentucky invasion and the battle of Stones River. He was severely wounded during the latter fight, but soon recovered and went on to command a brigade at Chickamauga. In July 1864, Clayton received a promotion to major general and assumed command of Stewart's division. During the Atlanta campaign, Clayton had three horses shot from under him during the fighting at Jonesboro. After the army's disaster at Nashville, General Hood commended Clayton for his rearguard action, which enabled the Confederates to retreat unmolested.[79]

In conjunction with Hill's movement east, Bragg departed Goldsboro that afternoon to assume command at Kinston. With the addition of Hill's Army of Tennessee contingent, Bragg's hastily assembled force at Kinston numbered about 6,100 infantry. Later that evening at the Samuel Howard house, Generals Bragg, Hill, Hoke, and Baker met to discuss their plans for defeating Cox. During the conference, Hoke proposed an assault against Upham's brigade. At first, both Bragg and Hill dismissed the idea, but Hoke persisted, expressing confidence in his division. For Bragg, executing Hoke's plan meant dividing his force in the face of a numerically superior enemy—a risky proposition at best. But for once, Bragg ignored the risks and decided to assume the offensive. A

78 *OR* 47, pt. 1, 1,086.

79 For biographical information on Clayton, the authors consulted Warner, *Generals in Grey,* 52-53.

successful attack might force Cox to fall back all the way to New Bern, thereby preventing or at least delaying Schofield's junction with Sherman.[80]

The agreed upon plan called for Hill to relieve Hoke's division along Southwest Creek no later than 5:00 a.m. the next morning. Once relieved, Hoke would then move his division to the right in order to strike the enemy's left flank. As a reserve, Bragg selected Hagood's brigade, still en route from Duplin County. While Hoke maneuvered into position, Hill would use Starr's artillery to pound the Federals and keep them occupied. Once Hoke had broken the enemy's line, Hill's Army of Tennessee contingent and Baker's Junior Reserves brigade would deliver the *coup de grace*, routing the Federals.[81]

The Confederate generals had just settled on what General Cox later described as a "boldly conceived" plan that would result in one of the South's last triumphs of the Civil War.[82]

---

80 See Appendix B for Confederate strength estimates. Barefoot, *General Robert F. Hoke*, 285; The Howard house stood near the intersection of Dover and Neuse Roads.

81 *OR* 47, pt. 2, 1,350.

82 Cox, *Military Reminiscences*, vol. 2, 428.

Chapter 5

"Colonel you are being flanked."

— *Unknown Civilian*

Hoke's Surprise

Early on the morning of March 8, D. H. Hill's infantry occupied the Southwest Creek trenches vacated by Robert Hoke's division. Hill commanded more than 2,500 infantry, which included his own division (Coltart's), Pettus's brigade, and the Junior Reserves. To facilitate Hoke's surprise attack at dawn, Hill's command was to make a spirited demonstration along Southwest Creek to divert the Federals' attention. Once Hoke's division had made contact with the enemy, Hill's infantry would "attack vigorously" across the creek and cooperate with his fellow North Carolinian. Bragg's written order offered little detail as to how he expected Hill to cooperate with Hoke. However, Hill's written account suggested that he discussed the upcoming attack with Hoke: "He expected to seize and hold the Lower Trent and Dover roads and . . . asked me to cut off the Yankee retreat on the British and Neuse roads."[1]

It is unclear if Bragg knew of Hoke's and Hill's agreed upon objectives for the assault. Because Bragg possessed a hands-off leadership style, he likely left the two generals to work out the details together. Fortunately, both Hill and Hoke were well acquainted with one another. The two had served together

---

1 OR 47, pt. 1, 1,087; pt. 2, 1,350. About mid-morning, Hagood arrived with the South Carolina contingent from his brigade. In accordance with Bragg's written order, Hagood acted as the reserve, subject to Hill's orders.

earlier in the war when Colonel Hill commanded the 1st North Carolina and Hoke served as a lieutenant in Company K. Historian Daniel W. Barefoot characterized the two men as "student and teacher," and once again the two commanders were together "to teach the Yankees one final lesson on the soil of their home state."[2]

Shortly after midnight, General Hoke's division began its movement. The darkness concealed a long detour through dense woods and swamps. Incessant rains had made the roads all but impassable. William "Bill" Loftin, a local citizen, guided the division on a "circuitous route" around the Confederate right, crossing Southwest Creek at the Upper Trent Road, en route to the Federal left flank.[3]

Hoke's command consisted of three infantry brigades: Clingman's, Colquitt's, and Kirkland's. Colonel John J. Hedrick's and Col. John D. Taylor's units arrived at Kinston before the rest of Hagood's brigade and were temporarily attached to other commands. Hedrick's men reported to Clingman's brigade and Taylor's troops were assigned to Baker's Junior Reserves brigade. With the addition of the 67th and 68th North Carolina, Hoke fielded about 4,500 infantry—more than half of Bragg's available force on March 8.[4]

Dawn brought welcome relief for both sides, after spending a cold and wet night in their defensive works. Conditions were even worse for soldiers on the front line, who had to make do without cooking fires because the flames drew attention from enemy sharpshooters. To the Federals' surprise, the morning passed quietly, as the Confederates seemed disinclined to initiate hostile actions. Soldiers of the 15th Connecticut not deployed on the skirmish line enjoyed the

---

2   Manarin et al., *North Carolina Troops*, vol. 3, 1-2, 51. Hoke served in Hill's 1st North Carolina at the battle of Big Bethel in June 1862, which resulted in a Confederate victory; Barefoot, *Lee's Modest Warrior*, 288.

3   A. M. Waddell Chapter, United Daughters of the Confederacy, "What Happened at Southwest Creek in the Spring of 1865"; Lieutenant Lamb of the 17th North Carolina wrote years later that Colonel Nethercutt, "who was familiar with the country," guided Hoke on March 8. See Wilson G. Lamb, "Seventeenth North Carolina Infantry," in Clark, *Histories*, vol. 2, 11; Henry C. Whitehurst, "H. C. Reminiscence," in Civil War Collection, North Carolina Department of Archives and History, Raleigh, NC, 8-11; Hagood, *Memoirs*, 351; Calder recorded in his diary that Taylor's contingent reached Kinston at 4:30 a.m. on March 8. Calder, diary, March 8, 1865.

4   Lamb, "Seventeenth North Carolina Infantry," in Clark, *Histories*, vol. 2, 11; See Table E, Appendix B, for Hoke's March 8 troop strength.

respite by boiling coffee—unaware that danger lurked in the woods to their south.[5]

On the Federal right, the 9th New Jersey and 23rd Massachusetts maintained an advanced position along the Lower Trent Road—approximately one mile forward of Palmer's main line on the British Road—to keep watch of the Confederates. Colonel Stewart of the 9th New Jersey spent a restless night, "satisfied that the enemy was in strong force and was preparing to make a sortie when daylight came." Fortunately for Stewart's soldiers, General Harland ordered the regiment withdrawn to Tilghman's plantation near the intersection of the British Road and railroad, shortly after dawn. Upon arriving, Stewart's men immediately constructed breastworks. Because the regiment lacked shovels and picks, they improvised with cups, plates, and bayonets. Like most other units in Palmer's and Carter's divisions, they had expected to make a rapid movement to Goldsboro and did not think they would need such pioneer tools.[6]

Two hundred men from Colonel Curtiss's Provisional command and two companies of the 132nd New York from Claassen's brigade occupied the line vacated by the 9th New Jersey. On Curtiss' right flank, Colonel Raymond's 23rd Massachusetts guarded the intersection of the Lower Trent and Neuse Roads— critical to preventing Confederate movement along either. Throughout the early morning, Raymond's soldiers had observed wagon trains traveling back and forth from the Confederate positions along Southwest Creek. Raymond and his men erroneously assumed all the traffic "was a general retreat of the rebels."[7]

Harland recognized the tenuous position Raymond's isolated regiment held. About 10:00 a.m., Harland ordered Lt. Col. Augustus B. R. Sprague of the 2nd Massachusetts Heavy Artillery to send forward a portion of his command to occupy a position on the Neuse Road and to connect with Raymond's right flank. Sprague dispatched Maj. William A. Amory and two companies—about half his command—in response to Harland's directive. Sprague accompanied

---

5 Thorpe, *History of the Fifteenth Connecticut*, 111.

6 Drake, *History of the Ninth New Jersey*, 275-276; OR 47, pt. 1, 985.

7 OR 47, pt. 1, 989-990. Companies E and I of the 132nd New York Infantry were deployed forward with Lieutenant Colonel Curtiss's command. Emmerton, *A Record of the Twenty-Third Regiment Mass.*, 244.

Amory and his men as they marched up the Neuse Road toward Raymond's position.[8]

At Palmer's headquarters, the general and his staff prepared to meet General Schofield at the railhead. Palmer did not anticipate any trouble from the Rebels, thinking they would remain on their side of Southwest Creek or withdraw, as reported by pickets of the 23rd Massachusetts. According to Lt. William Goodrich Jr., Palmer's aide-de-camp, the general left early that morning for the railhead. It is unclear whether Palmer notified Carter of his departure, even though it left Carter as the senior officer on the field.[9]

While Confederate preparations for the attack continued, Carter arrived at Upham's headquarters to inspect his brigade's position. During their meeting, a rider from the 12th New York Cavalry delivered a message to Carter stating that "negroes reported some 2,000 Rebels had passed down the Trent Road earlier that morning." Carter handed the message to Upham who immediately issued orders to counter the potential threat to his flank. Colonel Bartholomew relocated the 27th Massachusetts across the Dover Road to a blocking position on the British Road. Bartholomew's new position was several hundred yards to the left and rear of Major Osborn's 2nd Battalion. With Bartholomew's repositioning, Upham now had approximately 700 men located south of the Dover Road.[10]

A concerned Carter issued orders for Colonel Splaine's Third Brigade to send forward 200 men from the 17th Massachusetts to strengthen Upham's position at the intersection of the British and Dover Road. Carter also dispatched a courier to inform Cox of recent developments at the front. At the close of their meeting, Carter cautioned Upham to exercise "great vigilance."[11]

About 9:00 a.m., Hill's Confederates disturbed the morning calm with intermittent small arms and artillery fire. Colonel Starr's Confederate batteries kept the Federals entertained from their gun positions along Southwest Creek. Lieutenant Seymour's two-gun section of 12- pound Napoleon smoothbores

---

8   OR 47, pt. 1, 987. Only five of the regiment's ten companies: B, C, F, I, M, departed New Bern as part of Cox's Provisional Corps. On March 8, Sprague ordered Companies F and M to accompany Major Amory.

9   Thorpe, *History of the Fifteenth Connecticut*, 132. Palmer did not mention his absence from the front in his official report. See OR 47, pt. 1, 982.

10   OR 47, pt. 1, 994, 997; Thorpe, *History of the Fifteenth Connecticut*, 111.

11   OR 47, pt. 1, 994, 997.

Capt. Julius Bassett (seated in the middle), of Co. A, 15th Connecticut Infantry.
Courtesy of Buck Zaidel

from Battery I, 3rd New York Light Artillery replied in kind. Private Patrick McCourt, a new recruit in the 15th Connecticut, wanted to see the effect of the New Yorkers' artillery fire on the Confederate line. He climbed nearly twenty feet up a tree to get a better view, when suddenly "a shell came through the top of the tree making kindling wood of it." McCourt lost his grip and plunged to the ground. Every soldier in McCourt's company burst into laughter, but their merriment abruptly ceased when a second artillery round landed in their midst. The explosion showered Sgt. William Beecher with debris but left him otherwise unhurt. As Beecher wiped the dirt out of his eyes, he said, "I guess they are finding out where we are."[12]

A general engagement soon erupted that lasted for about two hours, resulting in minimal loss to either side. Sergeant Sheldon B. Thorpe of the 15th Connecticut was surprised more men were not wounded. "Fewer casualties than one would expect judging from the force in the front and volume of fire," wrote Thorpe. The sergeant's observation that the regiment's skirmish companies never "diverted a moment from the business they had on hand" highlighted the effectiveness of Hill's ruse to divert the Federals' attention away from Hoke's approach.[13]

During the diversionary engagement, the 15th Connecticut lost an experienced company commander, Capt. Julius Bassett of Company A—the first of seven the regiment would lose on March 8—as he passed along words of encouragement to his men. Sergeant Thorpe recounted that Bassett "repeatedly exposed himself by passing along the line almost within pistol shot of the

12 Calder, diary, March 8, 1865; Thorpe, *History of the Fifteenth Connecticut*, 246-247.

13 Ibid., 93.

Lt. Col. Walter G. Bartholomew,
27th Massachusetts Infantry
Wade Sokolosky Collection

enemy." During the skirmishing Bassett was mortally wounded, shot through both hips.[14]

As Carter rode back to his headquarters at Wise's Forks, he stopped to observe the position of Captain Cann's Company D, 17th Massachusetts at the British and Dover crossroads. Troubled by the company's ill-preparedness, Carter advised the captain to "throw up works for protection." Soon after departing Cann's location, Carter was overtaken by Maj. Roland R. West of the 12th New York Cavalry, who reported that "his pickets were being driven in at the bridge."[15]

Historical accounts indicate that Major West failed to first inform Upham of the cavalry debacle, and thus deprived him of additional time needed to shift his brigade toward the greater threat from the south. However, regimental historian Pvt. Thomas Kirwan of the 17th Massachusetts stated that Upham was aware of the reported Confederate movement. Kirwan wrote that his commander, Captain Cann, had warned Upham "twice that his Brigade was on the verge of being overwhelmed." Kirwan further noted that even if Upham had heeded the warnings, he probably lacked the time to make "proper disposition of his command for either defense or retreat."[16]

Carter meanwhile raced to his headquarters and dashed off a note to Upham, warning that the Confederates were indeed approaching on his flank. Apparently the messenger was killed or captured, because Carter never saw him again. Carter also scribbled a note to Cox advising him of the rapidly changing

14 Ibid., 112.

15 *OR* 47, pt. 1, 994.

16 Kirwan, *Memorial History to the Seventeenth Regiment Massachusetts*, 326; Upham submitted two separate reports after the battle, neither of which mentioned West's report of his cavalry being driven from their picket posts, nor Captain Cann's warnings. See *OR* 47, pt. 1, 997-999.

situation. Realizing that Upham's endangered brigade needed additional support, Carter ordered the 85th New York, which had just arrived from Roanoke Island, to report to Upham.[17]

On the British Road, a civilian approached Bartholomew and said, "Colonel, you are being flanked, you may expect them right in there any minute," pointing in the direction of the woods on the regiment's left flank. Bartholomew quickly ordered the regiment to change front so that his battle line faced the supposed threat. He ordered Company G, located on the regiment's right flank, to deploy as skirmishers. The ground to the regiment's immediate front rose slightly for 100 yards and then dropped off into a deep gulley. As Bartholomew moved forward to correct his skirmishers' positioning, he observed a formation of Confederates in the hollow. "The woods were full of them," he later wrote.[18]

While Upham and his commanders wrestled with the crisis developing around them, Cox and Schofield were en route to Palmer's headquarters. Cox had greeted Schofield earlier that morning at the railhead. At 10:00 a.m., Cox received word from Carter of the reported observation that "a heavy column of enemy had crossed the creek at the Wilmington Road and was moving toward the Upper Trent Road." The cavalry observing the Wilmington Road had "reported nothing," so Cox dismissed the account as "exaggerated." Nevertheless, he ordered Carter to push his cavalry in the direction of the Upper Trent Road to ascertain the truth and to have the remainder of his command at the ready.[19]

*   *   *

Shortly before 11:30 a.m., Hoke was ready to start his attack. Although he successfully captured a large number of enemy cavalrymen, the Federals surprisingly had yet to respond aggressively. Hoke summoned his brigade commanders for a last-minute "consultation." At the conclusion he ordered

17 OR 47, pt. 1, 994. The 85th New York, by general orders, was originally assigned to Palmer's division; however, upon reporting to Cox's headquarters for assignment on March 8, the regiment was assigned to Malloy's brigade of Carter's division. The 85th consisted of just two companies. The remaining nine companies were captured at the battle of Plymouth, N.C., in April 1864.

18 W. G. Bartholomew, "Battling Against Heavy Odds," National Tribune, August 1, 1902.

19 OR 47, pt. 1, 976. Schofield arrived at the railhead from New Bern the previous night.

Kirkland, whose brigade held the right of the line, to "extend his line still further to the right" to ensure that it struck the Federal left. Hoke and his subordinates rode in front of the assault column as it moved by the right flank "with no skirmish line out."[20]

General Hoke and his staff soon blundered into a knee-deep swamp. Suddenly, on the opposite side, a group of Federals rose up from the bushes and fired a volley into the startled Confederates, scattering Hoke and his entourage. According to one Tar Heel officer's account, Hoke did not immediately issue the command "forward into line," but instead displayed a calm and confident demeanor. With his hat raised in the air, Hoke shouted, "Make all the men cheer!" The effect was electrifying, as the Rebels sounded "like a tornado among the pines." Hoke's attack on Upham's brigade had begun.[21]

In his postwar reminiscence, Lt. Henry C. Whitehurst of the 67th North Carolina stated that his regiment deployed in advance of Hoke's brigades and engaged the Federals first. In describing the initial encounter, Whitehurst wrote:

> The regiment had but taken a few steps toward the front when the enemy heretofore silent and unseen rose from the bushes about fifteen or twenty yards in front and opened fire . . . along the whole line. For one moment there was wild confusion, and conflicting orders from the officers. The line scattered toward the rear. . . . [B]ut the cry "Rally-Rally" was heard near the colors."[22]

The startled Tar Heels regained their composure and reformed upon the unit's colors. The regiment then unleashed a volley toward the enemy and charged forward. Colonel John H. Nethercutt of the 66th North Carolina, temporarily attached to Hoke's staff, responded enthusiastically after he

---

20 Hagood wrote in his memoirs that Hoke's guns were heard about 11:30 a.m. See Hagood, *Memoirs*, 352; Charles G. Elliott, "Kirkland's Brigade, Hoke's Division, 1864-'65," in *Southern Historical Society Papers*, 52 vols. (Richmond, VA, 1895), vol. 23, 169-170; Elliot's reference to "Whitford's battalion of Rangers" implied the 67th North Carolina followed Hoke's mounted party.

21 Elliott, "Kirkland's Brigade," in *Southern Historical Society Papers*, vol. 23, 169-170.

22 Lieutenant Colonel Rufus W. Wharton of the 67th North Carolina corroborated Lieutenant Whitehurst's statement many years later when he recalled that the regiment was "in front" during Hoke's attack. See Rufus W. Wharton, "Sixty-seventh Regiment," in Clark, *Histories*, vol. 3, 708.

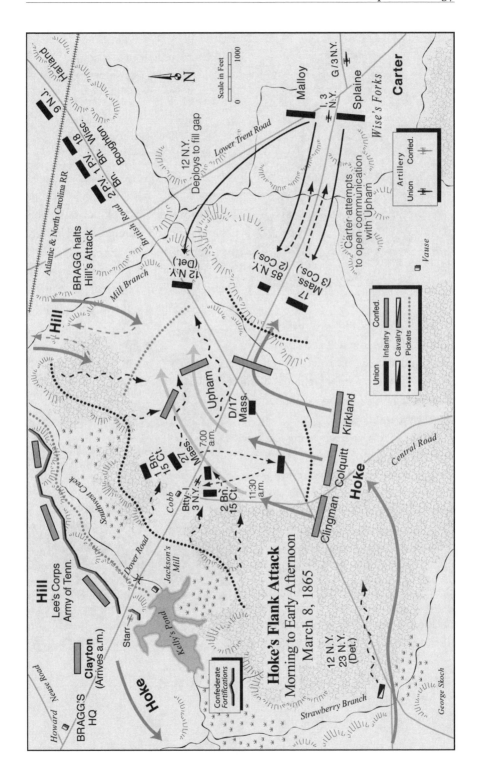

Hoke's Flank Attack
Morning to Early Afternoon
March 8, 1865

Top: Pvt. Josephus S. Morris, Company H, 67th North Carolina
State Archives of North Carolina

Bottom: Capt. John E. Mullally, Co. C, 17th Massachusetts Infantry
Wade Sokolosky Collection

observed the 67th North Carolina surge forward. The colonel raised his hat in the air and shouted, "By Heaven, they fight like devils."[23]

The 67th had much to prove on March 8, as the regiment had never participated in a general engagement.

Hoke's veterans did not have much faith in the regiment. "[T]heir bearing and conduct was narrowly watched," wrote Whitehurst, "while many disparaging predictions concerning them were indulged."[24]

As Hoke's infantry pressed the attack, Kirkland's line of battle struggled to maintain cohesion as it advanced through the densely wooded and swampy terrain. The 17th North Carolina, positioned on the brigade's right flank, drifted away from the main line because of thick underbrush. Kirkland ordered Pvt. G. L. Tonnoffski of the 17th North Carolina, a courier on the general's staff, "to go in search of the regiment." As Tonnoffski made

23 Henry C. Whitehurst, "Reminiscences," North Carolina Division of Archives and History, Raleigh, North Carolina, 8-11.

24 Ibid.

his way through the thick timber, he came within view of the Union line. He quickly changed direction and soon found the 17th, which he guided back into line.[25]

Despite the difficult terrain, the Confederates surged forward. Upon observing the thin Yankee picket line, the Southerners unleashed "a fearful volley of musketry" that sent Bartholomew's skirmishers scrambling for cover. His skirmish company stood no chance against the weight of Hoke's battle lines. They were quickly overwhelmed and driven back several hundred yards. One Massachusetts soldier on the skirmish line, Pvt. Edmond Pendleton, remembered that he and his comrades were still deployed in front when their regiment's main battle line responded with a volley. Caught between opposing firing lines, Pendleton and the others were forced to take an indirect route back to their regiment.[26]

The fast-moving Confederates soon enveloped the 27th Massachusetts' position. Private William P. Derby of the 27th described the action:

[W]e delivered a rapid and effective fire, causing their massed troops to recoil from our front. The Confederates covered our position with shrieking shot, amidst which Colonel Bartholomew moved back and forth along the line. 'You are doing well, boys; keep cool! Don't waste your ammunition!' shouted Bartholomew.[27]

As the Rebels pressed their advantage under a withering fire from the Bay Staters, the situation became desperate, but the Confederate battle line soon overlapped Bartholomew's flanks. The enemy's lines formed "nearly three-quarters of a circle around us," wrote a Massachusetts soldier. As his infantry received fire from the rear, Bartholomew had no choice but to fall back or risk capture.[28]

Above the roar of musketry, Private Derby heard his commander issue orders in a desperate attempt to stave off disaster. "Boys, I want to face you to the rear; march back a little, and turn around and give it to them again," Bartholomew shouted. "Keep cool and steady: About—Face!—Forward." As

---

25 G. L. Tonnoffski, "My Last Days as a Confederate Soldier," in *Confederate Veteran*, vol. 22, no. 2 (Feb. 1914), 68.

26 Edward Pendleton, "My Experience in the Army," Library of Congress, 23.

27 Derby, *Bearing Arms in the Twenty-Seventh Massachusetts*, 462.

28 Ibid., 462-463.

Maj. Eli W. Osborn,
15th Connecticut Infantry
Wade Sokolosky Collection

if on parade, the regiment executed the movement, moving in tight formation across the Dover Road and deploying in the field beyond the enemy's flanks. When the 27th Massachusetts had escaped the immediate threat, Bartholomew yelled, "Halt!" and the regiment faced about, unleashing a well-directed fire upon the attacking Confederates. Moments later, the Southerners responded with a volley that swept the Massachusetts regiment across its front and flanks. The Confederates surged forward yelling, "Surrender! Surrender!" Years later, a Massachusetts soldier described the scene at that critical moment. A "battle-cloud" of gunpowder smoke "covered the sky with its murky hue." Despite the calls for surrender, Bartholomew ordered the regiment to fall back a second time.[29]

Private Pendleton reached the line just as Bartholomew ordered the unit to fall back. A bullet struck Pendleton in his leg. He threw down his weapon and knapsack and "started to run for it." The private had barely taken a dozen steps when he was struck yet again in his ankle and arm. Unable to go any farther, Pendleton collapsed on the field, where he remained unattended until the next morning.[30]

Moments before Bartholomew's skirmishers were attacked, Upham received another dispatch stating that the Rebels were advancing up the British Road. As Upham scanned the message, musket fire erupted on his extreme left. Realizing the gravity of the situation, he dispatched adjutant Phillip C. Rand with orders directing Major Osborn to "change front with his battalion" to

29 Ibid.

30 Pendleton, "My Experience in the Army," 23.

meet the Confederate attack. No sooner had Osborn received the order than a bullet struck him as he buckled his sword. With Osborn wounded, Capt. George M. White of Company E assumed command. The 2nd Battalion executed its movement under fire and was able to deliver a volley that momentarily checked the Confederate advance.[31]

Lieutenant Seymour's section of Battery I, 3rd New York Artillery had fired only a few rounds when Upham ordered the gunners to limber up and report to him at the crossing of the British Road. The section's gun located on the road was able to quickly move out as ordered. As the crew rushed down the Dover Road, however, they discovered their egress blocked by Confederate infantry. In an "unceremonious charge," the artillerymen dashed through the Southerners, who wisely opened a path for the thundering horses. The Confederates "saluted the piece with a shower of bullets," mortally wounding one of the drivers, but the crew and their gun safely reached the main Federal line at Wise's Forks.

Seymour's second gun was not so fortunate. The gun was deployed off the road in difficult terrain, and the crew was delayed in limbering the piece. Before the New Yorkers had traveled 20 yards, the Confederates unleashed a devastating volley, killing several horses. With their limber immobilized, the artillerymen dismounted and sought cover in the woods. Five of Seymour's men were captured.[32]

The onrushing Southerners threatened to overrun Osborn's 2nd Battalion. White, not wishing to try "any more battalion drill," ordered the colors withdrawn to the Dover Road, about 100 yards from their current position. Once the colors were in place, planted on the remains of a rail fence along the edge of the woods, White commanded the battalion to "rally behind the fence."[33]

Confederate artillery supported Hoke's advancing infantry, firing from across Southwest Creek. Southern gunners positioned around Jackson's Mill witnessed the rout of Upham's Union brigade and quickly joined in the action. Lieutenant Halcott P. Jones of Dickson's Battery described the scene in his diary. "As they pass in confusion thro the field . . . we open on them," he

31 OR 47, pt. 1, 997, 999; Thorpe, *History of the Fifteenth Connecticut*, 94, 205.

32 OR 47, pt. 1, 997; Hall and Hall, *Cayuga in the Field*, 274.

33 Thorpe, *History of the Fifteenth Connecticut*, 112-113.

scribbled, "and as the shell burst amongst them it was beautiful to see them run and fall."[34]

The 27th Massachusetts was close on the heels of the Connecticut battalion. No longer able to hold their position, Bartholomew ordered his men to fall back toward the rail fence, where they discovered White's men lying down. "My men jumped the fence and faced about, and went to work," remembered Bartholomew. Unfortunately, the numerous new recruits in the 15th Connecticut were unreliable and many refused to fight when fear overtook them. As the senior officer present, Bartholomew tried to rally the green soldiers: "[S]ome of the old hands did get up and go to firing with my men."[35]

At the rail fence, the remnants of Bartholomew's and Osborn's commands made their last stand, firing volley after volley into the advancing Confederates. However, the besieged Federals were surrounded and under fire from the front, flank, and rear. Captain White thought there might be a chance of escaping north toward the railroad. He ordered the color bearers to make a break westward toward Colonel Tolles's headquarters at the Cobb house, hoping to prevent the regimental flag from being captured. After receiving a mortal wound, Cpl. George W. Manville, the 15th Connecticut's color bearer, made it as far as the house where he "handed his precious charge over to" Lt. Soloman F. Linsley. Soon afterward, Linsley and the colors were captured.[36]

Private Charles Baldwin and about a dozen others from the 15th Connecticut attempted to make a stand in a clump of pine trees. Seven men were shot down within seconds. Baldwin fired one shot before a Confederate bullet pierced his hat, and another struck a tree not far from his nose. Baldwin later stated, "I was so frightened that I think my hair had elevated [my] hat and it may have been the means of saving my scalp."[37]

As Bartholomew moved up and down the line, encouraging his men, a Minié ball shattered his leg and he crumpled to the ground in agony. Fearing

34 Jones, diary, March 8, 1865.

35 Bartholomew, "Battling Against Heavy Odds," *National Tribune*, August 1, 1902.

36 Thorpe, *History of the Fifteenth Connecticut*, 112-113, 213-214. The flag that Zachry's Georgians captured was a blue silk standard with no markings or insignia of any kind. This was because the regimental colors of the 15th Connecticut were sent home for repairs before the start of the campaign, and the U.S. Army had issued the regiment a plain blue silk flag as a temporary replacement.

37 Thorpe, *History of the Fifteenth Connecticut*, 247-248.

27th Massachusetts Infantry National Colors
Commonwealth of Massachusetts Art Commission

that their colors would be captured, Cpl. Lafayette Babb and Pvt. Leverett Clarke rolled the flags of the 27th Massachusetts on their standards and placed them beneath a rotten log. Moments later the two men were captured, but the Confederates never discovered the hidden flags. A month later, the unit's colors were recovered and taken back to New Bern.[38]

When the Rebels approached within 20 yards of Bartholomew's position, order disintegrated as the men took flight. "The enemy, quick to discern the temporary faltering of our fire, rushed upon us, and with one sweep crushed our column, and the conflict was over," recalled a Massachusetts soldier. According to Lt. Joseph W. Holmes, adjutant of the 27th Massachusetts, the engagement had lasted about 55 minutes from the opening volleys until Bartholomew's wounding.[39]

According to historical accounts, Colquitt's Georgians overran Bartholomew's position along the fence. Upon observing Bartholomew's injury, Adjutant Holmes immediately went to his fallen commander. While Holmes treated Bartholomew, the victorious Georgians surrounded the officers and divested their personal belongings. Colonel Charles T. Zachry, commander of Colquitt's brigade, arrived and reprimanded his soldiers for their egregious actions. As custom dictated, Zachry received Bartholomew's sword as a symbol of victory.[40]

---

38 Derby, *Bearing Arms in the Twenty-Seventh Massachusetts*, 464, 471.

39 Ibid., 464.

40 Ibid. Colonel Zachry assumed command of Colquitt's brigade shortly after Wilmington's evacuation. The 37-year-old farmer from Georgia had commanded the 27th Georgia since September 1862 and had earned the respect of his men. One fellow Georgian described Zachry "as amiable and a very brave officer." Allardice, *Confederate Colonels*, 412.

Col. Charles T. Zachry, 27th Georgia Infantry, acting commander of Colquitt's Brigade.

Thornton Jordan

*   *   *

While disaster befell Upham's left flank, another wave of Confederates immerged north of the Dover Road. Upon hearing Hoke unleash his attack, Hill's Confederates along Southwest Creek sprang out of their entrenchments and crossed the creek on logs and improvised bridges. Hill's infantry wasted no time getting across, aware that speed was the key to success. Once across the creek, Hill's command deployed for battle and pushed forward to cut off the Federals' retreat.

General Baker's Junior Reserves brigade spearheaded Hill's advance, crossing Southwest Creek south of the Neuse Road Bridge. Captain E. B. Vaughn of the 50th Alabama, commanding the skirmishers from Lee's Corps, pushed "boldly forward." Hill's Confederates found the woods nearly "impassable" in places. A Tar Heel officer wrote, "The undergrowth was matted and tangled so that it was almost impossible to get through." As officers struggled to maintain control of their battle lines, the simple task of identifying friend from foe proved difficult.[41]

Major Alexander McRae's 1st Battalion North Carolina Heavy Artillery, attached to Baker's brigade, deployed as skirmishers after reaching the opposite bank. McRae's adjutant, Lt. William Calder, wrote in his diary that "The men were perfectly green and the work of deploying them was very tedious." Until a few weeks earlier McRae's heavy artillery battalion had garrisoned the coastal defenses along the Cape Fear River and now served as infantry. As the Confederates moved forward, McRae's line "advanced with very good courage but exceedingly bad order," Calder observed.[42]

41 *OR* 47, pt. 1, 1,087; Calder, diary, March 8, 1865.

42 Calder, diary, March 8, 1865.

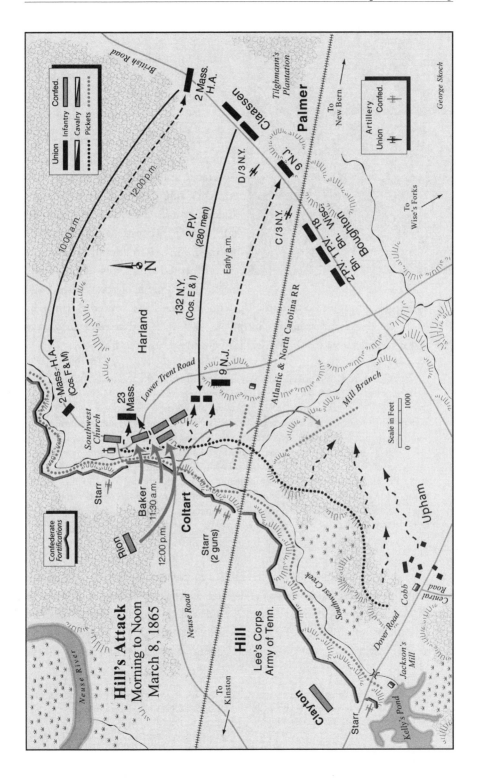

Lt. William Calder, adjutant, 1st Battalion
North Carolina Heavy Artillery
Courtesy of Robert Calder

McRae's skirmish line engaged the Federals in what one men called a "pretty spirited" encounter. As McRae's line executed a left oblique, Calder paused to organize stragglers and, in the process, lost sight of the battalion. Disoriented and unaware he had diverged from his unit, Calder pressed on and had a brush with death. "[E]xpecting every minute to come up with the line I discovered skirmishers firing on my right," he recalled "I tried in vain to learn whether they were friends or foes. I moved farther." Calder continued his account:

> . . . Being near a fence I looked over and not 60 yards from the fence was a Yankee skirmisher standing behind a tree. . . . This meeting opened my eyes, and I saw I was in front of our own lines and in rear of part of the enemies. I soon saw a line of skirmishers thrown out . . . and advance towards me. I thought it was time to retreat and moved quickly to the rear. Soon the Minnie balls were whistling around me, and I discovered I was being fired upon by our men. . . . I got into a ditch and thought upon my situation. If I remained where I was the enemy would capture me, if I advanced I might be shot by friends. Here was a dilemma. I quickly decided I would risk an advance towards our lines. As soon as I rose, two or three rifles were leveled on me, but I shouted 'A Friend' and waving my handkerchief succeeded in stopping them. I tremble now whenever I think of my narrow escape and devoutly thank God for his mercies towards me.[43]

To the north, where the skirmishing was particularly heavy, the Rebels encountered a determined Federal resistance. Curtiss's and Raymond's Union skirmishers, located west of the Lower Trent Road, doggedly held their position but eventually withdrew to their reserve line on the road. The initial attack by the Junior Reserves brigade pressed the Federal skirmish line back toward the

---

43 Ibid; On March 8, McRae's battalion of Red Infantry suffered two killed and five wounded. Isaac S. Tanner, Patient Registry Hoke's Division, Isaac S. Tanner Collection, Museum of the Confederacy, Richmond, Virginia, 137.

Lower Trent Road. "We fell back to the rail fence, and fought them," wrote a soldier from the 23rd Massachusetts. "They charged us three times, but they could not start us a hair." James A. Emmerton, regimental historian of the 23rd Massachusetts, noted the majority of the 27 losses the regiment suffered during the entire battle occurred in the skirmish companies on March 8. Along the Neuse Road, Sprague's timely arrival with two companies from the 2nd Massachusetts Heavy Artillery temporarily checked the Confederate advance along the critical route with a loss of only four men.[44]

After a "sharp skirmish" of about 30 minutes, the Federals effectively halted the advance of the Junior Reserves. For many of these young boys, this was their first opportunity "to see the elephant." Finding the Federal fire too much, an element of Baker's command broke and began to seek safety toward the rear. Despite Baker's protests, the frightened young Tar Heels continued to the rear where they were greeted with shouts of laughter from veterans of the Army of Tennessee. One Alabama sergeant yelled, "Go on back to moma boys we will take it from here." Hill reported later that "one regiment (the First, I think) broke, and the rest lay down and could not be moved forward."[45]

Long after the war, Col. Charles W. Broadfoot, commander of the 1st North Carolina Junior Reserves, challenged Hill's account of the Juniors' conduct during the March 8 assault. Claiming that Hill was "speaking from hearsay," Broadfoot argued that Hill was commenting on units that were not under his personal observation. "Had General Hill been writing of troops under his own command, or matters of his own knowledge," Broadfoot maintained, "his statement would be accepted." In fact, the Junior Reserves were under Hill's command, as Hill clearly stated in his report and as General Bragg indicated in his Special Order No. 57. In any event, Broadfoot claimed that a portion of the Junior Reserves, "misconceiving a command that was given to the skirmish line[,] did break and fell back some 150 yards," but at no time did they lie down and refuse to advance.[46]

---

44 *Salem Register* (Salem, MA), March 23, 1865; Emmerton, *A Record of the Twenty-Third Regiment Mass.*, 244; OR 47, pt. 1, 986-987.

45 Hagood, *Memoirs*, 353; *Southerner* (Tarboro, NC), July 11, 1867; OR 47, pt. 1, 1,087.

46 Charles W. Broadfoot, "Seventieth Regiment," in Clark, *Histories*, vol. 4, 19-20. For examples of the arguments and testimony to substantiate the conflicting claims, as well as information on the course of events in the battle, see Manarin et al., *North Carolina Troops*, vol. 17, 106-107.

Lt. Edwin C. Lineberry,
Company E, 1st Battalion Junior Reserves,
was badly wounded in the fighting at Wise's
Forks and died in a Raleigh hospital
on March 25, 1865.
State Archives of North Carolina

Hill directed Baker to hold his position and quickly ordered forward his only reserve, the 500-man South Carolina contingent of Hagood's brigade, to relieve the young Tar Heels. Simultaneously, Hill committed his remaining troops: Deas's, Manigault's, and Pettus's brigades from Lee's Corps, Army of Tennessee, which he personally led "around the swamp." The terrain's difficult nature channeled Hill's renewed attack in a southeasterly direction, forcing back the Union pickets between Carter's and Palmer's divisions. Hill noted that his flanking movement caused the Yankees to run "in the wildest confusion."[47]

North of the Dover Road on the Union left, Lt. Col. Samuel Tolles watched the fight along Southwest Creek from his headquarters at the Cobb House. Tolles was unaware of the disaster unfolding behind his position until the Confederates pressed Osborn's battalion back to the main road. Tolles gave the order to call in the skirmishers, but by then it was too late. General Hoke's Rebel infantry had already flanked the left of Tolles's skirmish line, causing it to give way.

Witnessing the Union rout from Southwest Creek, Capt. Minott A. Butricks's Company I and Lt. Solomon F. Linsley's Company K made their way to Tolles headquarters. Captain Butricks found Tolles near the Cobb house sitting on a five-rail fence with "lead flying freely" around him. "Well Captain what then devil does this mean," shouted Tolles. "It means for us to leave this place," replied Butricks. "It looks as if we wasn't wanted here." Moments later Tolles and the remnants of his command were swept along with the rest of

47 Hagood, *Memoirs*, 352; OR 47, pt. 1, 1,087.

Capt.. Samuel C. Kelly,
Co. E, 30th Alabama Infantry
Alabama Department of Archives and History,
Montgomery, Alabama

Upham's retreating brigade, which "ran plump into the net waiting to receive them."[48]

The rapid advance of D. H. Hill's infantry down the Lower Trent Road blocked Upham's route to safety. As a result, Captain Vaughan's skirmishers captured "about 300 prisoners," Hill noted. Vaughan described the Yankees' rout as "more complete than he had ever seen before." Captain Samuel C. Kelly of the 30th Alabama, commanding the skirmish line from Pettus's brigade wrote to his wife: "They were the easiest Yankees whipped I have ever seen and were well dressed."[49]

With luck and sheer determination, Colonel Upham and about 150 of his men escaped through the converging lines of Confederate infantry. One of the survivors, Pvt. Horace F. Farnsworth of the 15th Connecticut, had several close calls but successfully avoided capture. "I was not taken but had a slim escape," Farnsworth informed his wife. "I had to pop two over that were bound to have me."[50]

Colonel Upham eluded capture but the circumstances of his escape are not clear. According to his written report, he attempted to move toward the intersection of the British and Dover Roads after the attack on Bartholomew's position, but discovered "the enemy to have possession of that part of the field." Unable to go any farther, and his communication with subordinate

---

48 Thorpe, *History of the Fifteenth Connecticut*, 96.

49 *OR* 47, pt. 1, 1,087; Samuel C. Kelly to his wife, March 14, 1865.

50 Horace F. Farnsworth to Fannie Farnsworth, March 9, 1865, in Private Collection, Douglas W. Reynolds. Private Farnsworth estimated the number of survivors was no more than 160 men. This number increased the next day with the arrival of Company K, 15th Connecticut from New Bern. The entire 27th Massachusetts was either killed, wounded, or captured. Only seven members of the regiment detailed as part of the Ambulance Corps escaped capture. See Derby, *Bearing Arms in the Twenty-Seventh Massachusetts*, 465.

Corp. George Marvin,
15th Connecticut Infantry
Wade Sokolosky Collection

commanders cut off, Upham probably witnessed the disaster from some distance.[51]

One of Upham's soldiers, Private William H. Nichols of the 15th Connecticut, recounted that while returning to the front to recover his knapsack, he encountered remnants of the regiment running in panic toward the rear. Moments later, Nichols passed Upham riding on horseback, followed by Cpls. William H. Hubbard and George Marvin, with the national colors of the 15th Connecticut "fluttering in the wind." "With the aid of legs and luck," he explained, both men successfully eluded capture. Corporal Hubbard's calmness impressed Private Nichols, who later remembered that, "to see him you would think he was on parade, and the Johnnies were sending 'minnies' after him as fast as they could." Nichols's observation of the Confederate pursuit indicated that Upham probably waited until the final moments of the fighting to escape—and fortunately for the Union, he did so with the national colors.[52]

It was at this "critical moment" that General Bragg unknowingly lost his greatest opportunity for real victory. Major Francis S. Parker, Bragg's adjutant-general, delivered a note to General D. H. Hill ordering that officer to cease his attack and withdraw his command back to the Neuse Road. Hill was directed to then march northeast along the Neuse Road to where it intersected with the British Road, whereupon his infantry would proceed down the latter and successfully capture the retreating Union soldiers.[53]

---

51 *OR* 47, pt. 1, 999.

52 Thorpe, *The History of the Fifteenth Connecticut*, 101.

53 *OR* 47, pt. 1, 1,087; pt. 2, 1,078.

With more than 7,000 infantry poised to deliver the *coup de grace* to Cox's weakened and scattered forces, Bragg pulled Hill out of the fight. Hoke's recommendation to Bragg that Hill should execute the maneuver was nothing more than a reiteration of their previously agreed upon plan. With Hoke's physical location south of the Dover Road, he was likely unaware of Hill's success—Captain Vaughan's skirmishers in particular. Vaughan's ability to capture several hundred of Upham's men suggested that Hill had blocked the escape route.[54]

Bragg's decision to concur with Hoke's suggestion and merely pass it along indicated his lack of awareness of how the battle was unfolding. More importantly, it demonstrated Bragg's inability to provide decisive leadership when it was required. Bragg had been tormented by such missed opportunities throughout the war, and once again remained true to character.[55]

Surprisingly, the normally outspoken Hill offered no objection to the order, which had taken the head of his column at least five miles away from the battlefield. Perhaps the North Carolinian knew all too well of Bragg's reputation for seeking scapegoats. Hill obediently halted his attack and ordered his command to the Neuse Road. With Lt. Col. James H. Rion's South Carolinians from Hagood's brigade in the advance, Hill proceeded to march more than 2,000 veteran infantrymen on what proved to be a fool's errand.[56]

*   *   *

During the attack on Upham's brigade, Cox and Schofield were still en route to the front when they encountered General Palmer. Palmer had continued with his plan to meet the commanding general, despite the increased sounds of battle. Moments later, a courier reported that a large enemy column was moving between Upham's brigade and Carter's main line at Wise's Forks. Fortunately for Cox, the Confederates were unaware that a gap, at least half a mile wide, existed in the Union center. Cox recognized the gravity of the situation and acted swiftly to avert complete disaster. The generals and their

54 Ibid.

55 Arguably, one of Bragg's greatest missed opportunities came in September 1863 at the battle of Chickamauga, when he failed to pursue the routed Union army.

56 OR 47, pt. 1, 1,087; Hagood, *Memoirs*, 352.

staffs quickly rode forward to the front. Palmer's aide, Lieutenant Goodrich, remembered, "It was the hardest ride I have ever taken."[57]

Carter was instructed to reopen communication with Upham while simultaneously concentrating his division at Wise's Forks. Cox ordered Palmer to move a brigade to assist Carter and to make a vigorous demonstration toward Southwest Creek, hoping to deceive the Confederates. Lastly, General Ruger was ordered to move two of his brigades "at all speed" from Dover Station to Wise's Forks, and to follow with the third.[58]

Fortunately for the Federals, Hoke's attack briefly lost its momentum and unit cohesion as it bogged down in the swampy, heavily wooded terrain. In addition to the problem of difficult terrain, Hoke's commanders were burdened with hundreds of captured Union soldiers. These delays provided Cox and his commanders precious minutes to respond. When Hoke finally resumed pushing north along the British Road, his division unexpectedly encountered Union infantry emerging from the woods, threatening the right flank of Kirkland's brigade. General Kirkland halted and quickly reoriented his battle lines to meet the danger.[59]

Troops were deployed across Carter's and Palmer's divisional fronts to relieve Upham's beleaguered position and strengthen the weak Union center. On the Federal left, Carter ordered elements forward from Wise's Forks. Major William W. Smith and a battalion from the 17th Massachusetts marched west on the Dover Road, followed by Capt. Charles King's 85th New York.[60]

Lieutenant Martin Link of Company C, 85th New York remembered that the regiment arrived at Wise's Forks shortly before receiving Carter's orders. "The men had just had time to get dinner," wrote Link, when Major Smith's battalion from the 17th Massachusetts marched past en route to the front. Moments later, the New Yorkers received orders to follow behind Smith's formation.[61]

---

57 OR 47, pt. 1, 976-977; Thorpe, *History of the Fifteenth Connecticut*, 132.

58 OR 47, pt. 1, 949, 976-977.

59 Cox, *Military Reminiscences of the Civil War*, vol. 2, 436; Wilson G. Lamb, "Seventeenth Regiment," in Clark, *Histories*, vol., 11-12.

60 OR 47, pt. 1, 994, 999-1,000.

61 Martin Link, diary, March 8, 1865, Special Collections and Archives, Ralph B. Draughon Library, Auburn University, Auburn, Alabama.

Private William Hibbard of the 85th New York recalled moving toward the sound of the guns. "No one speaks as we marched out through the open lines and into the woods," wrote Hibbard. As the 85th New York marched past a Confederate prisoner being escorted to the rear, all eyes turned to look at the Southerner as he passed the column. The Union guard yelled to the New Yorkers: "plenty for you to do in there, boys." The Confederate prisoner, with his head bowed and in a low voice shot back, "Yes, plenty for you to do."[62]

An uneasy feeling gripped the New Yorkers as they entered the woods along the Dover Road. "A caisson with three limping horses and a sergeant riding on the limber holding a wounded gunner in his arms" flew past them, remembered Hibbard. "Wounded men were straggling back, dying men, dead men, the sharp spit of the balls, and we are where 'there is plenty to do,'" wrote Hibbard, echoing the prophetic words of the Rebel prisoner.[63]

Captain King's 85th New York joined Major Smith's Massachusetts battalion already formed on the left side of the Dover Road. The New Yorkers deployed above the road, connecting with the 17th Massachusetts. The New Englanders greeted King's men with some ominous news. "Upham and his command, with a section of artillery, had just been captured, a little to our front," wrote a New York soldier.[64]

With both regiments formed in line, the Union infantry advanced cautiously toward Upham's former position. The Federals discovered a "few Rebel skirmishers in front" who quickly retreated at the sight of the advancing line of battle. Captain King ordered Link to deploy a line of skirmishers and "see what is in our front!" Within minutes, Link's soldiers encountered a Confederate skirmish line. "My men acted well, we passed a lively fire for some minutes," Link recorded in his diary.[65]

South of the Dover Road, Smith's Massachusetts skirmishers emerged from the thick underbrush into an opening, where they discovered an abandoned gun at the intersection of the British and Dover Roads. Captain James Splaine of Company A, 17th Massachusetts suggested to Smith that they

---

62 . W. Neighbor, *Neighbor's Home Mail: The Ex-soldiers' Reunion and National Camp-fire*, Issue 2 (Princeton, NJ, 1874), 181.

63 Ibid.

64 Kirwan, *Memorial History to the Seventeenth Regiment Massachusetts*, 327; Neighbor, *Neighbor's Home Mail*, 181.

65 Link, diary, March 8, 1865.

attempt to regain possession of the gun. Smith concurred and ordered Captain Splaine to proceed with his company. Splaine and his men rushed forward, and while under fire cut the harnesses off the dead horses. The brave Union soldiers had nearly succeeded in recovering the piece when "the long gray lines seemed to rise out of the ground."[66]

From the opposite side of the clearing the Confederates rushed out of the woods toward the gun. A desperate fight for the gun ensued with "bayonets and clubbed muskets." Upon witnessing Company A's plight, Major Smith "sent forward on the double-quick" two companies commanded by Captains Charles O. Fellows and John E. Mullally. To Company A's surprise and disappointment, the two companies "were charged upon by a whole regiment of the enemy," and Splaine's men were forced to fall back.[67]

After securing the lone gun, the Confederates pressed their advantage but were met with repeated volleys from the two Union regiments. Despite their stubborn resistance against the ever-increasing number of Confederates, the Federals grudgingly fell back toward Wise's Forks. "I could tell by the firing from the Massachusetts Battalion that they were driving them back," recalled Link, who observed that a "large body" of Rebels moved toward the right. Realizing he could not hold his position he ordered his men to withdraw. Link instructed the front line to retire "the proper distance" while the second line covered their retreat. When the first line was in place, the second line fired a volley then fell back joining the first, forming on the regiment.[68]

While Smith and King contested the Rebel advance, Carter received the grim news of the fate of Upham's brigade. One of Upham's staff officers had managed to escape the Confederate trap and successfully reached Carter's headquarters. The officer reported that "nearly the whole" of Upham's brigade had been lost. Carter immediately rode forward "to learn for him-self the true state of affairs."[69]

Shortly after Carter's departure, Cox arrived at the vicinity of Wise's Forks. Prior to Ruger's arrival, Cox ordered Colonel Savage "to check" the Confederate advance in the center with his cavalry, and available troopers were

---

66   OR 47, pt. 1, 1,000; Kirwan, *Memorial History to the Seventeenth Regiment Massachusetts*, 328; Neighbor, *Neighbor's Home Mail*, 181.

67   Kirwan, *Memorial History to the Seventeenth Regiment Massachusetts*, 328; OR 47, pt. 1, 1,000.

68   Link, diary, March 8, 1865.

69   OR 47, pt. 1, 994.

Capt. Joseph M. Fish,
Co. A, 12th New York Cavalry
Libraries of Stevens County,
Kettles Falls, Washington

rushed to the endangered area. The New Yorkers dismounted to establish a hasty defensive line that momentarily succeeded in securing the threatened sector.[70]

Captain Fish of the 12th New York Cavalry spurred his way forward with his company and a section of flying artillery. Fish was proud of Company A's two 12-pound mountain howitzers, which he jokingly referred to as "pop guns." As Fish galloped past the 17th Massachusetts, he could not stop himself from boasting, "Wait until I get out there with my 'pops' then you will hear some noise and see some fun."[71]

Meanwhile, along the Dover Road, "a crashing of the underbrush ahead" signaled a renewed Confederate attack. Carter's two lone regiments greeted the Rebel advance with a volley that forced the Southerners to fall back and regroup. However, as suddenly as the firing stopped, it started once again. From a haze of smoke, an explosion of musket fire greeted the Federals. "I hear the 'thupp' of a striking ball," recounted Hibbard, who watched in horror as wounded comrades fell around him. "One by one our ranks are thinned." The ghostly image of a Confederate line of battle emerged from the dense smoke. The Southerners advanced with "a long line of bayonets" against the beleaguered Union position. Hoke's battle line was so close that all the Federals could do was fire "one last volley, fairly in their faces," observed a New York

---

70 Ibid., 977; Cox, *Military Reminiscences of the Civil War,* vol. 2, 436-437.

71 Kirwan, *Memorial History to the Seventeenth Regiment Massachusetts,* 326. It is unclear by whose direction and at what time Captain Fish moved forward. Flying artillery was an unofficial Civil War term that also meant "light" or "horse" artillery, a reference to the high maneuvering speeds of these batteries.

soldier, and those that were able "skedaddled" in the direction of Wise's Forks.[72]

Hibbard of the 85th New York described the spirited engagement as they withdrew toward the crossroads:

> We would run a few rods, and settle down like a bevy of frightened quail, behind trees and stumps. We hear them coming, and look nervously to the priming of our rifles. Some draw the ram rods from the pipes and place cartridges between their teeth that they may reload in desperate haste. Nearly all of us un-sling our knapsacks and drop them to our feet, that the arms and shoulders may be unencumbered.[73]

As the 17th Massachusetts and 85th New York retreated to the main Union line they encountered hastily constructed earthworks occupied by a detachment commanded by the 17th's Lt. Malcum Sillers. As the regiments passed, Sillers's men fired a few volleys into the advancing Confederates before falling back. This slowed the Rebels long enough to allow the two regiments to safely reach the Federal entrenchments at Wise's Forks. "They cheered us as we came in," Link later recorded in his diary. General Carter, who was present as the Union infantry came back through the line, expressed to Link his relief upon their safe return. "You done well to get back," shouted Carter. "When I heard the firing I did not expect to see you return."[74]

Captain Fish and his section of mountain howitzers were not so fortunate. Despite his earlier boast, Fish's artillery accomplished little, and in the process lost his prized pop-guns—two of the three artillery pieces the Federals lost on March 8. In addition to losing the guns, Fish's command was routed, with the captain numbered among the wounded. During the fight, a Confederate bullet struck Fish in "his mouth and knocked out a number of his teeth." One of Fish's men spied the Confederate who had shot the captain and returned the favor. Wounded, the offending Southerner dropped his rifle and slumped over a tree limb.[75]

---

72 Neighbor, *Neighbor's Home Mail*, 181.

73 Ibid.

74 *OR* 47, pt. 1, 1,000; Kirwan, *Memorial History to the Seventeenth Regiment Massachusetts*, 328; Link, diary, March 8, 1865.

75 Kirwan, *Memorial History to the Seventeenth Regiment Massachusetts*, 326; *Daily Journal* (New Bern, NC), May 27, 1886. In 1886, Fish returned to the place where he was wounded and cut "several sticks from the branches to take home" as souvenirs of his brush with death.

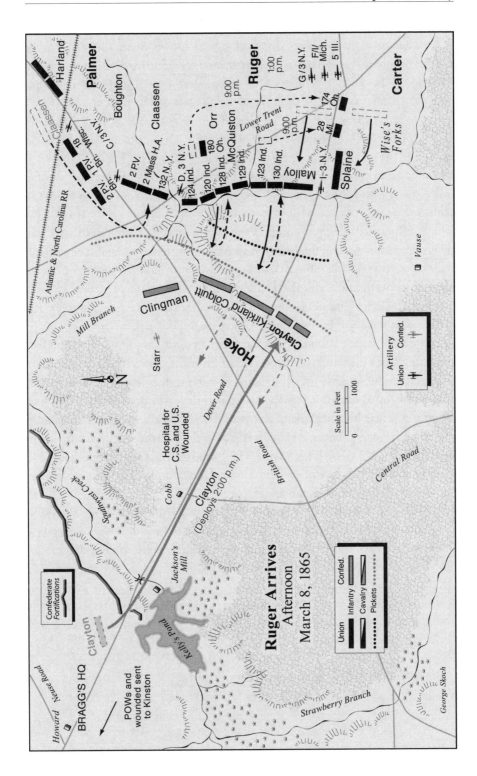

Ruger Arrives
Afternoon
March 8, 1865

Simultaneous with Carter's fight along the Dover Road, General Palmer arrived back at his headquarters and began strengthening his division's position. Unsure of the impact of the Confederate attacks on his division, Palmer ordered his aide Goodrich to move along the line in the direction of Wise's Forks to see if there had been "any disaster to us." Goodrich only traveled a short distance before he came under artillery fire. As an officer on horseback, Goodrich presented a tempting and viable target. Moments later, a Rebel shell burst "in front of and over" him. Goodrich came through unscathed, but his horse was not so fortunate, as the shrapnel tore "a piece from my good mare's flank."[76]

As Goodrich scouted south, Palmer issued orders to consolidate his division's position along the British Road. He drew in his vulnerable right flank maintained by Harland's First Brigade, so that it occupied a slight rise in the terrain just north of the railroad. Palmer shifted regiments toward the division's left flank, held by Colonel Boughton's Third Brigade, thus extending his line farther south toward the vulnerable Union center.[77]

During Palmer's absence from the front earlier that morning, Harland had prudently taken the initiative to consolidate his badly scattered regiments. After their successful repulse of the Junior Reserves, the forward elements of Claassen's and Harland's brigades maintained their positions along the Lower Trent and Neuse Roads. Harland recognized his brigade's "long and necessarily weak" position, and became concerned about the "considerable" Confederate force in his front and on his left flank. He wisely ordered Colonel Sprague's 2nd Massachusetts Heavy Artillery and Colonel Raymond's 23rd Massachusetts withdrawn to the British Road line.[78]

Sprague withdrew Major Amory and his two companies from along the Neuse Road and reported with the entire regiment to brigade headquarters. For unknown reasons, Harland's initial order to withdraw failed to reach Raymond. Throughout the initial Confederate attacks, the 23rd Massachusetts had maintained its position near the Neuse Road Bridge, isolated and alone. Raymond deemed the position critical, and had earlier warned Harland that it could not be held without reinforcement. Finally, at 2:00 p.m., orders reached

76 Thorpe, *History of the Fifteenth Connecticut*, 133.

77 *OR* 47, pt. 1, 982.

78 Ibid., 985.

Raymond directing the regiment back to the division's main line. The 23rd fell back unmolested and occupied a position to the right of the 9th New Jersey.[79]

Palmer instructed Colonel Claassen to advance his brigade (minus Curtiss's detachment on the Lower Trent Road) from the Union right toward Jackson's Mill. Claassen had advanced less than a half mile when Confederates were observed on the Dover Road and the brigade's right flank. Wisely, Claassen ordered a withdrawal to a position along the British Road, where his command occupied a line to the left of Boughton's brigade.[80]

Throughout the morning Boughton's Third Brigade had occupied the division's left flank. In response to initial attacks and a tenuous position, Boughton ordered the left of his line refused (or angled back) across the British Road, where it constructed temporary barricades. During this time, Sprague's 2nd Massachusetts Heavy Artillery reported to Boughton and was placed on the brigade's far left. Claassen's brigade arrived and extended line held by the artillerymen, anchoring the far left of Palmer's division.[81]

Palmer's extension of his line farther south occurred just as General Hoke renewed his attack. Claassen's brigade had only partially established its new defensive position when Confederate infantry, several hundred yards in front, suddenly emerged from the woods. Confederate artillery preceded the advancing infantry with a tremendous barrage of shot and shell. A "brisk fight" ensued, but the Union line held firm. During the engagement, Capt. Stephen Van Heusen's Battery D, 3rd New York Light Artillery deployed its four 3-inch ordnance rifles in support of Claassen's infantry. Heusen's gunners were exposed to "a galling fire of musketry and cannon shot" that resulted in the loss of several of the battery's horses.[82]

Confederate infantry also appeared in front of Boughton's brigade, but seemed disinclined to press the attack upon the Federals' hastily constructed earthworks. To counter the potential threat, two sections from Capt. William E. Mercer's Battery C, 3rd New York Light Artillery arrived to bolster the brigade's position. Boughton employed Mercer's guns to cover the open field in

79 Emmerton, *A Record of the Twenty-Third Regiment Mass.*, 245; OR 47, pt. 1, 986-987.

80 OR 47, pt. 1, 982, 990; Thorpe, *History of the Fifteenth Connecticut*, 132. Schofield had accompanied Palmer and Goodrich on their way back toward the front, and upon arriving, the department commander continued down the line in the direction of Wise's Forks.

81 OR 47, pt. 1, 982, 987, 992.

82 OR 47, pt. 1, 990; Hall and Hall, *Cayuga in the Field*, 272.

Col. Horace Boughton
Wade Sokolosky Collection

front of his brigade. One section was deployed on the British Road, and the remaining section near the brigade's right flank.[83]

Lieutenant Goodrich arrived just as the fighting erupted in front of Boughton's and Claassen's brigades. The staff officer dismounted and continued along the division line, where he discovered a Union battery with its guns silent. "Half the guns were pointed to the front and the other half facing southwest," observed Goodrich. Looking toward the southwest he witnessed "one of the prettiest sights in all my army experience." A Confederate brigade had formed into line about 100 yards away. Goodrich asked the officer in charge of the battery, "Why do you permit this formation in your front without an effort to drive it back." The officer responded that he was waiting for orders. "Open fire immediately with canister on those Rebels, by order of Palmer," snapped Goodrich. The battery jumped into action and forced the Rebels to take cover.[84]

Although the Union artillery succeeded in disrupting the Confederate infantry's advance, it failed to silence the Rebel batteries. Starr's gunners promptly replied and all but silenced the Union guns. Boughton later wrote, "I had hoped that all these pieces would silence the rebel battery, but was disappointed." Five of the six Union guns employed were disabled. In addition to the guns, Mercer's Battery C lost five men and two horses.[85]

As Palmer's division successfully held off repeated Confederate attacks, to their left at the Union center Colonel Savage's thin line of dismounted cavalry stubbornly held its ground. Fortunately for the New Yorker troopers, a long

83 *OR* 47, pt. 1, 992.

84 Thorpe, *History of the Fifteenth Connecticut*, 134.

85 *OR* 47, pt. 1, 992; Hall & Hall, *Cayuga in the Field*, 274.

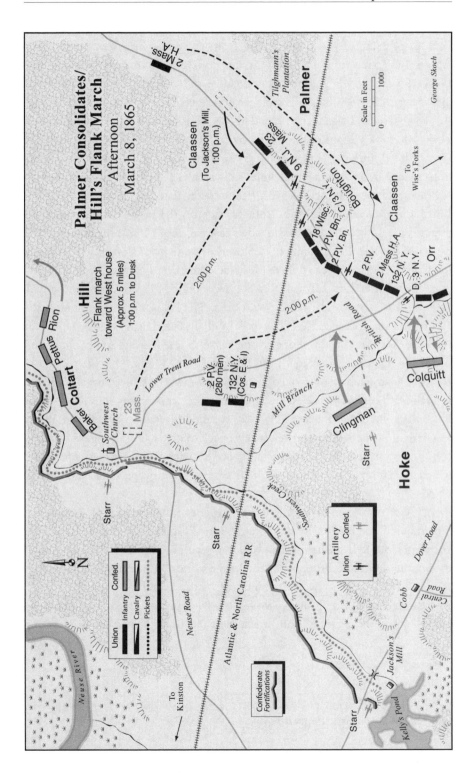

Palmer Consolidates/ Hill's Flank March
Afternoon
March 8, 1865

column of infantry was approaching from the rear—help was on the way. About 1:00 p.m., after marching at the double-quick for about five miles, General Ruger's First and Second Brigades arrived at the front and deployed into the gap between Palmer's and Carter's divisions.

Ruger's First Brigade, commanded by Col. John M. Orr, arrived at Wise's Forks and took a position along the Lower Trent Road. With no time to waste, Orr ordered three of his regiments forward into line to relieve Savage's horsemen and to connect with Palmer's division. The 124th Indiana, as the lead regiment, established the link with Palmer's left flank, followed by the 120th Indiana in the center, and the 128th Indiana on the brigade's left flank. Orr retained the 180th Ohio as the brigade's reserve, about 100 yards in rear of the center of the line. Each regiment deployed a company of skirmishers to check the Confederate advance while the brigade constructed earthworks.[86]

Shortly after Orr's arrival, Ruger's Second Brigade, commanded by Col. John C. McQuiston reached Wise's Forks. The brigade's lead regiment, the 129th Indiana, followed by 123rd and 130th Indiana, deployed to the left of Orr's brigade. McQuiston sent a strong skirmish line forward under command of Lt. Col. Dewitt C. Walters of the 123rd Indiana.[87]

McQuiston's brigade arrived without a moment to spare. Captain William L. Day of Company K, 123rd Indiana remembered swinging into line "where the bullets were the thickest." As Day steadied his ranks, Pvt. David Bailey reached into his pocket and threw away a pack of cards. Observing his soldiers' actions, Day asked, "What the hell are you throwing your cards away for?" To which Bailey replied, "I don't want to be killed with a pack of cards in my pocket."[88]

"We were moved up hastily in time to check the advance of the rebels," remembered an Indiana soldier. The Union skirmishers advanced and soon encountered a Rebel skirmish line "charging with a yell." The Federals forced the Southerners back through the "thick pine woods." Emerging into a clearing, the Hoosiers observed two Rebel lines of battle several hundred yards away. The Confederates fired a heavy volley but McQuiston's veterans stubbornly held their ground. Private John R. Miller of the 123rd Indiana later described

86 OR 47, pt. 1, 949, 942.

87 OR 47, pt. 1, 949.

88 William S. Kaler, *Roster and History of the One Hundred Twenty-Third Regiment, I. V. I. in the War of the Rebellion* (Rushville, IN: 1899), 50-51.

the fight to his father: "I had that day just 50 fair shots at a distance of less than 300 yards and if I didn't hurt anybody, why there is no virtue in powder, and lead and Springfield rifles."[89]

The timely arrival of two fresh Union brigades effectively eliminated the threat to the Union center. Just west of the Lower Trent Road, Ruger's two brigades formed a line on a rise fronted by Mill Branch. Using the terrain to their advantage, the Indiana regiments constructed a formidable line of breastworks. Unlike Carter's and Palmer's divisions, Ruger ordered his brigades to carry their pioneer tools until wagons were available. Each brigade carried "at least 100 axes, 100 spades or shovels and 25 pickaxes."[90]

Private Moses Sisco of the 123rd Indiana missed the afternoon fight, having been detailed in the rear. While away from the front he observed groups of New England soldiers wandering in without their weapons. Later, when Sisco returned to his regiment, he found to his surprise the 123rd Indiana "in possession of some brand new rifles." As he admired the shiny weapons, others in the regiment commented that "them Feather Bed soldiers from New Bern had run like sheep" at the sight of the Confederates emerging from the swamp.[91]

The arrival of Ruger's two brigades compelled Bragg to reinforce Hoke. By mid-afternoon, Hoke's attack had lost momentum as his infantry faced increased resistance along Cox's vastly strengthened line. Bragg wanted to continue attacking but did not have enough infantry at his disposal. He had already committed most of his force. All that remained was General Clayton's division from the Army of Tennessee. Clayton's undersized command was typical of many from the Western army, numbering only 416 men.[92]

During the morning, Clayton had arrived at the Kinston rail depot and immediately marched to the front. Arriving at the battlefield, his two Georgia brigades were held in reserve behind the Confederate defenses near Jackson's

---

89 John R. Miller to his father, March 14, 1865.

90 OR 47, pt. 2, 656.

91 Sisco, *Personal Memoirs*, 71.

92 Henry D. Clayton, "Report from H. D. Clayton, Clayton's Division, to Major J. W. Ratchford, March 15, 1865," in Henry De Lamar Clayton, Sr. Papers, William Stanley Hoole Special Collections Library, University of Alabama, Tuscaloosa, Alabama. Hereafter cited as "Clayton's Battle Report." Clayton reported that he went into the battle with only 396 men, 20 less than what Hill reported. For the purposes of this study, the authors chose to use Hill's reported strength; OR 47, pt. 1, 1,088.

Mill. At 2:00 p.m., Bragg ordered Clayton to cooperate with Hoke by attacking east toward Wise's Forks. As Clayton moved down the Dover Road, his Georgians soon encountered the Federal main line. Clayton prudently refrained from assaulting the strong position, opting to engage in a lively skirmish.[93]

On the Neuse Road, Hill's command continued northeast toward its out-of-the-way objective. So far the march had proved uneventful with no sign of the enemy. At 4:30 p.m., Hill's column arrived at the West house, near the intersection of the Neuse and British Roads. General Hagood ordered Colonel Rion's South Carolinians to picket the British Road and scout southeastward toward the enemy. Rion soon returned "without meeting even a straggler."[94]

As Hill patiently waited for the sight of fleeing Yankees, a rider arrived with orders from Bragg. The commanding general directed Hill to attack south along the British Road, provided it was not "too late to accomplish anything before dark." If Hill thought an attack imprudent, Bragg granted him the option to return to Southwest Creek.[95]

Hill called a meeting with his commanders to weigh their options. Only General Baker advised to attack, while the others "thought it too late and too hazardous." Perhaps Baker's lone suggestion to attack stemmed from wanting to provide his Junior Reserves an opportunity to redeem their earlier performance. With Hill's command isolated from the main Confederate force, several miles from the bridge over Southwest Creek, and with Union cavalry reportedly patrolling on the Neuse Road to their rear, Hill opted to countermarch down the Neuse Road toward Kinston.[96]

As Hill's infantry retraced its steps, a heavy rain mixed with sleet fell upon the formations, adding misery to a wasted foray. During the return march, Hill received further orders from Bragg directing him to cross the bridge over Southwest Creek on the Neuse Road and move south to the crossing near Jackson's Mill. Hill was then to report to Hoke for further orders.

About midnight, Hill's command arrived in the vicinity of Jackson's Mill, where it was directed to occupy a position alongside Hoke's division next to the British Road. Hoke's and Hill's deployment east of Southwest Creek reflected

93 OR 47, pt. 1, 1086; Clayton, "Clayton's Battle Report."

94 OR 47, pt. 1, 1,087; Hagood, *Memoirs*, 352.

95 Hagood, *Memoirs*, 352.

96 OR 47, pt. 1, 1,087.

Bragg's decision to employ an echelon style of defense, with the majority of his infantry deployed along the first line, and a smaller force held in reserve along the second line. Baker's Junior Reserves returned to their former position behind the creek, where they unceremoniously spent the remainder of the battle in a reserve role.[97]

Despite the day's lost opportunity, Bragg remained positive about what his hastily assembled force had accomplished. That evening, Bragg informed Generals Lee and Johnston of his success. "We captured three pieces of artillery and several hundred prisoners. The number of his dead and wounded left on the field is large. Our own loss, thanks to Providence, is comparatively small. Major-Generals Hill and Hoke have exhibited their usual zeal, energy, and gallantry in achieving this result. Our troops behaved most handsomely."[98]

Although the commanding general remained upbeat, Bragg's foot soldiers exhibited "mixed emotions." Lieutenant Fabius H. Busbee of the 3rd North Carolina Junior Reserves remembered the "mingled sensations of elation and anxiety" that one of his fellow officers exhibited. Their joyous victory on March 8 was tempered by the unwelcome news of Federal reinforcements advancing from Wilmington and of Sherman's approach toward Fayetteville.[99]

Such feelings of reservation were held not only by those in the army, but also by North Carolina civilians. Forty-one-year-old Catherine Ann Devereaux Edmondston of Halifax did not admire Bragg. Upon learning of the victory at Kinston, Edmondston wrote in her diary that "our joy is dampened by the fact that Bragg . . . will be sure to . . . lose the fruit of a victory gained by him."[100]

Analysis of March 8, 1865

The return of General Hill's command to the defenses along the British Road marked the end of Bragg's offensive operations on March 8. The Confederates' initial success waned with the onset of evening. Bragg, unable to

---

97 Calder, diary, March 8, 1865; *OR* 47, pt. 1, 1,087; Hagood, *Memoirs*, 354.

98 *OR* 47, pt. 1, 1,078.

99 Edwards and Rowland, *Through the Eyes of Soldiers: The Battle of Wyse Fork*, 45; Fabius H. Busbee, "The Junior Reserves Brigade," in Clark, *Histories*, vol. 4, 591.

100 Beth G. Crabtree and James W. Patton, eds., *Journal of a Secesh Lady: The Diary of Catherine Ann Devereaux Edmondston 1860-1865* (Raleigh, NC, 1979), 676.

exploit his gains, allowed the Federals precious time to adjust their lines and prepare for another attack. Cox's Union army had survived a near catastrophe.

From the Union perspective, a lack of credible intelligence, poor tactical employment of units, and the lack of unit cohesion within Carter's and Palmer's divisions contributed to the scare for the Federals. On the Confederate side, Bragg's failure to aggressively follow up his early success resulted in a lost opportunity to possibly turn back the Federal advance on Goldsboro.

From the commencement of the march from New Bern, the Federals executed an aggressive offensive that relied on intelligence based on rumors, the skill of the cavalry, and a general knowledge of the area. Throughout the war, Union forces from New Bern had frequently conducted small-scale raids toward Kinston, and had grown accustomed to the Confederates' defenses and tactics. During such operations, engagements with the Rebels amounted to nothing more than brief skirmishes until they reached Southwest Creek. As Cox's Provisional Corps advanced toward Kinston, the Confederates remained true to character, lulling the Federals into a false sense of security.

Up until March 5, Cox believed the Confederate threat to be insignificant and "of questionable reliability." This changed the following day with the arrival of Colonel Claassen's brigade at Wise's Forks, and the subsequent reporting of General Hoke's presence. On the morning of March 8, local civilians reported a large Confederate formation moving around the left flank. The Union cavalry reported the same, based on information received from similar sources. Cox dismissed the reports as "rumors," trusting the cavalry to confirm or deny. Mistakenly, Cox placed too much trust in the ability of his horse soldiers.[101]

Why did the cavalry fail to provide timely information on enemy movements? Due to a lack of primary source material, the answer remains a mystery after 150 years. For reasons unknown, Colonel Savage left no post-battle report for operations concerning the 12th New York Cavalry. Consequently, it remains uncertain which units were responsible for guarding the lower crossings of Southwest Creek. Possible clues exist within the individual service records of Savage's troopers. The 12th New York Cavalry, including the attached companies from the 23rd New York Cavalry, lost a total of 80 men during the entire battle, 73 of which were reported captured or missing. Forty-eight of the captured (65 percent) were in Company H, 12th New York Cavalry and Company A, 23rd New York Cavalry on March 8. The

---

101 Cox, *Military Reminiscence of the Civil War*, Vol. 2, 435.

Capt. Robert B. Hock,
Co. F, 12th New York Cavalry,
captured on March 8, escaped four days later.

U.S. Army Military History Institute

excessive number of men bagged from these two companies indicates they were likely responsible for picketing the crossings south of Upham's position. Service records reveal that Company H had 38 men captured on March 8, and Company A had 10 captured. Interestingly, neither unit recorded any men wounded, and only one soldier, Lt. Augustus Pittman of Company H, was killed.[102]

What is known is that the cavalry failed to properly post the crossings and provide the early warning. Hoke's men surprised and captured the majority of the Federal troopers posted along the Upper Trent Road. Cox later commented that the cavalry had grossly neglected its duty, "so badly done" it had resulted in the rout of Upham's brigade.[103]

Unit cohesion is extremely important in combat, reflecting the trust individual soldiers or regiments have in one another to perform their duty. Due to the Provisional Corps' hasty creation, Carter's and Palmer's divisions suffered from a lack of unit cohesion. These divisions were a "melting pot" of units cobbled together from Union garrisons in eastern North Carolina, strengthened with raw recruits and furloughed soldiers.

Another significant weakness in Cox's command was a lack of veteran field units in Carter's and Palmer's divisions. Thanks to garrison duties, the majority of these regiments had grown unaccustomed to the rigors of campaigning.

---

102 The 23rd New York Cavalry consisted of only two companies and served its entire term of service, from July 1863 to July 1865, in the state of North Carolina, attached to the 12th New York Cavalry. In January 1865, Company B reported the majority of its personnel dismounted. These men were unavailable during the battle and remained at New Bern. Men that had horses were assigned to Capt. Emory Cummings, Company A.

103 Ibid., 932; OR 47, pt. 1, 932, 62.

Many were badly understrength, but the assignment of hundreds of raw recruits to the divisions only exasperated the problem.

As a result, Union commanders made two tactical errors that, if properly exploited by the Confederates, could have resulted in disaster. First, Carter deployed Upham's brigade well in advance of the rest of the division. Upham was left isolated, separated by almost two miles from other Union brigades posted at Wise's Forks. Second was a lack of coordination for mutual defense between Carter's and Palmer's divisions, resulting in a large and dangerous gap between the two commands.

On March 7, when Upham's brigade relieved Claassen's at the intersection of the British and Dover Roads, Upham chose a different strategy than his fellow brigade commander. According to Carter's official report, Upham was "to guard the British road, south of the Dover road, and the country between it and Southwest Creek." Unlike Claassen, who only deployed a small security element forward of the British Road, Upham posted the majority of his brigade beyond the road—about 800 yards beyond Claassen's former position.

While Upham deployed his brigade in a textbook manner, it was grossly over extended. By pushing this brigade so far forward, it lacked sufficient numbers to cover the area along Southwest Creek while also trying to connect with the skirmishers from Palmer's division. Moreover, Upham had deployed approximately half of his brigade as skirmishers, greatly diminishing the strength of his main line.

The brigade's position was well beyond supporting distance of friendly forces. Carter visited Upham's headquarters on the morning of March 8, but incredibly neither commander recognized the brigade's tenuous position. Carter and Upham were well aware of the rumors circulating about a possible threat from the south, yet the position of Upham's brigade remained unaltered. The only adjustment made was to reposition an undersized regiment to protect Upham's left flank from the potential threat. For his part, Carter offered only cautionary words of advice to "use great vigilance," and ordered a small detachment from the main line to picket the British and Dover Roads. Both commanders apparently placed their faith in the Federal cavalry and its ability to provide ample warning. However, it is doubtful that an early warning from the cavalry would have changed the outcome.[104]

104 Ibid., 993-994.

Cox's perception of Upham's rout was unambiguous. His journal entry for March 8 read: "The mischief was caused by the lack of care and the inexperience of that brigade. They had been two years doing garrison duty, and could not believe there was any danger till it was upon them." Years later, with the benefit of hindsight, Cox questioned the placement of Upham's brigade when he wrote, "Upham seems to have marched the whole of his brigade to Jackson's Mills and to have left only a picket post at the British road." Surprisingly, Cox seemed to not hold Carter accountable as Upham's senior commander, and retained him as a division commander for the remainder of the campaign.[105]

In defense of his commander, Captain White of the 15th Connecticut wrote years later faulting Carter for Upham's misfortune. White suggested that it was the senior officers who were negligent. No senior officer expected "that there would be any serious fighting," let alone having to fend off an attack. White stated that Carter, "feeling secure in his position," did not make the necessary adjustments to protect his division, and never realized his "stupid blunder" until it was too late. [106]

On the morning of March 8, Generals Carter and Palmer disregarded security with regard to a mutual defense. They seemingly trusted their thin skirmish lines posted along Southwest Creek to provide proper security, while neglecting to ensure a sufficient link between the remaining brigades of both divisions. Because the two division commanders failed to confirm that their units were connected, the large gap in the Union center remained undefended until the arrival of Ruger's division later that afternoon. The Federals escaped a calamitous error by sheer luck and Bragg's lack of situational awareness.

It is important to note that on March 7, Carter's and Palmer's divisions were focused on offensive movements toward accomplishing Cox's objective of seizing the three bridges over Southwest Creek. In carrying out these orders, the divisions moved along separate routes without mutually supporting one another, and creating separation. When operations ceased that evening, the lead brigades from each division established hasty positions: Upham's brigade

---

105 *OR* 47, pt. 1, 932. Cox's assessment is only partially correct regarding the experience level of Carter's regiments. For example, the 27th Massachusetts Infantry had extensive combat experience, as recent as 1864, having fought in several engagements during the Bermuda Hundred and Petersburg campaigns with the Army of the James; Cox, *Military Reminiscence of the Civil War*, vol. 2, 432.

106 Thorpe, *The History of the Fifteenth Connecticut*, 103.

astride the Dover Road near the Jackson's Mill crossing, and portions of Harland's brigade along the Lower Trent Road, close to the railroad and Neuse Road crossings. Because the division commanders expected to resume operations the next day to seize the bridges, both generals failed to rectify the gap.

If Carter and Palmer exhibited questionable leadership abilities, the same can be said of General Bragg, who bears sole responsibility for arguably the greatest blunder committed by the Confederates on March 8. Bragg's hands-off approach to command left him unaware of Hill's success in blocking the retreat of Upham's soldiers toward the railroad, and the subsequent threat Hill posed to the gap between Palmer's and Carter's divisions. Bragg lost his greatest opportunity for complete victory when he halted Hill's supporting attack, and unwittingly diverted 2,000 veteran infantry away from the fight to "make many captures" of refugees from Upham's brigade.[107]

Despite Bragg's failures, his two principal subordinates, Generals Hoke and Hill, exhibited a spirit of cooperation that ensured the Confederates' initial success. Hill successfully drew the Federals' attention away from Hoke's flank movement, and when the time came to attack, Hill did so aggressively. Unfortunately for Hill, his fighting ended early on March 8. Regardless of Hill's secondary role, the North Carolinian deserves much credit for adhering to General Johnston's request "to forget the past." Hill acted honorably and cast aside his personal feelings toward Bragg—at least for the time being.

D. H. Hill's fellow Tar Heel, General Hoke, deserves credit for delaying Cox's initial advance on March 7, thus preventing the Federals' seizure of the Southwest Creek defensive line. It was Hoke who formulated the bold plan resulting in the rout of Upham's brigade—despite the doubts of his fellow generals. Throughout the day, Hoke maintained constant pressure on the Federals as his men struggled to maintain unit integrity while operating in difficult terrain. On March 8, Hoke clearly lived up to this reputation as an excellent division commander

Hoke's surprise attack, which had begun so favorably, failed because Bragg lacked the numbers to exploit his initial success. Had Hill's command remained on the battlefield and cooperated with Hoke, the Confederates might have driven a wedge between Palmer's and Carter's divisions, threatening the latter's

---

107 *OR* 47, pt. 1, 1,087.

two remaining brigades at Wise's Forks. Victory slipped through their hands, however, and the March 8 battle ended in a draw.

It is difficult to measure the total number of losses suffered by both sides on the first day of battle. Confederate reports are non-existent, and Union reports encompass the entire three days of fighting. With regard to Union operations, the single greatest loss on March 8 occurred in Upham's brigade. Cox's final report from the campaign listed a total of 889 losses from the brigade—11 killed, 50 wounded, and 828 missing (93 percent). One can assume the number wounded was actually higher, as the report fails to account for wounded soldiers taken prisoner by the Confederates. Interestingly, the total of 828 officers and men captured from Upham's brigade was not as large as the Confederates claimed—in some cases as many as 1,500. Not counting Upham's brigade, the total number of Union losses in Carter's and Palmer's divisions was 185 men, as both divisions assumed a primarily defensive role following Upham's rout. By the end of the day on March 8, Cox had suffered approximately 1,100 losses throughout his entire corps.[108]

On the Confederate side, the patient registry of Hoke's chief surgeon, Isaac S. Tanner, indicated that losses within the division were not significant. Tanner's numbers are consistent with Bragg's message late on March 8, in which he informed Generals Johnston and Lee, "Our own loss . . . is comparatively small." As the Confederates were primarily the aggressors, their losses were probably between 200 and 300 men. Regardless of the actual figure, Bragg remained committed to maintaining the offensive.[109]

The Confederate success on March 8 came at a cost in senior officers. Bragg's casualty list included Col. James H. Neal of the 19th Georgia, who was shot through the head while leading his regiment against Upham's brigade, and Col. John J. Hedrick of the 40th North Carolina, who was severely wounded in the thigh—an injury that sidelined him until April 1865.[110]

*　　*　　*

108　*OR* 47, pt. 1, 61-62. Throughout the three-day battle, Palmer lost a total of 127 men, with Carter losing 58.

109　Tanner, Patient Registry, 135-139; *OR* 47, pt. 1, 1,078.

110　*OR* 47, pt. 1, 1,078; *Atlanta Intelligencer*, May 4, 1866; File of Col. John J. Hedrick, *Records of Confederate Soldiers Who Served During the Civil War, Compiled Service Records of Confederate Soldiers Who Served in Organizations from the State of North Carolina*, M270, roll 72, Records Group 109, National Archives.

With the day's fighting at an end, it remained for the two armies to care for their wounded and bury their dead. Throughout the day Confederate surgeons had treated the wounded from both sides at the Cobb house. The residence and surrounding property were transformed into a makeshift hospital. As a prisoner of war, Private Baldwin of the 15th Connecticut assisted Southern doctors in caring for the Federal wounded. In one instance, the resourceful Union soldier traded a "fine pen knife" to one of the Confederate surgeons for some morphine. Later, Baldwin came upon a Frenchmen from Company E with both hips shattered. "Oh, sergeant, do shoot me, do shoot me," cried the Frenchmen. Baldwin gave the man a dose of morphine, "his way to death was made easy."[111]

Baldwin's quick thinking resulted in temporary duty with his wounded comrades. Confederate soldiers had attempted to usher Baldwin away to Kinston with the other prisoners. Baldwin was pleading with his captors when General Bragg and his staff rode by the Cobb house. Seeing an opportunity, Baldwin called out to the passing general. When Bragg heard the captive, he turned in the saddle to see what the commotion was all about. The quick-thinking Baldwin saluted Bragg and asked if he could "stay with my brother." Bragg replied, "Yes, and if any one disturbs you, tell them you are here by order of General Bragg." A surgeon on Hoke's staff later gave Baldwin a pass to remain on the field.[112]

In addition to the Cobb house, the Confederates established a temporary collection point near Jackson's Mill for the triage of wounded. The walking wounded crossed Southwest Creek where Surgeon Tanner had established the field hospitals belonging to Hoke's division. The more seriously wounded were transported by ambulance or wagon.

Despite their earlier success on the battlefield, the Confederate rear area was soon discovered to be wholly vulnerable to Union cavalry, especially the unguarded wagon trains bearing the wounded. Late in the afternoon, a detachment from the 12th New York Cavalry launched a little-known raid between Southwest Creek and Kinston. It is unclear whether the bold operation was officially planned, or whether it was simply initiated by daring Union troopers. Either way, the mounted thrust proved successful. The Federal

---

111 Thorpe, *History of the Fifteenth Connecticut*, 248.

112 Ibid.

Confederate surgeon Stiles Kennedy,
8th North Carolina Infantry
Courtesy of Bill Bowers

cavalry captured a number of Rebels, including Surgeon Stiles Kennedy of the 8th North Carolina Infantry and five ambulances.[113]

Later that evening it began to rain again and the wounded were moved to the Cobb house porch. Baldwin noticed Cpl. George W. Manville of Company E, 15th Connecticut, who sat on the porch with his back against the house. Baldwin approached him to check his wounds: "His breast was exposed, and I saw in it a ghastly hole, from which blood oozed at every breath."[114]

Not all of the wounded were fortunate enough to receive immediate care. Many were grievously injured and unable to move. As the fighting shifted to other parts of the battlefield, the fallen had been left behind. Some waited for help for hours, bleeding and suffering from exposure to the elements. Private Pendleton of the 27th Massachusetts remained on the field all the night and was not recovered until the following morning.[115]

Captain Bassett of the 15th Connecticut was brought off the field and placed in one of the small cabins outside the Cobb house. Baldwin discovered the young officer in a terrible state. Realizing death was near, the private

---

113 *Old North State* (Beaufort, NC), March 14, 1865; File of Surg. Stiles Kennedy, *Compiled Service Records of Confederate Soldiers Who Served in Organizations from the State of North Carolina*, M270, roll 185, Records Group 109, National Archives. Kennedy's service record indicates that he was captured on March 8, 1865. After a brief stay at the Confederate prisoner of war camp at Point Lookout, Maryland, Union authorities paroled Kennedy on March 30, 1865.

114 Ibid.

115 Pendleton, "My Experience in the Army." 24.

brought water to ease the man's parched throat. With many requiring care, Baldwin left to attend others.

About 10:00 p.m., wagons arrived along with orders to move the wounded "Yanks" to Kinston. Baldwin assisted in loading the wagons, finishing by 1:00 a.m. Before departing, Baldwin paid one last visit to the shanty where he had left Bassett. "I saw him outside, dead, and divested of his uniform."[116]

116 Ibid., 249.

Chapter 6

"The roar of musketry sounds like thunder"

— *Lt. Geo. F. Stewart, 124th Indiana*

The Tide of Battle Turns

The inhabitants of Kinston awoke on the morning of March 9 to find their town overwhelmed by wounded soldiers—the aftermath of the previous day's fighting.

Throughout the night, Confederate and Union casualties arrived from the front—some on foot and others in wagons and carriages. Bragg's medical director, Surgeon T. G. Richardson, used homes, businesses, and churches to accommodate the growing number of wounded, but these accommodations were inadequate. Lacking proper facilities, Richardson prepared to evacuate them westward. He telegraphed the staff at Goldsboro's Confederate General Hospital No. 3 to "prepare for 300 wounded, in addition to your present accommodations." Since 1862, the Confederate army had operated two hospitals in Goldsboro: General Hospital No. 3, a multistory brick building located in the former Wayne Female College, and Wayside Hospital No. 4, a large wood-frame structure located at the fairgrounds near the railroad.[1]

---

1   Tyndall, *Threshold of Freedom*, 103; Edwards and Rowland, *Through the Eyes of Soldiers: The Battle of Wyse Fork, Kinston, North Carolina March 7-10, 1865*, 84; OR 47, pt. 2, 1,851; The Rebel army established a third hospital in Goldsboro for men infected with smallpox prior to the Wise's Forks battle. We know little about the facility's role in treating the wounded from Kinston. Wayside Hospital No. 4 was just one in a network of hospitals established in the spring of 1862 along the "wayside," i.e., the major rail lines throughout the South. "Waysides" offered food and minor medical care for Confederate soldiers traveling on furlough.

Confederate General Hospital No. 3, Goldsboro, N.C.
Wayne County Public Library, Goldsboro, N.C.

Throughout March 9, the Confederates at Kinston evacuated hundreds of injured men to Goldsboro via the Atlantic & North Carolina Railroad. When a troop train arrived from Smithfield, the wounded were loaded onto the cars for the return trip, which enabled Richardson to clear all except those too weak or too grievously injured to travel. Sergeant Baldwin of the 15th Connecticut offered a revealing account of the suffering endured during the evacuation process:

> Toward night there was a sudden commotion. Officers were hurrying to and fro, and soon orders came to move all he wounded to a train of box cars that stood on the track not far away. It seemed to me little short of downright murder, but at it I went, lifting the poor fellows into the old baggage wagons and then into the filthy cars, and not until 8 o'clock was the last sufferer loaded. That night was one of unutterable horror. There was no light in the cars, and before the train reached Goldsboro, it stopped and started at least twenty times, and at every start a jerk was given that sent a thrill of agony from one end of the train to the other. In the car where I was I could distinctly hear the

broken bones grate at such times. I felt as if I would shoot the engineer if I could, for it seemed to me he did it from sheer cruelty.[2]

Kate Sperry, a Confederate nurse at General Hospital No. 3, recalled the confusion that befell Goldsboro with the arrival of so many wounded. "Been a battle near Kinston . . . per consequences wounded have just been pouring in the town, wounded Yanks, too," she wrote. "They are established at Court House and the slightly wounded of our men sent to the Fair Grounds and the worst cases here." Wounded Federals were hospitalized at the fairgrounds as well, including Major Osborn and several wounded comrades from the 15th Connecticut. The men had to endure a painful ride from the railhead to the fairgrounds hospital, "in a springless wagon without bed or blanket."[3]

The influx soon overwhelmed Goldsboro's hospitals and prompted the Confederates to send casualties to points farther west on the North Carolina Railroad: Raleigh, High Point, Greensboro, and Charlotte. Among the 21 wounded admitted to the Wayside Hospital in High Point on March 9 were three severely injured Union soldiers from the 27th Massachusetts. The Confederate medical service's ability to transport wounded from Kinston to High Point in just one day—a distance of 150 miles—is surprising, given the unreliability of the railroad in March 1865.[4]

In contrast with Bragg's timely evacuation of his March 8 casualties,

Confederate Nurse Kate Sperry
*Fred Barr Collection, Stewart Bell, Jr. Archives Room,
Handley Regional Library, Winchester, VA*

2   Thorpe, *History of the Fifteenth Connecticut*, 251.

3   Kate S. Sperry, diary, March 8, 1865, in Personal Papers Collection, The Library of Virginia, Richmond, VA; Thorpe, *History of the Fifteenth Connecticut*, 251.

4   Barbee Hospital Registry, March 9, 1865, High Point Public Library, High Point, NC; The Barbee Hotel served as a wayside hospital from September 1863 through May 1865. The hotel was located across from the North Carolina Railroad freight depot in High Point.

Cox's wounded required up to three days to reach Foster General Hospital in New Bern—a distance of less than 30 miles. This delay occurred for two reasons. First, the Federals at Wise's Forks were located ten miles from an operational railroad. Second, Cox's Provisional Corps lacked the usual complement of wagons and ambulances found in comparable U.S. Army organizations. Because each division had only 10 wagons, field hospitals had to retain casualties for hours and even days.[5]

Worse yet for Cox, the lack of transportation affected the Federals' resupply operations. On the morning of March 9, Pvt. Charles A. Tournier of Battery A, 3rd New York Light Artillery awoke "wet to the skin . . . cold and hungry." Because his brigade's supply wagons had failed to return to the front, Tournier and his comrades went without food for more than 24 hours. The famished Tournier scoured the ground where the battery's horses had just fed for dropped kernels of corn. He then boiled the corn and devoured it. "This is the first time I ever ate the leavings of an animal," wrote Tournier, "but it tasted good."[6]

Tournier's desperate action epitomized the problem that Cox and his commanders faced in feeding their men—a situation which grew worse each day. The heavy fighting on March 8 compounded the problem, as ammunition resupply and the evacuation of wounded competed for the corps' limited transportation. Cox later wrote that on March 9, "We husbanded our resources, for our ammunition was running short and the roads through the swamps were nearly impassable."[7]

In response to General Johnston's reinforcement of Bragg, Schofield directed Cox to "remain on the watchful defensive" and await Gen. Darius Couch's arrival with two additional divisions from the XXIII Corps. Schofield's order weighed heavily on Cox, for it might well have prevented him from

---

5 *OR* 47, pt. 1, 932; Forty-four percent (35 of 80) of the Union wounded from March 8 required three or more days to reach Foster General Hospital in New Bern. Records of the Adjutant General's Office, 1762-1984, Field Records of Hospitals, 1821-1872, Records Group 94, Foster General Hospital Registry, March 1865, National Archives, Washington, D.C. Hereafter cited as Foster General Hospital Registry, March 1865; Core Creek Station was 12 miles along the railroad from Southwest Creek.

6 Tournier, diary, March 9, 1865.

7 *OR* 47, pt. 1, 932; pt. 2, 747, 749. At noon on March 9, Cox sent a message to Capt. Amos S. Kimball in New Bern about trying to locate a delayed ammunition train containing 250,000 rounds; Cox, *Military Reminiscences*, vol. 2, 440.

reaching Goldsboro before Sherman. To Schofield's credit, he did not hide the bad news but kept his superiors informed of the situation at Wise's Forks. On the morning of March 9, Schofield wrote to Grant, "We can make no further progress until General Couch arrives." Schofield's caution was based on his assumption that Bragg would remain on the offensive, and that Johnston was concentrating his army at Kinston. Although Schofield was mistaken about Johnston's true intent, he was wise to assume the defensive pending Couch's arrival.[8]

By March 9, Cox had stretched his supply line to the limit. Until the railroad was repaired closer to the front, an advance toward Goldsboro would entail great risk. He confronted an enemy of unknown strength that displayed an eagerness to fight. The Provisional Corps' poor performance on March 8—Ruger's division notwithstanding—revealed to Schofield the unreliability of the units in Cox's command. In a letter to Grant, Schofield gave a brutally frank assessment of Palmer's District of Beaufort units, describing them as "little better than militia."[9]

To keep Sherman updated, Schofield sent a concise message describing the setback at Wise's Forks: "The enemy has checked our advance. . . . A portion of Johnston's force is here, and I presume the rest will be concentrated in my front." Schofield also revealed his uncertainty of reaching "Goldsboro or even Kinston" before Sherman. He promised to "work as far forward as I can and put the railroad in order as far as I go."[10]

While Schofield pondered strategic and operational challenges, Cox sought to prevent another disaster on the order of Upham's rout. He could at least rest assured his corps was protected by strong entrenchments. The Federals had dug fortifications throughout the night of March 8-9 with lines of abatis across their front and cleared fields of fire, thus creating a formidable obstacle to any attacking force. Cox's fortified line stretched more than two miles in length, with Palmer's division holding the right, Ruger's the center, and Carter's the left.

---

8   OR 47, pt. 2, 743-744; Cox, *Military Reminiscences*, vol. 2, 440; OR 47, pt. 2, 743-744; In his memoirs, Cox noted that he and Schofield exaggerated the strength of the Army of Tennessee: "We were necessarily wholly ignorant of the causes which had reduced the divisions from the West." Cox, *Military Reminiscences*, vol. 2, 444.

9   OR 47, pt. 2, 743-744.

10 Ibid., 744.

Palmer's division was entrenched along the British Road, where it defended the railroad toward New Bern. Palmer's position had one critical weakness. It failed to secure the Neuse Road several miles to the north, leaving the corps' right flank and rear area vulnerable to Confederate incursions. General Harland's First Brigade held the extreme right of Palmer's line in the vicinity of the Tilghmann farm. Just north of the railroad, Harland placed the 9th New Jersey and the 23rd Massachusetts along the road. On Harland's left, Colonel Boughton's Third Brigade entrenched south of the railroad in a blocking position across the British Road. Boughton deployed his units from right to left: the 18th Wisconsin, the First and Second Provisional Battalions, and the 2nd Massachusetts Heavy Artillery. To Boughton's left, Colonel Claassen's Second Brigade, comprising the 132nd New York, and Lt. Col. Frank S. Curtiss's 2nd Provisional Regiment, occupied the division's left flank.[11]

To Palmer's left, Ruger's veteran division from the XXIII Corps defended the center, but more importantly, it protected the Lower Trent Road—vital to maintaining a line of communication throughout the corps' line. Ruger's division consisted of two brigades. Colonel John M. Orr's First Brigade held the right of the line, with the 124th, the 120th, and the 128th Indiana regiments posted from right to left. Orr held the 180th Ohio in reserve. On the left, Col. John C. McQuiston's Second Brigade connected with Carter's division just north of the Dover Road. From left to right, McQuiston's brigade consisted of the 130th, the 123rd, and the 129th Indiana regiments.[12]

Carter's division anchored the corps' left flank near Wise's Forks, linking Carter to Ruger's and Palmer's divisions via the Lower Trent Road, affording the Federals the advantage of interior lines. The Dover Road served as a Union supply route running from Wise's Forks back to the railhead. To hold the left flank, the Federals had to hold onto Wise's Forks. Since March 7, Carter's division had occupied the crossroads. Carter had initially placed his brigades several hundred yards west of Wise's Forks in order to block the Confederate advance along the Dover Road. However, Carter's initial defensive alignment failed to address a potential enemy advance from the south via the Lower Trent Road. This left Wise's Forks and the corps' rear area dangerously exposed.

11 The 2nd Massachusetts Heavy Artillery was detached from Harland's brigade and remained with Colonel Boughton's command throughout the remainder of the battle.

12 *OR* 47, pt. 1, 942-944, 949-953; John R. Miller to father, March 14, 1865, in http://www.civilwararchive.com.

Since the evening of March 8, Cox had sought to bolster his vulnerable left flank. He ordered Carter to refuse his left so that his line ran parallel to the Dover Road and then cut back toward the Lower Trent Road. The division's line thus resembled the letter "L," with Col. Adam G. Malloy's First Brigade posted north of the Dover Road and Lt. Col. Henry Splaine's Third Brigade joining on Malloy's left and angling toward the Lower Trent Road.[13]

Malloy's brigade consisted of three hastily-formed Provisional battalions and the recently attached 85th New York. Splaine's Third Brigade fielded two under-strength infantry regiments, the 17th and 25th Massachusetts, and Battery A, 3rd New York Light Artillery, which now served as infantry. Because Splaine's brigade lacked the manpower to extend to the Lower Trent Road, Col. John S. Jones and 439 men of the 174th Ohio from Ruger's division arrived on the evening of March 8 to lengthen Splaine's line.[14]

*   *   *

As Cox's soldiers strengthened their defenses, General Bragg—aware of Couch's approach from Wilmington—sought to strike the Federals before reinforcements arrived. In short, "time was of the essence." Displaying his usual lack of tactical imagination and situational awareness, Bragg chose once again to attack the Federal flank while maintaining pressure on the center, evidently unaware that the enemy's position was far stronger than it had been the previous day.[15]

Bragg selected the Union right (Palmer's division) as his target and assigned Hoke's division to carry out the operation. Hill's Army of Tennessee contingent would maintain a supporting role. Bragg emphasized to Hoke and Hill that the "attack must be vigorous and determined, as success must be achieved." The Confederate commander, however, failed to strengthen the crucial force in his attack plan—Hoke's division. On the morning of March 9, Hoke had only three brigades on hand: Kirkland's, Colquitt's, and Clingman's. Hagood's brigade

---

13 *OR* 47, pt. 1, 978, 994-995.

14 Ibid., 956, 995-996.

15 Edwards and Rowland, *Through the Eyes of Soldiers: The Battle of Wyse Fork, Kinston, North Carolina March 7-10, 1865*, 47; Bragg biographer Judith Lee Hallock claims that the general "lacked imagination, a serious drawback that caused inflexibility during crises." See, *Braxton Bragg and Confederate Defeat*, vol. 2 (Tuscaloosa, AL, 1991), 268.

remained attached to Hill's Army of Tennessee contingent. Without Hagood's men, Hoke's striking force fielded an estimated 4,000 men.[16]

Bragg's orders failed to mention Baker's Junior Reserves brigade. The Juniors remained in the trenches along Southwest Creek and were "not subject" to Hill's orders. Hagood's and Baker's brigades numbered approximately 2,100 men, yet Bragg allowed them to remain idle throughout the day. Relegated to a supporting role, Hill's troops held the Confederates' advanced position along the British Road, creating a diversion to cover Hoke's movement.[17]

By the morning of March 9, the Southerners had constructed a line of breastworks that paralleled the British Road down to Mill Branch. From there, the works angled sharply back toward Southwest Creek and the railroad, running parallel with Mill Branch. Facing the railroad, Hagood's brigade occupied the position nearest to Southwest Creek. On Hagood's right stood the two brigades from Hill's (Coltart's) division: Manigault's and Deas's. To the southwest and along the British Road, Pettus's Alabama brigade went into position, followed by Jackson's and Stovall's brigades from Clayton's division. Featherston's brigade from Maj. Gen. William W. Loring's (Jackson's) division, of Stewart's Corps, was posted on Clayton's right.[18]

During the night of March 8, Featherston's brigade, commanded by Col. Wallace B. Colbert of the 40th Mississippi, had arrived at Kinston and marched immediately to the battlefield. Featherston's brigade consisted of seven understrength Mississippi regiments, and fielded about 200 to 300 men. Colbert's command was the first of three brigades from Loring's division to arrive. The two remaining brigades arrived on March 9.[19]

16 *OR* 47, pt. 2, 1,359-1,360; Hagood, *Memoirs*, 354; See Appendix B, Table E for the estimated strength of Hoke's division on March 9. The estimated 4,000 men included the 67th and 68th North Carolina.

17 *OR* 47, pt. 2, 1,359-1,360; Bragg's low opinion of Hagood and the brigade's large number of "Red Infantry" may have influenced Bragg's decision to relegate him to a supporting role; The First Battalion Junior Reserves may have participated on March 9. For a more detailed discussion describing the possible role of the Junior Reserves on March 9, see Manarin et al., *North Carolina Troops*, vol. 17, 105-108.

18 Pettus's brigade was the only unit from Maj. Gen. Carter L. Stevenson's division, of Lee's Corps, to fight in the battle; Loring, who was sick, remained at Greensboro as his division continued forward to Smithfield. Colonel James Jackson, commander of Scott's brigade, assumed temporary command of Loring's division. Loring recovered sufficiently a week later to participate in the battle of Bentonville. Albert Q. Porter, diary, March 9.

19 Colonel Colbert was mortally wounded at the battle of Bentonville.

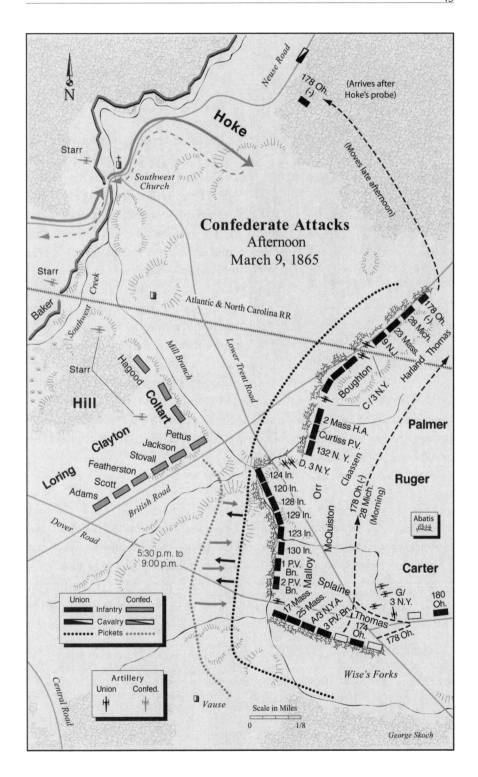

N

Neuse Road

Hoke

178 Oh. (-)

(Arrives after Hoke's probe)

(Moves late afternoon)

Starr

Southwest Church

Starr

Baker

Southwest Creek

Confederate Attacks
Afternoon
March 9, 1865

Atlantic & North Carolina RR

178 Oh. (-)
28 Mich.
23 Mass.
9 N.J.
Boughton
C/3 N.Y.
Harland
Thomas

Mill Branch

Lower Trent Road

2 Mass H.A.
Curtiss P.V.
132 N.Y.

Palmer

Hill

Hagood

Coltart

Starr

Claussen

Pettus

Jackson

Stovall

Clayton

Featherston

Scott

Adams

Loring

British Road

D. 3 N.Y.
124 In.
120 In.
128 In.
129 In.
123 In.
130 In.
1 P.V. Bn.
2 P.V. Bn.

178 Oh. (-)
28 Mich. (-)
(Morning)

Ruger

Abatis

Dover Road

5:30 p.m. to
9:00 p.m.

Orr

McQuiston

Malloy

Splaine

Carter

G/ 3 N.Y.

180 Oh.

17 Mass.
25 Mass.
A/3 N.Y.A.
3 P.V. Bn.

Thomas
174 Oh.

178 Oh.

Union	Confed.
Infantry	
Cavalry	
Pickets	

Central Road

Artillery
Union   Confed.

Vause

Wise's Forks

Scale in Miles
0   1/8

George Skoch

Lt. Albert T. Goodloe,
35th Alabama Infantry
Confederate Veteran

Scott's brigade, commanded by Capt. John A. Dixon of the 12th Louisiana reached Kinston about noon. Dixon commanded an estimated 350 men, of whom 235 belonged to the 12th Louisiana. The rest were all that remained of five depleted Alabama regiments. Lieutenant Albert T. Goodloe of the 35th Alabama remembered that upon reaching Kinston the brigade "with the upmost promptness marched forward four miles to the front," where they occupied a position along the British Road. Later that afternoon, Adams's brigade, commanded by Lt. Col. Robert J. Lawrence of the 14th Mississippi, arrived at the front. Adams's brigade, consisting of six understrength Mississippi regiments, fielded no more than 300 men.[20]

*   *   *

At daylight, Hoke's division left its position along the British Road and marched back toward Kinston, crossing the bridge over Southwest Creek and moving down the Neuse Road "around the enemy right with a view to attack." Shortly after dawn, the Union skirmishers of Colonel Orr's First Brigade discovered the Confederates had abandoned their advanced position of the

---

20 Captain Dixon assumed command of Scott's brigade in the absence of Colonel Jackson and remained in that position through the battle of Bentonville. Albert Q. Porter, diary, March 9; The strength estimate for Scott's brigade is from Email correspondence between the author and R. Hugh Simmons, July 12, 2005; Albert T. Goodloe, *Confederate Echoes, A Soldier's Personal Story of Life in the Confederate Army from the Mississippi to the Carolinas* (Washington, D.C., 1893), 61-62.

previous night. Companies B and G of the 124th Indiana moved forward to investigate the enemy's sudden disappearance. After the Hoosiers had proceeded almost a quarter-mile, they discovered the Confederates had withdrawn and occupied a stronger position atop a hill. Unwilling to relinquish the ground his men had gained, Orr ordered his skirmish companies forward, where they occupied the abandoned Southern works and fortified them with barricades.[21]

A short time later, the Army of Tennessee's skirmish line opened a spirited musket fire to draw attention away from Hoke's movement. Captain William P. Howell of the 25th Alabama, commanding the skirmishers from Zach Deas's brigade, described the subsequent fighting on March 9 as "considerable," and had it not been for his "heavy leather haversack," a Yankee bullet might have dealt him a mortal wound. Captain Howell's advanced position was located "in a swamp with thick undergrowth" only a short distance from the Federals. Because of the heavy terrain, Howell recalled that "we could not see whether it was a mere picket line or a line of battle."[22]

Colonel Toulmin, commanding Deas's brigade, was eager to gain intelligence on the Union position to his front. Toulmin ordered Howell "to send a man up a tree to ascertain the strength of the enemy's line." Knowing the danger inherent in such a task, Howell was troubled by the order. Howell's concern for the welfare of his men conflicted with his duty to carry out the directive. "I hesitated to obey that order," wrote Howell, "Because I knew if the enemy should happen to spy a man in or up a tree, they would be sure to shoot him at once."[23]

Howell decided on a course that solved his leadership dilemma. "I called the men up who were not on duty and informed them of the order, stating that I did not desire to force any man to do so, without his consent, but made this proposition: that if any of them would volunteer to go up a tree, a Yankee for to see, I would relieve him from further duty that day and he could go back to the regimental camp and rest." Surprisingly, one of the two "Galvanized Yankees"

---

21 Hagood, *Memoirs*, 354; OR 47, pt. 1, 943, 946. Major Henry S. Gibson of the 124th Indiana Infantry estimated that a distance of 100 to 150 yards separated the opposing skirmish lines.

22 William P. Howell, Manuscript, "History of the 25th Alabama Infantry 1861-1865," Alabama Department of Archives and History, Montgomery, Alabama, 46-47.

23 Ibid., 47.

assigned to his company accepted the duty—a soldier Howell had not expected to volunteer.[24]

Howell's Company I contained two New Yorkers known as "Allen and Jones." Both had opted to serve in the Confederate army rather than suffer in a Southern prison. One of them stepped forward and volunteered to ascend the tree. Although he made "no new discovery," the lucky soldier escaped without drawing the attention of his former Union comrades. Howell was impressed by the man's show of bravery. However, "not very long after," both "Galvanized Yankees" slipped away, never to be seen again.[25]

For General Palmer's men picketing the division front, the firing erupting south of their position increased their anxiety. Aware of Hill's failed attempt on the Federal right the previous day, Palmer's soldiers anticipated an attack. By mid-morning, the pickets reported a Confederate troop movement approaching the division's right flank.[26]

Cox perceived increased firing along the Union center as merely a demonstration to draw attention from the flanks, and he notified Palmer at 8:30 a.m. to "watch your right." Cox's message seemed apologetic: "I extremely regret the inconvenience of our position, but regard it our duty to maintain it till it becomes manifestly untenable." Cox also discussed with Palmer the worst-case scenario of having to "unite all our forces at Gum swamp again." It was at first unclear why Cox sent the message.[27]

Palmer's response an hour later seemed to reveal the reason. Palmer reported the presence of Confederates "massing at some point on our right." He informed Cox of two of the enemy's probable courses of action. "We must expect either an attack on our right soon, or that the enemy will give us the 'go-by' and move on our communication."[28]

Palmer's suggestion of a Confederate "go-by" into the corps' rear area was a valid concern. However, Palmer failed to answer Cox about what he had done to mitigate the possibility of such an attack—a question Cox had asked two

24 Ibid.

25 Ibid., 48.

26 OR 47, pt. 2, 749-750; Cox wrote many years later that Hill's aborted attempt to attack the Federal right on March 8 also "gave an exaggerated impression of the enemy's strength." Cox, *Military Reminiscences*, vol. 2, 439.

27 OR 47, pt. 1, 982-983.

28 Ibid., pt. 2, 750.

hours earlier at 6:15 a.m. Cox also asked, "What did you send over to the Neuse Road, and . . . have you any intelligence from there?" The corps commander recognized the vulnerability and reminded Palmer of their discussion the previous night "as to the imperative necessity of watching and, if possible, guarding the Neuse Road crossing of the creek."[29]

In all likelihood, Palmer lost his nerve and began to invent reasons to withdraw his division—again displaying a lack of determination when facing difficulties. The report of Confederates massing on his flank clouded Palmer's judgment, largely because of his respect for Hoke, which made him excessively cautious. In any event, Palmer hoped to avoid the same disaster that had befallen Carter's division the day before.

In response to the enemy threat to the Union right, Cox ordered Ruger to reinforce Palmer. At 10:00 a.m., Ruger sent his Third Brigade, commanded by Col. Minor M. Thomas, to bolster the threatened flank. After a brisk hour-long march, Thomas arrived at Palmer's position with the 178th Ohio and 28th Michigan. Palmer ordered Thomas's two regiments to occupy a position on the division's right, where the veteran soldiers began throwing up works.[30]

Cox did not allow Palmer's anxiety to distract him from the rest of the corps. During the morning, Cox received definitive proof that he faced not only Hoke's division, but elements of Lee's and Stewart's corps. Reinforcements from the Army of Tennessee indicated that the enemy had no intention of abandoning the battlefield. Cox assumed that Bragg would again seek to exploit the Union left flank occupied by Carter's division.[31]

The corps commander ordered Carter to shift his line parallel with the Dover Road and extend it to block the Lower Trent Road south of Wise's Forks. A 150-man detachment from Malloy's brigade, under Capt. William Howard, relocated to the left of the 174th Ohio and allowed the Federals to reach the road. The survivors of the 15th Connecticut's March 8 debacle had begun to return and assisted in constructing earthworks and abatis. Near the southern fork of the Dover and Lower Trent Roads, Carter deployed nine

---

29 Ibid., 749; Other than cavalry patrols, Palmer had not complied with Cox's guidance, and did not comply until late on the afternoon of March 9. Palmer ordered the 178th Ohio to fortify and guard the Neuse Road. See, OR 47, pt. 1, 957.

30 OR 47, pt. 1, 940, 954. The 28th Michigan was detached from McQuiston's Second Brigade.

31 Ibid., 978.

12-pound Napoleon smoothbores from Batteries I and G of the 3rd New York Light Artillery. Later that evening, the 180th Ohio from Ruger's division arrived and went into reserve along the Dover Road, just east of Wise's Forks near Ruger's division field hospital.[32]

*   *   *

By late afternoon, Hoke's division was in position to attack Palmer's division. At 4:20 p.m., Bragg notified Hill by courier "that [at] any moment Hoke's guns may be heard." Due to the paucity of Confederate accounts of Hoke's operations on March 9, little is known about how the division deployed against Palmer and what ultimately transpired.[33]

Rather than attack the Yankee position, however, Hoke withdrew his brigades. Historians rely upon Hill's post-battle report as a source for Hoke's cancelled March 9 attack. Unfortunately, Hill's account was brief and provided few details. He stated that Hoke found "the Yankees strongly intrenched and did not attack." After withdrawing, Hoke returned his division to the works along the British Road, where it occupied a position on the right of Hill's Army of Tennessee contingent. For Bragg, Hoke's "feeble" attempt eliminated any hope of the Confederates repeating the success of the previous day.[34]

The official accounts submitted by Palmer and his brigade commanders described March 9—aside from late-night skirmishing—as uneventful, which confirms that Hoke did not attack. Palmer reported that "with the exception of some slight skirmishing on my left . . . the enemy did not disturb us." General

---

32 Ibid., 932, 943, 956, 948, 994-995. Regimental historian Thorpe stated that on March 9, the survivors from March 8 and Captain Munson's Company K—the latter having arrived from New Bern that afternoon—were employed constructing earthworks along the Trent Road. The regiment's exact position on Splaine's line is unknown, but several sources suggest that it was close to the Trent Road, which is consistent with Splaine's attempt to reach the road. According to Thorpe, the regiment mustered for duty seven officers and 219 enlisted men on March 10. Thorpe, *History of the Fifteenth Connecticut*, 104; Horace F. Farnsworth to Fannie Farnsworth, March 9, 1865, Douglas W. Reynolds, Jr., private collection. Private Farnsworth of the 15th Connecticut estimated the surviving number at no more than 160 men on March 9; General Ruger estimated the hospital was one half-mile down the road from Wise's Forks. OR 47, pt. 1, 940; The 180th Ohio left one company on the First Brigade's skirmish line when ordered to support Carter's division. OR 47, pt. 1, 943.

33 OR 47, pt. 2, 1,360.

34 Barrett, *The Civil War in North Carolina*, 288; Barefoot, *General Robert F. Hoke*, 289; OR 47, pt. 1, 1,087; Hagood, *Memoirs*, 354; Manarin et al., *North Carolina Troops*, vol. 12, 273.

Harland, whose brigade occupied the extreme right of the Union line and would have sustained the brunt of Hoke's attack, neglected to mention anything about March 9 in his official report.[35]

About 5:30 p.m., in conjunction with Hoke's operations against the Federal right, Hill launched his diversionary attack against Ruger's and Carter's divisions. Hill ordered Capt. Edward B. Vaughan of the 50th Alabama, commanding the skirmish line of Lee's Corps, to advance against the Federals. In contrast with Hoke, Vaughan's operation appeared more resolute and determined—especially to the Federals confronting him. Ruger later noted that Hill's Confederates "pressed the skirmish line pretty severely a number of times and seemed to [be] meditating an attack."[36]

Lieutenant Col. Reuben C. Kise of the 120th Indiana commanded the skirmish line of Orr's brigade. Throughout the day, Kise's skirmishers engaged the Confederates in "occasional sharpshooting" as the latter attempted to draw attention from Hoke. "[J]ust after dark," the Rebels "launched a heavy attack on the picket line" and forced one of the skirmish companies form the 128th Indiana to withdraw. Lieutenant Col. Jasper Packard, commander of the 128th Indiana, observed the company's sudden movement to the rear but his remaining Hoosiers "bravely stood to their posts, firing to their flank, and held the enemy in check" until he ordered a second company forward in support.[37]

Orr's commissary officer, Lt. George F. Stewart, described the fighting on March 9 as "hard." Stewart recalled that at one point he was four miles to the rear collecting supplies at the railroad, and the roar of musketry sounded to him "like thunder" that could be heard above a driving rain. An amusing mishap involving Colonel Kise occurred along Orr's skirmish line that night. About 9:00 p.m. the Confederates attacked, and as Kise ran up and down the line encouraging his men, he tumbled into an old well. According to First Sgt. David W. Smith of the 120th Indiana, the ground the skirmishers occupied had once been a Confederate camp with a number of shallow wells. Unable to climb out unassisted, Kise shouted for help but could not be heard above the noise of

35 OR 47, pt. 1, 983-986; Analysis of Union hospital records reveals that Palmer's division suffered minimal casualties on March 9. Foster General Hospital admitted 14 wounded Union soldiers on March 9, three of whom were from Palmer's division. RG 94, Foster General Hospital Registry, March 1865.

36 OR 47, pt. 1, 940; Malloy placed the time of Hill's attack at "about 5:30 p.m."

37 Ibid., 943, 947.

Col. Willard Warner, 180th Ohio Infantry
U.S. Army Military History Institute

combat. After the firing had died down, Kise's men rescued their uninjured leader.[38]

Later that evening, Lt. Col. Hiram McKay of the 180th Ohio, wet from the rain and weary from the day-long fight, decided to slip to the rear for a cup of coffee. As he withdrew from the line, McKay was severely wounded in the groin and died four days later. McKay's death deeply affected those who had known him. His regimental commander, Col. Willard Warner, characterized McKay as "brave, cool, and skillful as an officer of three years' experience in all grades from private to his present rank." Maj. John T. Wood of the 180th Ohio wrote his wife, "The Col. & myself are like two children since [McKay] was gone."[39]

Confederate activity increased sharply along Palmer's front during the night, principally in the area of Claassen's and Boughton's brigades. The skirmishing occurred at intervals and became "brisk" at times. Boughton stated that the attacks along his front had "little effect." The 3-inch ordnance rifles of Captain Mercer's Battery C, 3rd New York Light Artillery repelled the Southerners with "a few . . . well directed" shots.[40]

South of Ruger's division, the Confederates' diversionary attacks against Carter's division were intense. Splaine reported that his Third Brigade skirmish line was "sometimes driven by the enemy and sometimes driving him," with neither side gaining an advantage. Private Thomas J. Carey of the 15th Connecticut recorded in his diary: "The Rebels Opened on our front early. . . . We have been hard at work making breastworks of fallen trees and brush, dirt.

38 George F. Stewart to Sallie Stewart, March 9, 1865; David W. Smith, "Hovey's Babies," *National Tribune*, Dec. 29, 1887.

39 *OR* 47, pt. 1, 948-949; John T. Wood to wife, March 12, 1865, in Civil War Miscellaneous Collection, U.S. Army Military History Institute, Carlisle, Pennsylvania.

40 *OR* 47, pt. 1, 992.

The Rebels tried hard to force our lines through the day and night. Did Not Do It."[41]

Colonel Malloy's First Brigade skirmishers stopped the Confederate attack with a "well-directed volley, driving them back in confusion." However, the Southerners regrouped and attacked again, this time capturing Malloy's advanced position. Malloy refused to yield. About 9:00 p.m. he reinforced his skirmish line, drove off the Confederates, and recaptured their rifle pits.[42]

Private William Fifer, a replacement soldier destined for Sherman's army and temporarily assigned to Malloy's brigade, proudly informed his mother about the fight on March 9—his first time in combat:

> I have seen the elephant. . . . The rebs drove our pickets in and then we ware ordered out to retake the rifle pits. We went and took the pits. I fired 20 rounds at them at first. They raised the yell but the hoosiers fed them on led. Instid of running they scadalded [skedaddled]. We built works all nite and laid in the ditch raining all the time.[43]

In conjunction with the Army of Tennessee's demonstration, Confederate artillery from Starr's battalion subjected the Federal left to a "vigorous shelling." The Union batteries stationed near Wise's Forks were ordered not to fire in order to conserve their limited supply of fixed ammunition. Eager to quiet the annoying Rebel gunners, Lieutenant Richardson of Battery I, 3rd New York Light Artillery, approached General

Captain William E. Mercer, Battery C,
3rd New York Light Artillery
U.S. Army Military History Institute

41 OR 47, pt. 1, 1,000; Thomas J. Carey, diary, March 9, 1865, in the Southern Historical Collection, Manuscripts Department, Wilson Library, University of North Carolina at Chapel Hill.

42 OR 47, pt. 1, 996.

43 William Fifer to mother, March 17, 1865.

Col. Adan G. Malloy
U.S. Army Military History Institute

Carter and several other senior officers gathered just behind his gun line. Lieutenant Richardson advised his division commander "that our guns could shut up the rebels in short order." Before Carter could respond, General Schofield appeared and politely assured Richardson, "You all will have business enough to-morrow."[44]

*   *   *

Despite General Hoke's aborted attack, the aggressive Bragg remained confident and even eager to strike Cox's Union army again. Sometime before evening, and probably after the cancelled assault against the Federal right, Bragg and Hoke met to formulate a plan of attack for the following day. D. H. Hill was not present at this meeting, but Bragg's courier directed that general to "confer" with Hoke regarding the proposed offensive maneuver. In order to bolster the attacking force, Bragg instructed Hill to return Johnson Hagood's brigade to Hoke's division. Bragg further ordered Hill to hold the Army of Tennessee in its present position during the upcoming attack.[45]

Sometime after 6:15 p.m., Bragg modified Hill's assignment for the next day. Hill reported that Bragg directed him "to co-operate" with Hoke by making a strong demonstration against the enemy but "not to attack the main line of the Yankee earth-works." Bragg based this order on the belief expressed by officers of the Army of Tennessee that their men would refuse to attack

---

44 Hall and Hall, *Cayuga in the Field*, 274; It is unknown which batteries from Starr's battalion provided the artillery support in conjunction with D. H. Hill's demonstration. Lieutenant Jones from Company E (Dickson's Battery) recorded in his diary for March 9: "Lay all day at the mill. Hoke moved on the right of the enemy, but was so well prepared that the troops withdrew without attacking." Jones, diary, March 9, 1865.

45 *OR* 47, pt. 2, 1,360.

earthworks, owing to the army's disastrous experience during the previous campaign in Tennessee.[46]

Several factors influenced General Bragg's willingness to attempt a third assault. First, the morale among the troops remained high, spurred on by their success on March 8. Second, for the past three days, Bragg had stalled Cox's advance while sustaining only minimal losses. In response to Governor Zebulon Vance's offer to send additional medical support to Kinston, Bragg replied, "[O]ur loss is so small as not to require [it]."[47]

The final factor was General Johnston's decision to send additional units from the Army of Tennessee. Johnston dismissed his earlier concerns about reinforcing Bragg's operations at Kinston, and now appeared emboldened by the promising success on March 8. In hopes of achieving an even greater victory, Johnston ordered "any officer commanding troops arriving at Smithfield . . . [to] proceed immediately to Kinston." Johnston's decision was risky—General William T. Sherman's large Union army was closing in on Fayetteville—and it deviated from his plan to concentrate his scattered forces at Smithfield.[48]

Bragg initially rejected the idea of receiving substantial reinforcements. Throughout March 9, Col. John B. Sale, Bragg's assistant adjutant general, had traded messages with Lt. Col. Archer Anderson, his counterpart on Joe Johnston's staff. At first, Sale indicated that Bragg desired no more than the 1,000 men from Alexander P. Stewart's Corps. By 5:45 p.m., Bragg had changed

---

46 Ibid., pt. 1, 1,088; The courier's message that D. H. Hill received was written at 6:15 p.m., which implied that General Bragg modified the order sometime after having written the note and the Army of Tennessee's attack the following day.

47 Ibid., pt. 2, 1,363.

48 Ibid., 1,356. General Johnston sent the message at 6:30 a.m. on March 9, having arrived at Fayetteville, where he met with Gen. William J. Hardee. Johnston had abandoned his plan to oppose General Sherman along the Cape Fear River, leaving Hardee to contend with Sherman's army unsupported. Johnston directed that Hardee delay Sherman, which would buy time for the Confederate concentration at Smithfield. Wade Hampton's cavalry would form the rear guard at Fayetteville, allowing Hardee time to safely withdraw his infantry and artillery across the river and move north. Johnston also instructed Hardee to keep his corps between Sherman and the city of Raleigh, delaying the Yankees' march without placing his command at any undue risk. Once he confidently ascertained Sherman's ultimate objective—Raleigh or Goldsboro—Hardee was to move to block any threat against the capital and await further reinforcements from Smithfield. If Sherman moved toward Goldsboro, however, Hardee would move to support Bragg.

his mind, and requested instead that Johnston "hurry forward all troops to Kinston. Operation there not closed."[49]

Bragg's not wanting additional forces is puzzling. Commanders in combat typically demand more resources. Bragg, however, may have been unsure of his next move. Bragg's biographer, Judith L. Hallock, describes the March 9 dispatches as indicative of "his usual battlefield confusion and lack of focus." However, the 30 minutes between Colonel Sale's last message and Bragg's dispatch to Hill regarding the next day's proposed attack indicates that Bragg made his decision after Hoke had called off his flank maneuver. Only then did Bragg make obtaining reinforcements a priority.[50]

*   *   *

As the skirmishing diminished to sporadic musketry, the exhausted soldiers on both sides seemed content to settle down for the evening. The night was cold and wet, and the men sought warmth from a woolen blanket or a small campfire. For some, their work had just begun. Back along the Dover Road, surgeon Alonzo Garwood of Ruger's division "received wounded through the night." The doctor recorded that he had "been operating on the wounded and sending them back to N. B. [New Bern]." Despite the day's intense skirmishing, casualties had been relatively few for the Federals—a benefit of fighting behind prepared works.[51]

According to several accounts, the Confederates sustained relatively few losses, despite being on the offensive. Most documented casualties occurred in units fighting under Hill's command. General Hagood reported that his brigade was "engaged in heavy skirmishing all day," but suffered only five casualties— all wounded in action. In Marcellus Stovall's Georgia brigade, the only recorded

49 Ibid., 1,350, 1,355, 1,356, 1,359-1,360; Historian Timothy W. Auten maintained that Bragg thought "as long as he remained on the offensive and simply replaced his losses, his rebel forces would remain victorious." See Timothy W. Auten, *The Battle of Wyse Fork: North Carolina's Neglected Civil War Engagement*, 126.

50 Hallock, *Braxton Bragg and Confederate Defeat*, 251; Cox later summarized Bragg's operations on March 9: "a delay in testing conclusions with us was due, in part no doubt, to the fact Stewart's corps of the Army of Tennessee was en route to him." Cox, *Military Reminiscences*, vol. 2, 441.

51 Garwood, diary, March 9, 1865; Foster General Hospital admitted 14 Union wounded soldiers on March 9. RG 94, Foster General Hospital Registry, March 1865.

Maj. John N. Slaughter,
34th Alabama Infantry
*Alabama Department of Archives and History,
Montgomery, Alabama*

losses occurred in the 42nd Georgia, which suffered three men wounded, including Lt. John O. Medlock, the commander of Company A. Lieutenant Col. C. Irvine Walker, commanding the 10th South Carolina of Arthur Manigault's brigade, was wounded in the hand and evacuated from the battlefield. Colonel Walker was the highest ranking casualty from the Army of Tennessee.[52]

That night, Pvt. Thomas Smyrl of the 34th Alabama suffered a horrific death—not from enemy fire but from a tree. Smyrl's brigade commander, Lt. Col. John C. Carter, had just completed an inspection of Manigault's brigade and returned to his former regiment for a few hours' sleep. He found the regiment's commander, Maj. John N. Slaughter, and Private Smyrl already lying under a tent-fly. Carter rolled out his blanket next to them and quickly fell asleep.[53]

Unbeknownst to the three men, the tree they slept under had been damaged earlier by artillery fire. A strong gust of wind caused the tree to fall upon the slumbering soldiers. The massive trunk crushed the skull of the 36-year-old Smyrl, killing him instantly. Carter escaped the accident with minor injuries. Robert Smyrl, Thomas's younger brother, was at the regimental hospital when his brother was killed. Hours later he learned of his sibling's demise and wrote his mother and sister. "It has become My Painful Duty to

---

52 Hagood, Memoirs, 354-355; *Atlanta Weekly Intelligencer*, April 17, 1865; File of Lt. Col. Cornelius I. Walker, *Compiled Service Records of Confederate Soldiers Who Served in Organizations from the State of South Carolina*, (M267), roll 245; Captain Robert Z. Harllee of Company D assumed command of the 10th South Carolina with Walker's departure. Walker would not return to the regiment until after the battle of Bentonville.

53 Robert Smyrl to mother, March 10, 1865, Civil War Soldiers Letters, Alabama Department of Archives and History, Montgomery, Alabama; Hagood's departure from the Army of Tennessee's line along Mill Branch required Colonel Carter to reposition his men.

state to you this morning I have just returned from the grave of my own Dear Brother." Later that day, Robert Smyrl constructed a wooden coffin, and with the help of several soldiers, buried his brother Thomas on the Wise's Forks battlefield, far away from their Alabama home.[54]

54 Ibid.

Chapter 7

"The worst place that I ever was in my life."

— *Pvt. James O. Keel, 17th North Carolina*

Bragg's Final Strike

A cold, predawn rain marked the end of an already miserable night for soldiers on both sides. Earlier in the evening, Lieutenant Calder of the 1st Battalion North Carolina Heavy Artillery spent time in Kinston seeking rations for the men. The lieutenant returned to the Mill Branch line about 1:00 a.m., exhausted and hoping for a few hours' sleep. At 3:00 a.m., General Hagood ordered the brigade into formation, for it was moving to rejoin the rest of General Hoke's division. With Hagood's departure, Bragg sent the 67th North Carolina from Hoke's position back to D. H. Hill's to occupy the vacated trenches along Mill Branch.[1]

Before sunrise, General Hoke's division was on the move. With Hagood's return, the North Carolinian commanded all four of his brigades for the first time at Wise's Forks. With the addition of the 68th North Carolina, Hoke fielded the strongest Rebel force on the battlefield—about 4,400 men. Bragg looked to Hoke's division to lead the attack for the third consecutive day.[2]

---

1   Calder, diary, March 10, 1865; *OR* 47, pt. 2, 1,360.

2   It is unclear what the 68th North Carolina's brigade assignment was throughout the battle of Wise's Forks. Regimental historian John E. Evans described the unit's participation in the battle in one sentence: "Our regiment was in the division of General Hoke and several of the regiment were killed and wounded." See John W. Evans, "Sixty-eighth Regiment," in Clark, *Histories*, vol. 3, 722; See also Manarin et al., *North Carolina Troops*, vol. 15, 523-524.

Surprise would be crucial to Hoke's success, and he used the waning hours of darkness to conceal his movement from the Federals. He marched his brigades south along the Cobb (or Central) Road and then turned east, executing a cross-country movement toward the Lower Trent Road. Hoke halted the division near the Wooten house after a relatively easy route on the Cobb Road. "Everything passed off quietly and safely until we reached Mrs. Wooten's house," wrote a Confederate officer. The closeness to the Federals required the Southerners "to be very cautious." Hoke worried that as the division moved farther south, a large undefended area would separate his command from Hill's line along the British and Dover Roads. To prevent a possible Federal counterattack through this area, Hoke ordered Hagood to leave a detachment along the route to act as a blocking force.[3]

Hagood assigned Colonel Taylor's 275-man battalion the mission of guarding the area along the Cobb Road. Taylor reported to Major Davis of Hoke's staff for instructions. Davis identified the Wooten house as a reference and instructed Taylor to hold that point "at all costs" should the attack fail and the enemy attempt to cut off Hoke's retreat. Taylor promptly deployed his "Red Infantry" and awaited the outcome of Hoke's attack. In the meantime, Mrs. Wooten welcomed a group of Taylor's officers into her home, where they warmed themselves in her parlor.[4]

Once the division exited the Cobb Road and began moving east, Hoke's men struggled through the "pocosons and dense pine forests" characteristic of the region. Mr. Wooten aided Hoke in negotiating the difficult terrain and by late morning, the division reached the Lower Trent Road. Once again, Hoke had succeeded in maneuvering his command onto the flank of the enemy undetected. Fault for this reality was again placed on Colonel Savage and his 12th New York Cavalry, who had been assigned the dual mission of finding the enemy and, more importantly, providing early warning against potential threats. The day before, Cox had prudently ordered Savage to post videttes well beyond the Union left flank, all the way down to the Upper and Lower Trent Roads. Mounted patrols also operated along the routes to the south to locate the enemy

3 Calder, diary, March 10, 1865.

4 The major may have been Maj. David S. Davis from the 66th North Carolina. John D. Taylor, "War Recollections of Col. John D. Taylor," in John Douglas Taylor Papers, North Carolina Division of Archives and History, Raleigh, North Carolina, 5-6; Calder, diary, March 10, 1865.

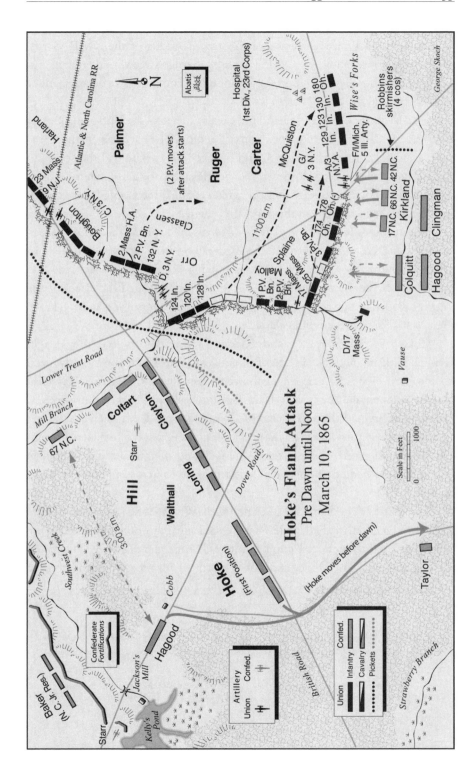

Hoke's Flank Attack
Pre Dawn until Noon
March 10, 1865

and make contact with General Couch's two divisions of the XXIII Corps, which were approaching via Onslow County. Savage's New Yorkers failed to locate Couch, but they did report the location of a company-size detachment of Confederate cavalry on the Cobb Road.[5]

On March 10, Cox had ordered the cavalry to patrol the Upper and Lower Trent Roads southeastward to the town of Trenton. The corps commander was eager to make contact with Couch and believed his cavalry had the southern approaches well covered. However, the videttes were too far down the Lower Trent Road to detect Hoke's division, which enabled the Confederates to slip between the cavalrymen and the main Union line.[6]

By late morning, Hoke had concealed his division in the dense woods several hundred yards south of the Federal position at Wise's Forks. In preparation for his attack, Hoke deployed his division *en echelon* with two brigades in front and two in back. This formation mitigated the effect of the thickly wooded terrain on maintaining command and control and allowed Hoke to mass his force at the point of attack.

Hoke selected Colquitt's and Kirkland's brigades to lead the assault. General Kirkland and his brigade of three North Carolina regiments advanced on the right along the axis of the Lower Trent Road. Clingman's Tar Heel brigade, commanded by Col. William Devane, followed Kirkland in support. Colonel Zachry and the Georgians of Colquitt's brigade attacked on the left several hundred yards west of the road. General Hagood's brigade of South Carolinians advanced in rear of Zachry. Hoke's line of battle stretched for half a mile, from the center of Splaine's Union brigade to across the Lower Trent Road.[7]

The focus of the battle on March 10 was Wise's Forks. Because it was a crucial intersection, the Federal left flank rested squarely upon it. Located in the center of a partially cleared knoll, the terrain rose about 20 feet above the surrounding area. The Dover and Lower Trent Roads crossed on the crest of the knoll, which provided the Federals a commanding position against possible

---

5 Hagood, *Memoirs*, 354; Elliott, "Kirkland's Brigade," in *Southern Historical Society Papers*, 170-172; Auten, *The Battle of Wyse Fork*, 141. A pocoson (also spelled pocosin) is a low, wooded swamp in an upland coastal region; *OR* 47, pt. 2, 748, 770.

6 Ibid.; On the morning of March 10, 1865, Couch was located 13 miles south of Richlands, N.C., Which is about 43 miles from Kinston. *OR* 47, pt. 2, 751.

7 Hagood, *Memoirs*, 354.

enemy advances from the south or west. The ground sloped gently in both directions for several hundred yards until it reached the low-lying area adjacent to Mill Branch.

Dense woods concealed the Federal line south of the Dover Road. In accordance with General Cox's orders, the Union soldiers had constructed abatis in front of their earthworks. A soldier from Hoke's division later described the manmade obstructions as "small pines, which had been cut down, lapped over each other and their limbs trimmed and pointing in our direction." The weakest point on the Federal defensive line was at the southern fork of the Lower Trent and Dover Roads. A thin skirmish line manned by the 180th Ohio prevented Hoke from cutting across the Dover Road and reaching the Federal rear.[8]

In short, the Federals could not have asked for better terrain to defend against an attack from the south. Wise's Forks was ideally suited for artillery, with the open area to the rear of the main line commanding the southern approach along the Lower Trent Road. On this knoll, Carter had deployed Capt. William A. Kelsey's Battery G, 3rd New York Light Artillery with its six 12-pound Napoleons. Along the Lower Trent Road he posted Lieutenant Seymour's two-gun section from Capt. William M. Kirby's Battery I, 3rd New York Light Artillery. The partial clearing in front of the Union line afforded the Yankee artillerymen an excellent field of fire against approaching Rebel formations.[9]

Shortly after 10:30 a.m., the "rattling fire of musketry on the Lower Trent Road" signaled the Federal's response to the Confederate advance. Rebel skirmishers emerged from the woods closely followed by lines of battle, which one Yankee officer described as "a perfect cloud of regiments and brigades." The Confederate attack may have surprised the Federals, but Hoke's infantry soon discovered that there would be no repeat of its easy success against an ill-prepared enemy two days earlier. This time, the Federals were ready for them.[10]

---

8   George M. Rose, "Sixty-sixth Regiment," in Clark, *Histories*, vol. 3, 697-698.

9   Hall and Hall, *Cayuga in the Field*, 275; Lieutenant Seymour's one-gun section from Battery I, 3rd New York, remained near Malloy's brigade along the Dover Road.

10 OR 47, pt. 1, 932; Hall and Hall, *Cayuga in the Field*, 275. Hoke's initial attack likely occurred sometime after 10:30 a.m. Cox telegraphed Schofield at that time reporting, "No rebels on the Lower Trent Road." *OR* 47, pt. 2, 770.

Union skirmishers from Splaine's brigade, comprising the 174th and 180th Ohio, confronted the advancing Confederates. Despite the masses advancing from the woods, the Union soldiers stubbornly held firm, buying time for the regiments along the main defensive line while Cox and Ruger rushed additional infantry and artillery to the threatened left flank.

From Battery A's position on the far left of Splaine's brigade, Private Tournier described the initial Confederate attack as "the most fierce at the right" against the 17th and 25th Massachusetts, while his battery "saw no rebels in front." Lieutenant John Chapman of the 180th Ohio recorded a similar observation in his diary on March 10: "Skirmishing on the right quite heavy. At 11:00 a.m. Rebs opened on the left, trying to flank us."[11]

On Splaine's right, Capt. James Tucker of the 25th Massachusetts commanded the skirmish line. A fellow officer of the 25th, Capt. Arthur P. Forbes, commanded the left wing of the skirmishers, which received the brunt of Colquitt's attack. Bleeding profusely from a serious neck wound suffered early in the engagement, Forbes refused to leave his post on the skirmish line.[12]

Despite the gallantry of the Union skirmishers, their position became untenable when the full weight of Colquitt's brigade bore down upon them. The "overwhelming masses" of five Georgia regiments—numbering more than 1,000 men—forced Captain Tucker to withdraw his skirmishers to the main Federal entrenchments. As they withdrew, Forbes finally collapsed from a loss of blood. Several fellow New Englanders carried the unconscious officer back to the main line. Despite the enemy's superior numbers, Tucker's skirmishers suffered few casualties thanks to the excellent cover provided by the woods.[13]

After brushing aside the annoying Yankee skirmishers, Zachry's Georgians resumed the advance and the Confederate formations began receiving incoming artillery fire. With Tucker's skirmish line out of the way, Lieutenant Seymour's remaining 12-pound Napoleon near the Dover Road opened fire on the Georgia troops "with every variety of missiles in the calendar," as one artillery officer later described it.[14]

---

11 Tournier, diary, March 10, 1865; *Hutchinson News* (Hutchinson, KS), April 8, 1933.

12 Denny, *Wearing the Blue in the Twenty-Fifth Mass.*, 417; *OR*, 47, pt. 1, 995.

13 Denny, *Wearing the Blue in the Twenty-Fifth Mass.*, 417.

14 Hall and Hall, *Cayuga in the Field*, 275.

Brig. Gen. William W. Kirkland
Courtesy of Library of Congress

The Georgians pressed on as the 17th and 25th Massachusetts waited behind their breastworks. When the Confederates came into effective musket range, the Federal infantry fired volley after volley into the Southern formations. The lethal combination of artillery and small arms fire forced Zachry to withdraw his brigade to the cover of the woods. An officer from Colquitt's brigade, Capt. Thomas J. Marshall of the 6th Georgia, recorded in his diary: "Moved around on his [the enemy's] left flank again on the 10th but failed to carry his works," the line "being strongly entrenched."[15]

After the repulse of Colquitt's brigade, the fighting intensified on the Union far left where the 174th and 180th Ohio defended the Lower Trent Road. A battalion of sharpshooters from the 66th North Carolina, commanded by Capt. William T. Robinson of Company D, preceded Kirkland's brigade. Robinson's sharpshooters and Federal skirmishers from the Ohio regiments traded musket fire, with neither side gaining an upper hand.[16]

As Kirkland had not brought his entire brigade into the fight before the repulse of Zachry's Georgians, Cox gained precious minutes to reinforce the Union line in front of the oncoming Tar Heels. The uncoordinated attacks launched by the two lead Confederate brigades proved costly to Hoke, as Kirkland faced a greatly strengthened Union position unsupported. In response to Kirkland's initial attempt to push back the Federal skirmishers, Hoke ordered him to advance his entire brigade. Captain Charles G. Elliott, a member

---

15 Thomas J. Marshall, "Diary of Thomas Jefferson Marshall from June 1863 to May 1865," in *Confederate Reminiscences and Letters 1861-1865* (Georgia Division United Daughters of the Confederacy, 2001), vol. 20, 25. Co-author Wade Sokolosky has documented 21 losses (wounded or captured) in Colquitt's brigade during the March 10 attack.

16 Elliott, "Kirkland's Brigade," in *Southern Historical Society Papers*, vol. 23, 172; Denny, *Wearing the Blue in the Twenty-Fifth Mass.*, 417.

of Kirkland's staff, recalled that Hoke ordered Kirkland "to feel the enemy, but not to attack the breastworks."[17]

General Kirkland advanced his North Carolinians in *en echelon*. He deployed the 42nd North Carolina on the right, while the 17th North Carolina and remaining companies of the 66th North Carolina held the left and center. A rain-swollen ditch, which was part of Mill Branch, separated Kirkland's Tar Heels from Colquitt's brigade. The wooded terrain that had provided excellent cover for the Federal skirmishers now served to hinder Kirkland's ability to observe the movement of Colquitt's brigade on his left. Unsure of Colquitt's progress, he dispatched courier G. L. Tonnoffski to "tell [Colonel Zachry] that we have driven in the picket line of the enemy and can hear nothing from him."[18]

Tonnoffski, however, failed to reach Colonel Zachry. As he headed to the left, the Confederate private observed Federal infantry supported by artillery, which Kirkland's brigade would soon encounter. Tonnoffski immediately returned to report his findings to Kirkland. The general repeated his order, telling the private to "go and find Colquitt and deliver my message." Once again, the private failed to reach General Colquitt's brigade. In what was essentially a no-man's-land, Tonnoffski found himself caught between the Federals' retreating skirmish line and main works, where he soon fell into enemy hands.[19]

Cox used the advantage of interior lines to shift units from other parts of the battlefield and bring them to bear against Kirkland. In a brief span of 25 minutes, Cox telegraphed General Palmer twice for reinforcements to bolster the threatened Union left. He first called for a regiment, but minutes later directed Palmer to send a brigade "if [the enemy] is quiet in your front." Cox's second telegram to Palmer betrayed his anxiety over the possible loss of Wise's Forks due to Hoke's sudden appearance on the Union left. Cox went so far as to

17 Elliott, "Kirkland's Brigade," in *Southern Historical Society Papers*, vol. 23, 170-172. General Hoke presumably issued similar orders to Colonel Zachry. As an experienced division commander, Hoke almost certainly would not have allowed one brigade to advance unsupported.

18 Tonnoffski, "My Last Days As A Confederate Soldier," in *Confederate Veteran*, 68. It is important to note that Private Tonnoffski wrote his account 49 years after the 1865 battle. Private Eli E. M'Gee, a fellow courier on General Kirkland's staff, refuted parts of Tonnoffski's account. *Confederate Veteran*, vol. 22, no. 5 (May 1914), 213.

19 *Confederate Veteran*, vol. 22, no. 5 (May 1914), 213.

instruct Palmer to warn Schofield "not to leave the train to come to the front this morning."[20]

The additional units allowed Cox to extend the infantry line farther east beyond the Lower Trent Road and Hoke's right flank. Cox later wrote that the repositioning of regiments to the left occurred "with not a minute to spare." He also pulled units from Ruger's division, and Carter likewise shifted troops from his division. Captain Russell's Battery A, 3rd New York Light Artillery also shifted to the left. "There was a great cry on our left," wrote Private Tournier of Battery A. "Our company was then ordered to the left on double quick time. As we ran under the low branches of the trees, my blanket caught fast and I lost it. The Rebels were pouring voley after voley of bullets just over our heads cutting the small limbs and leaves so they came falling down around us."[21]

The New Yorkers occupied a line of hastily constructed breastworks, which Tournier described as "two small logs, one on top of the other making a protection about 1 foot and 6 inches in height, behind which we dropped." Captain Russell's men were in a tight situation, having reached their new position just as the Confederates pressed the attack. Tournier believed that he and his comrades "would have been driven out had it not been for a battery of 12 pound steel cannon that came in our line and commenced pouring their shot and shell into the advancing Rebels."[22]

In addition to Carter's two batteries, Ruger sent Capt. Andrew M. Wood's 5th Independent Illinois Battery and Capt. Byron D. Paddock's Battery F, 1st Michigan Light Artillery to the threatened Federal left. Paddock' battery raced down the Lower Trent Road to "an open field in front of a heavily timbered swamp." The battery had just unlimbered its four 3-inch ordnance rifles when Paddock observed the Rebels "pouring out into the clearing like a swarm of bees."[23]

---

20 OR 47, pt. 2, 772; In response to Cox's request for additional units, the 9th New Jersey from Harland's brigade, the 2nd Regiment of Provisionals from Claassen's brigade, and the 28th Michigan from Thomas's brigade were sent to the left. All three units arrived too late to assist in Hoke's repulse.

21 Ibid., pt. 1, 932-933; Tournier, diary, March 10, 1865.

22 Tournier, diary, March 10, 1865.

23 Byron D. Paddock to Hattie, March 13, 1865, in Johnny Craig Young Collection, East Carolina Manuscripts Collection, J. Y. Joyner Library, East Carolina University, Greenville, North Carolina.

Col. John C. McQuiston
U.S. Army Military History Institute

Ruger received Cox's permission to shift one of his brigades from the center. At 11:00 a.m., Colonel McQuiston's Second Brigade marched rapidly to the left, leaving its skirmishers in place.[24] While en route, McQuiston's brigade passed by Ruger's headquarters. Private Moses Sisco of the 123rd Indiana observed the general "dancing around like a chicken with its head off, as the bullets were flying around like hail." The veteran soldiers could not resist poking fun at the general, yelling "lay down Ruger, grab a root." The soldiers' comments stung. After the battle, Ruger considered preferring charges against the regiment but wisely reconsidered.[25]

The area behind the Federal lines afforded shelter for neither man nor beast—the artillery horses in particular suffered severely due to their exposed positions. An Ohio sergeant recalled how the bullets "flew quite thick several times." General Cox himself experienced a near miss by an errant Confederate round. As Cox and Brig. Gen. George S. Greene sat upon their horses observing the battle, a bullet struck Greene's mount, killing the animal. Cox described his location as a "hot place." Several staff officers lost their horses to enemy fire. An orderly lost an arm to a shell, and two others were wounded.[26]

Upon reaching the Union left flank, McQuiston deployed his three regiments. The 130th Indiana occupied the brigade's extreme left, followed by the 129th Indiana in the center and the 123rd Indiana on the right, adjacent to the 180th Ohio. With McQuiston's arrival, the Union line extended almost one

24 *OR* 47, pt. 1, 940, 973.

25 Ibid.

26 Joseph J. Brown to Rosa, March 13; *OR* 47, pt. 1, 973; Cox, *Military Reminiscences*, vol. 2, 442; The 64-year-old Greene was the oldest Union general officer at the battle of Wise's Forks. An 1823 graduate of West Point, Greene served with distinction at Sharpsburg, Chancellorsville, and especially at Gettysburg. Wounded in October 1863, Greene was en route to Sherman's command. Warner, *Generals in Blue*, 186-187.

quarter-mile east of the Lower Trent Road, diminishing the threat to the Union rear. Ruger ordered McQuiston "to advance a skirmish line well extended to the left," beyond the 180th Ohio's skirmishers to locate the Confederate right flank. McQuiston entrusted Maj. Irvin Robbins of the 123rd Indiana to carry out the division commander's order. Robbins moved forward with Company C of the 123rd, Companies H and I of the 129th, and Company D of the 130th Indiana.[27]

Despite the Federals' stubborn resistance, Kirkland continued to press his attack. He assigned two staff officers to assist in maintaining communication with the regiments on either flank. Captain Elliott accompanied Lt. Col. Thomas H. Sharp's 17th North Carolina, and Maj. Lucius J. Johnson rode forward with Col. John E. Brown's 42nd North Carolina. Kirkland remained in the center, behind the 66th North Carolina, commanded by Maj. David S. Davis.[28]

As Kirkland's Tar Heels advanced, Mr. Wooten approached Elliott and said, "Captain, your brigade has not gone far enough to the right, and Hoke is doing wrong to attack here." The guide's warning, however, had come too late. Instead of feeling the enemy's position, Kirkland's brigade delivered a "resolute and determined attack." On Kirkland's left, the 17th North Carolina cheered as Capt. George B. Daniel and Lt. Wilson G. Lamb of Company F urged their men forward by waving their swords. "As soon as our line emerged from the woods," recalled Elliott, "we ran up against a very strongly-intrenched line of the enemy, obstructed by trees they had cut down, and supported by artillery."[29]

The situation was the same across the entire brigade front. Adjutant George M. Rose of the 66th North Carolina recalled: "For some reason our lines were not extended sufficiently far to our right and [the enemy's] left, and when the charge was made we found that the enemy had prepared for us with

27 OR 47, pt. 1, 941, 949-952.

28 Elliott, "Kirkland's Brigade," in *Southern Historical Society Papers*, vol. 23, 170-172; Rose, "Sixty-sixth Regiment," in Clark, *Histories*, vol. 3, 697. Because of Colonel Nethercutt's knowledge of the area, he served as Hoke's chief of staff. Major Davis assumed command of the 66th North Carolina in Nethercutt's absence.

29 Elliott, "Kirkland's Brigade," in *Southern Historical Society Papers*, vol. 23, 170-172. Thirty years after the war Elliott wrote, "I have heard that Hoke censored [censured] Kirkland for making the disastrous charge . . . but did not hear of it at the time." In his postwar memoir, General Hagood did not mention any censure on the part of Hoke toward Kirkland; See Hagood, *Memoirs*, 354-355.

Maj. John T. Wood, 180th Ohio Infantry
U.S. Army Military History Institute

his breastworks." Rose's observation reveals the dire situation confronting Kirkland's exposed right flank due to the Federals' oblique fire.[30]

Along the Lower Trent Road, Col. John S. Jones's 174th Ohio and the 178th Ohio were prepared to meet Kirkland's assault. Jones remembered that his Ohioans had put their picks and axes to good use. "Hoke's division could not have struck our line in any [other] position . . . [that would] have been more to our advantage and to their discomfort."[31]

In a letter to his mother, Maj. John T. Wood of the 180th Ohio described the repulse of Kirkland's attack:

> Our Regt. did splendidly. . . . [W]hen the Rebels made their last-charge we occupied a very trying position being entirely unprotected by works of any kind, but the Rebels fire was very wild, while ours was most deadly, causing them to go to the rear on the double quick. . . . I felt the responsibility of the lives of 700 men greatly, but as the Rebs were driving in our skirmishers & saw the countenances of the men . . . I felt safe as our skirmishers fell back on us and the Rebel line appeared we greeted them with a shout and such a warm Reception that we threw them into confusion & success was easy.[32]

Some Union soldiers lost their composure in the face of the Confederate onslaught and broke for the rear. Two men from Capt. Paddock's Michigan battery abandoned their posts during the battle. When the fugitives returned,

---

30 Rose, "Sixty-sixth Regiment," in Clark, *Histories of the North Carolina Regiments*, vol. 3, 697-698.

31 John S. Jones, *History of the 174th O.V.I. and the Roster of the Regiment* (Marysville, OH, 1894), 20; *OR* 47, pt. 1, 956. Sixty men from Company A of the 178th Ohio reported to Jones at 9:00 a.m. on March 10.

32 John T. Wood to mother, March 13, 1865, in Civil War Miscellaneous Collection, U.S. Army Military History Institute, Carlisle, Pennsylvania.

Paddock had them tied "to a tree so that . . . we will know where to find them."
Other men were simply nervous and forgot how to properly fire their weapon.
"My left hand neighbor forgot to take the ram rod out of his gun," recalled a
New Yorker, "so when he fired the gun it burst about six inches down from the
top and the man went over backwards. He was not badly hurt, but kept close to
the ground and did not shoot any more."[33]

The Union infantry received plenty of help from artillery in repulsing the
Confederate attack. The March 10 battle with Hoke arguably belonged to the
long arm of Cox's command. For the first time at Wise's Fork, the Federals
employed their artillery with maximum effectiveness. Withdrawal of the
skirmish line allowed the four Union batteries to train their deadly fire on the
advancing Confederates. The swampy and wooded terrain prevented Hoke's
artillery from deploying, and the Federal gunners operated without fear of
counter-battery fire.

Concentrated against Kirkland's and Clingman's brigades were as many as
18 Union guns, more than half of which were 12-pound Napoleons. Their
close-range fire devastated the Confederate infantry. The Napoleon was the
workhorse of Civil War field artillery, valued above all for its effectiveness in
firing canister rounds. When used against charging infantry, the brass Napoleon
could be devastating.[34]

Placed hub-to-hub across the Lower Trent Road, the Federal guns fired
shell and canister into the advancing North Carolinians. Private Tournier
recalled the terrible effects of the massed artillery fire "mowing [down] both
men and trees." Exploding shells shattered countless trees, transforming wood
fragments into lethal projectiles. Falling trees also posed a danger. One tall
specimen fell atop Cpl. John A. Wilhelm of the 42nd North Carolina. The
severely wounded corporal was captured during the Federal counterattack.
Another fell upon Pvt. Lewis Sanderson of the 66th North Carolina, wounding
him as he lay on the ground. Thirty-nine years after the battle, the *Charlotte News*
ran a story about a cannonball embedded in a tree from the battlefield that
damaged a saw blade in a local mill. "The trees in that section seem to be loaded

---

33 Tournier, diary, March 10, 1865.

34 Dean Thomas, *Cannons: An Introduction to Civil War Artillery* (Gettysburg, PA, 1985), 28;
Accounts indicate that the 5th Illinois Independent Battery fielded six guns. However, the type
of guns is undetermined.

Col. John M. Nethercutt,
66th North Carolina Infantry
State Archives of North Carolina

with cannon balls," the newspaper reported, "as this is only one of numerous instances where cannon balls have been found in logs from Wise's Forks."[35]

Several Union rounds injured friend as well as foe. According to Colonel Jones of the 174th Ohio, "some of our men were injured by our own artillery, which was too far in the rear and persisted in firing, although warned that they were injuring our men." The six Napoleons of Battery G, 3rd New York Light Artillery probably fired the errant rounds.[36]

In any event, Kirkland's troops could not withstand the combined firepower of the Federal infantry and artillery. Seeing this, and in an effort to spur his men on, Colonel Nethercutt of the 66th North Carolina guided his mount to within close range of the Union field works. Despite the heroic leadership displayed by Nethercutt and other Confederate officers, Kirkland's attack stalled. "I succeeded in coming out unhurt but it was the worst place that I ever was in my life," Pvt. James O. Keel of the 17th North Carolina wrote his wife. Another Tar Heel observed, "The troops on the left of our line did not seem to take in the situation, and did not come to our support, and we were compelled to fall back."[37]

35 Tournier, diary, March 10, 1865; *Carolina Watchman* (Salisbury, NC), March 13, 1865; Manarin et al., *North Carolina Troops*, vol. 15, 382. Private Sanderson's pension record indicated that he was wounded "by a tree falling across him that was shot off by a Ball."; *Charlotte News* (Charlotte, NC), August 7, 1902.

36 Jones, *History of the 174th O.V.I. and the Roster of the Regiment*, 20-21.

37 Rose, "Sixty-sixth Regiment," in Clark, *Histories*, vol. 3, 697; James O. Keel to Susan, March 11, 1865, in Private Collection, Gray Ezzard; Elliott, "Kirkland's Brigade," in *Southern Historical Society Papers*, vol. 23, 170-172; Rose, "Sixty-sixth Regiment," in Clark, *Histories*, vol. 3, 697.

The storm of lead and iron projectiles forced the Confederates to hug the ground for cover or risk annihilation. A Tar Heel from the 66th North Carolina wrote that when his regiment "was within fifty yards of the enemy, it was ordered to lie down to protect itself from the galling fire from the [Union] breastworks."[38]

On Kirkland's left, Captain Elliott informed Colonel Sharp of the 17th North Carolina "to hold their position" while he sought out Kirkland for reinforcements. Elliott found the brigade commander and reported the 17th's predicament. Kirkland ordered the staff officer to direct Sharp to "hold our line" while the general went "to Hoke for help." The unfortunate staff officer never reached Sharp's position. "Instead of finding friends," recalled Captain Elliott, "I rode into the advance skirmish line of the enemy, as the woods were very thick." With a flair for the dramatic, Elliott recounted his brush with serious injury or death:

> Four of them halted me and inquired who I was. The shells and bullets were still falling fast around us and my captors were dodging and did not make me dismount. I took advantage of this, told them to 'put down their guns and go with me or we would all be killed.' They foolishly did this and we started toward the rear, or away from the danger, as we thought. Suddenly we came upon a Federal regiment in line of battle. My captors made signals not to shoot and seemed delighted to find friends (mistaking the Rebs for fellow Yanks). I turned my mare and ran off in the opposite direction, both spurs in her flanks. A volley from their skirmishers passed me without harm and I made 'excellent' time through briers and thickets and over a very wide ditch, and most happily emerged into an open field in front of Colquitt's Georgia brigade. They met me with cheers and laughter, seeing how I was 'running.' And I rejoined my brigade which had been rallied and reformed in line.[39]

The Federal line of battle that Elliott encountered had launched a bold counterattack against General Kirkland's exposed right flank. Earlier, Major Robbins of the 123rd Indiana had completed his reconnaissance east of the Lower Trent Road and found no Confederates opposite the left wing of the Federal skirmish line. With Cox's consent, Ruger ordered McQuiston "to advance the left of the skirmish line, double up the skirmish line of the enemy and attack him in the flank if possible." To increase the shock of the attack, McQuiston ordered his former regiment, the 123rd Indiana commanded by Lt.

---

38 Ibid., 697-698.

39 Elliott, "Kirkland's Brigade," in *Southern Historical Society Papers*, vol. 23, 171.

Maj. Irvin Robbins, 123rd Indiana Infantry
Wade Sokolosky Collection

Col. Dewitt C. Walters, to advance four companies of skirmishers in support of Robbins.[40]

The Federal guns fell silent as a lone Union soldier stepped into the road waving "the Stars and Stripes back and forth," signaling the artillery to cease firing. Moments later, bugle calls sounded as Robbins ordered an advance. With perfect timing, the Hoosiers launched a furious charge into the stunned Confederates. The Federal counterattack struck just as Kirkland "found the fire from the breastworks in his front . . . more than he could live under."[41]

Shortly after Robbins's advance upon Kirkland's flank, Colonel Jones ordered forward Maj. William G. Beatty and two companies of the 174th Ohio. Beatty reported that his small detachment "picked up many stragglers and 132 Enfield rifles," while Jones counted 30 dead Rebels and a large number of wounded lying in front of his works.[42]

Terrified North Carolinians scattered left and right as Robbins's battle line rolled up Kirkland's flank. Ruger later described the Confederate retreat as "a quick and disorderly flight." The Federals had caught Kirkland's men off guard, with the 42nd North Carolina on the right absorbing the initial shock. Colonel Brown was unable to reform his Tar Heels in time to turn and meet the Federals. The regiment lost more than 100 men captured, including Major Johnson of Kirkland's staff. Sixteen-year-old Pvt. Taylor Whitley of Company H suffered a terrible wound in his left thigh that prevented him from escaping. In their haste, Whitley's fleeing comrades abandoned the youth—one of many

40 *OR* 47, pt. 1, 941, 949, 951,

41 Sisco, *Personal Memoirs of Moses Aaron Sisco*, 72; *OR* 47, pt. 1, 941.

42 Ibid., 956.

wounded Confederates captured by the enemy. Whitley did not recover and died on April 12, 1865, at Foster General Hospital in New Bern.[43]

The Yankees had wrecked Kirkland's brigade. Those fortunate enough to escape retreated into the woods. The remainder quickly surrendered. "Long strings of them were coming continually over the works near our colors," recalled Colonel Jones of the 174th Ohio, "glad to get out of the way of the deadly missiles that were mowing down their comrades." Private Sisco of the 123rd Indiana wrote in his diary: "A big Johnie raised up from behind a log and another one stepped from behind a tree. We brought our guns to our shoulders. One of the boys said, 'come here Johnie.' They at once threw up their hands, dropping their guns and came to us."[44]

Other Southerners feigned death and lay among their fallen comrades. Private James O'Connell and another soldier from the 130th Indiana were searching the Rebel dead when they happened upon two men lying under a log. "As we bent over to take their weapons," recalled O'Connell, "we learned they were playing possum." The Confederates jumped up and struck the two Union soldiers in the head with their rifles. Before losing consciousness, O'Connell heard gunshots. He later learned that several comrades had killed the two Confederates before they could finish off the unconscious O'Connell and his partner.[45]

While Robbins's attack routed Kirkland's Confederates, Colonel Splaine ordered his younger brother, Capt. James Splaine of the 17th Massachusetts, to strike the left flank of Colquitt's brigade with a company-sized skirmish line. Captain Splaine's effort, however, failed to stampede the Georgians as Robbins had done to the North Carolinians. Hoke's attack on the Union left flank had failed. The division suffered irreplaceable losses, particularly in Kirkland's brigade. General Hagood described Hoke's casualties on March 10 as "the chief loss" sustained by the Confederate army in the battle of Wise's Forks. Kirkland's three North Carolina regiments had endured devastating Union artillery fire, followed by an overwhelming Federal counterattack, losing more than 300 men. Because of its location on the right flank, the 42nd North

43 Manarin et al., *North Carolina Troops*, vol. 10, 190-288; File of Pvt. Taylor Whitley, *Compiled Service Records of Confederate Soldiers Who Served in Organizations from the State of North Carolina*, M270, roll 185, Records Group 109, National Archives.

44 Jones, *History of the 174th O.V.I.*, 20-21; Sisco, *Personal Memoirs of Moses Aaron Sisco*, 72.

45 Lawrence, *Grandfather's Civil War Diary*, 275-276.

Carolina lost more than 150 men—the heaviest loss of any Confederate regiment.[46]

In describing the losses of the 66th North Carolina, Adjutant Rose wrote that when the regiment withdrew, it left "a large number of men . . . dead and dying on the field." Rose's account is an exaggeration. During the three days of fighting, the 66th lost 92 men—16 wounded (two mortally) and 76 captured. The disproportionate number of prisoners casts doubt on Rose's description.[47]

Hoke was fortunate. In anticipation of renewed Confederate attacks elsewhere along the line, Cox had ordered the Federal counterattack halted at the Lower Trent Road, which allowed Kirkland to withdraw his battered brigade to the safety of the woods. Had Robbins' attack continued, the damage could have been much worse.[48]

Defeated, Hoke withdrew his division westward to its original position along the British Road. Throughout the morning, from its position near the Wooten house, Colonel Taylor's detachment from Hagood's brigade had anxiously awaited news of Hoke's flanking movement. The sound of small arms and artillery fire was so loud that Taylor believed "the line of battle did not seem more than a few hundred yards from me." Soon afterward, "stragglers came running in," recalled Taylor, "who were stopped until I received an order to let them pass."[49]

Despite the mad scramble to the rear, causing concern for the safety of his own soldiers, Taylor maintained his position on the Cobb Road. The colonel soon observed Hoke approaching at a leisurely pace, "as cool as if he had been on dress parade." Hoke ordered Taylor to fall back with the rest of the division. According to Lieutenant Calder, an officer in Taylor's command, "The division returned to the lines and we soon had our little tent pitched and fine fires going. But there was no rest for the wicked and orders came as soon as we got comfortable, to move off." Taylor had received orders to make camp on the

---

46 OR 47, pt. 1, 1,000; Hagood, *Memoirs*, 354-355; Manarin et al., *North Carolina Troops*, vol. 10, 190-288; Capt. James A. Blackwelder of Company F, 42nd North Carolina listed 19 soldiers lost during the battle: one killed, three wounded, and 15 captured. *Carolina Watchman* (Salisbury, NC), March 13, 1865. See also, *Daily Conservative* (Raleigh, NC), March 20, 1865.

47 Rose, "Sixty-sixth Regiment," in Clark, *Histories*, vol. 3, 697-698; Manarin et al., *North Carolina Troops*, vol. 15, 305.

48 OR 47, pt. 1, 933, 949-950.

49 Taylor, *War Recollections*, 6.

Kinston side of Southwest Creek. "We marched about 2 miles to this side of Cobb's Mill," Calder continued, "and bivouacked in an old field."[50]

Shortly after 12:30 p.m., renewed fighting broke out. Cox's instincts had proved correct. No sooner had Hoke's attack been repulsed than the thunder of battle erupted along Ruger's front north of Wise's Forks. Cox noted in his journal: "I check our men in pursuit, fearing an attack elsewhere. Sure enough it comes in a very few minutes." Union skirmishers from Ruger's division desperately held onto their advanced positions against an attack from D. H. Hill's Confederates. Cox believed that the enemy had misinterpreted the sounds of rejoicing emanating from Wise's Forks. "Our men raised a shout at their success," wrote Cox, "and the enemy, thinking apparently that it was a signal for their having beaten us, rushed in on Ruger's center with a will and a yell."[51]

Cox immediately shifted his attention to the new threat—the Army of Tennessee. General Hill and Maj. Gen. Edward C. Walthall had carried out Bragg's order to cooperate with Hoke "by making a strong demonstration" along their front. Troops from the XXIII Corps once again faced their old adversary from the Western Theater. Union veterans would later recall that the fight at Wise's Forks on the afternoon of March 10, 1865, was as fierce and desperate as any of their previous battles in Georgia and Tennessee.[52]

---

50 Taylor, *War Recollections*, 6; Calder, diary, March 10, 1865.

51 *OR* 47, pt. 1, 933.

52 Ibid., pt. 2, 1,088; Joshua Fraser to brother and sister, March 13, 1865, in Indiana Historical Society, Indianapolis, Indiana.

Chapter 8

"Kise saved our colors and our scalps as well"

— *Sgt. Joseph Edmonds, 120th Indiana*

So We Meet Again

Just before dawn, as General Hoke moved to turn the Union left, the opposing skirmish lines along the British Road broke the morning stillness with a burst of musketry. In front of General Loring's division, Capt. Isaac J. Rogers of the 27th Alabama commanded 60 skirmishers. Rogers recalled spending most of the night "forming my line in the dark." A cold rain began to fall just before sunrise, and he shivered under his blanket, feeling "wet, cold and hungry." Awakened by the firing, Rogers hurried forward to assess the situation and received a severe wound in his right foot. He spent the remainder of his service moving from one Confederate hospital to another.[1]

The firing along the skirmish line proved insignificant, for the Federals displayed no inclination to seriously press forward. As a precaution, General Hill ordered the skirmish line doubled along the front. Captain Henry Dickson's battery of Starr's battalion moved to the Army of Tennessee's line along the British Road. Dickson placed Lieutenant Jones's section along Mill Branch and deployed the battery's remaining guns farther to the left along the railroad.[2]

---

1 Harry Vollie Barnard, *Tattered Volunteers: The Twenty-Seventh Alabama Infantry Regiment, C.S.A.* (Northport, AL, 1965), 67.

2 *OR* 47, pt. 1, 1,088; Jones, diary, March 10, 1865. It is unclear whether Bragg, Hill, or Starr gave the order to relocate the battery.

Maj. Gen. Edward C. Walthall
Alabama Department of Archives and History,
Montgomery, Alabama

General Edward C. Walthall arrived that morning from Smithfield with 354 men from A. P. Stewart's Corps. Accompanying Walthall was William A. Quarles's brigade, led by Brig. Gen. George D. Johnston, and a pair of Arkansas regiments from Daniel Reynolds's brigade led by Col. Henry G. Bunn, commander of the 4th Arkansas.[3]

The 33-year-old Walthall was a respected leader with considerable combat experience. A native of Holly Springs, Mississippi, Walthall studied law and later became a district attorney. As Mississippi organized for war in April 1861, he joined the 15th Mississippi, and within a few weeks became the regiment's lieutenant colonel. In January 1862, Walthall received his baptism of fire at Mills Springs, Kentucky, where the Confederates suffered a major defeat. A rising star in the Army of Tennessee, Walthall rose to brigade and ultimately division command as the army fought in the Chickamauga, Chattanooga, and Atlanta campaigns. Following the defeat at Nashville, Walthall and Maj. Gen. Nathan Bedford Forrest commanded the Army of Tennessee's rear guard, holding back the pursuing Federals and enabling the shattered army to withdraw unmolested into northern Mississippi. At Wise's Forks, Walthall assumed command of the contingent from Stewart's Corps, which now consisted of his and Loring's divisions. On the morning of March 10, the two units totaled barely 1,000 men.[4]

---

3   OR 47, pt. 2, 1,368; Robert P. Bender, ed., *Worthy of the Cause for Which They Fight: The Civil War Diary of Brigadier General Daniel H. Reynolds* (Fayetteville, AR, 2011), 281n. Johnston reported that Quarles's brigade fielded 91 men a week later at the battle of Bentonville, while Reynolds reported that his brigade numbered 150 men. See, OR 47, pt. 1, 1,104-1,105.

4   Warner, *Generals in Gray*, 325-326; Bradley, *Last Stand*, 165; OR 47, pt. 2, 1,354-1,355. It is unclear whether Walthall's command fell under General Hill's authority on March 10. Hill commanded the Army of Tennessee contingent, but his command status may have changed

Sgt. William Trousdale,
Co. E, 48th Tennessee Infantry,
was killed on March 10, 1865.

Confederate Veteran

Captain Joseph Love of the 48th Tennessee Infantry, part of of William Quarles's brigade, recalled that after arriving at Kinston, "We left the train, marched some 2 miles beyond the little village, took position on the extreme right, [and] halted a while at some unfinished breast-works, awaiting orders." The welcomed arrival of Quarles's brigade extended D. H. Hill's battle line farther south along the British Road.[5]

The Army of Tennessee's attack would be in *en echelon*, beginning with Henry Clayton's division from S. D. Lee's Corps on the left and the two divisions from A. P. Stewart's Corps on the right. Three experienced major generals and a pair of brigadiers led eight brigades totaling 1,700 men—the equivalent of a single average brigade in the Army of Tennessee during the Atlanta campaign.

From left to right, Clayton's division consisted of Edmund Pettus's Alabama brigade (on loan from Carter Stevenson's division), followed by John K. Jackson's and Marcellus Stovall's Georgia brigades. D. H. Hill's division under Colonel Coltart, along with the 67th North Carolina—numbering about 1,260 men—remained in their defenses along Mill Branch. To the right of Clayton's division, Stewart's Corps formed a line of battle, with Loring's division on the left and Walthall's division on the right. Led by Colonel Jackson, Loring's division consisted of Adams's brigade on the left, Scott's brigade in the center, and Featherston's brigade on the right. Walthall fielded only Quarles's

---

with General Walthall's arrival on March 10. It is probable that Walthall and Hill led separate commands under Bragg's direction.

5   Jill K. Garrett and Marise P. Lightfoot, *The Civil War in Maury County, Tennessee* (Columbia, TN, 1966), 230.

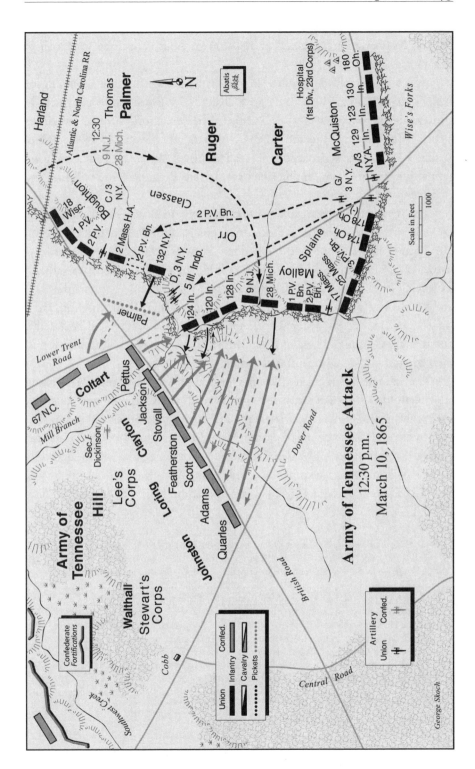

Army of Tennessee Attack
12:30 p.m.
March 10, 1865

George Skoch

brigade, as Reynolds remained at Kinston to police the town and collect stragglers.[6]

By late morning, the familiar sounds of battle signaled the beginning of Hoke's attack. Captain Love and Sgt. William Trousdale stood by the roadside awaiting news from the sergeant's older brother, Lt. Wilson Trousdale, who was a courier for General Johnston. The two men did not have long to wait. "Gen. Walthall was seen approaching," recalled Love, "and the order he gave Johns[t]on was the same he received from Gen. Bragg . . . you will find the enemy in your front."[7]

The Army of Tennessee left its trenches along the British Road and formed ranks in preparation for the attack. One Tennessean remembered, "We took our place in line and received the orders, 'Forward March.'" Arrayed in two battle lines, the Army of Tennessee contingent crossed the British Road, advancing toward the enemy. Clayton's report for the battle suggests that Hill and Walthall advanced their commands simultaneously. "In moving forward," wrote Clayton, "I was ordered to guide to the right upon Genl. Walthall's command." On the other side of the British Road, the two commands found their progress hindered by difficult terrain.[8]

The natural obstructions played a crucial role in how the Confederate attack unfolded. Between the British and Lower Trent Roads, the area consisted of low-lying swamps, fallen timber, and thick underbrush that impeded movement and dissolved unit cohesion. The Federals could not have asked for a more favorable position to defend. Ruger's entrenched line was located on a slight rise along the eastern bank of Mill Branch, which followed the Lower Trent Road. A branch of that creek ran the entire length of the Union line.

---

6   Hill's division fielded 562 men. *OR* 47, pt. 1, 1,088. The 67th North Carolina mustered about 700 men. *OR* 47, pt. 2, 1,424; Because the Army of Tennessee maintained the same position along the British Road throughout March 9, the authors assume that as additional brigades from Stewart's corps arrived, they formed on the right of the previous brigade. Clayton's account of the battle on March 10 identified the brigade alignment in Lee's Corps, and stated that Stewart's Corps was on the right. Bragg, however, ordered Walthall to leave a unit in Kinston to round up stragglers. *OR* 47, pt. 2, 1,360. General Reynolds's diary entry for March 10 stated that his two regiments arrived in Kinston but did not participate in the battle. The authors assume that Walthall assigned Col. Henry G. Bunn and the two Arkansas regiments to provost duty at Kinston. Bender, ed., *Worthy of the Cause for Which They Fight: The Civil War Diary of Brigadier General Daniel H. Reynolds*, 281n.

7   Garrett and Lightfoot, *The Civil War in Maury County, Tennessee*, 230.

8   Ibid.; Clayton, "Clayton's Battle Report."

Heavy rains had recently transformed the sluggish stream into a vast swamp. In crossing, the Army of Tennessee's assault degenerated into an uncoordinated advance by individual brigades, with their carefully aligned battle lines breaking up into ever-smaller fragments. On Hill's far left, the progress of Pettus's brigade slowed to a crawl. To the south, Walthall's line struggled "some 100 yards through a pond or lagoon 2 or 3 feet deep." Once Pettus's Alabamians had emerged from the muck, the general halted his command to reform, while Clayton's two Georgia brigades continued to press forward, separating the Alabamians from the Georgians.[9]

On clearing the swamp, the Army of Tennessee troops came under fire from Federal skirmishers. The sheer weight of Confederate numbers soon forced the skirmishers in blue back to Ruger's main line. Mill Branch was a formidable barrier, and it forced the Confederate formations to drive toward the center of the Union defensive line. As the Southerners soon discovered, Ruger had selected an excellent location for his defense, described by one Southern officer as "hidden by a dense growth or underwood." Ruger's veterans had occupied the high ground west of the Lower Trent Road since the afternoon of March 8 with ample time to prepare well-constructed earthworks.[10]

The departure of McQuiston's brigade to the Wise's Forks area, however, had significantly weakened Ruger's Federal line. To compensate, Ruger ordered Colonel Orr's First Brigade, located on the division's right, to extend its line to the left. Orr was now in a dangerous position, having to defend a two-brigade front with just three infantry regiments. A Hoosier from the 124th recalled: "we could only touch the next man to us at arm's length." Colonel Allen W. Prather, commander of the 120th Indiana, reported that his regiment had to cover 250 yards of trench line in single rank. During the previous two days, Orr's men had performed well. On this day, his veterans would face their greatest challenge since coming to North Carolina.[11]

---

9 Clayton, "Clayton's Battle Report"; *Garrett and Lightfoot, The Civil War in Maury County, Tennessee*, 230.

10 Ibid.

11 Orr was a 35-year-old farmer from Connersville, Indiana. Wounded in 1863, he returned in time to participate in the Atlanta campaign and the battles of Franklin and Nashville in Tennessee, which earned him a promotion to colonel. Six months after the war, Orr committed suicide with a gunshot to the head. OR 47, pt. 1, 942; David W. Smith, "Hovey's Babies," *National Tribune*, Dec. 9, 1887; OR 47, pt. 1, 945.

Col. John M. Orr
Wade Sokolosky Collection

Clayton's division made first contact with Orr's brigade because of the proximity of Lee's Corps to the main Union line. As the Confederate battle lines approached the rise, Orr's Hoosiers unleashed several volleys into the Southerners. The Georgians of Stovall and Jackson's brigades found themselves "warmly engaged," as they exchanged fire with the entrenched Federals. First Sgt. David W. Smith of the 120th Indiana remembered that the 120th's skirmishers had just reached the safety of the main works when "a strong line of battle was discovered advancing against us. . . . They charged with desperate determination to the creek, within a few feet of our works, but the 'Babies' with undaunted courage stood firm to their work, and the Johnnies were forced to retreat."[12]

In response to the Confederate attack across Orr's front, Cox once again exploited his interior lines by shifting units to the endangered center. He moved infantry and artillery from Palmer's and Carter's sectors, but the redeployments took time, leaving Orr's brigade to handle the Confederate assault alone.[13]

Following their repulse, the Georgians reformed ranks and continued to exchange fire with the Federals. It was an unequal contest, with the Federals fighting in relative safety behind their earth-and-log parapets while the Confederates made easy targets in the open. As their casualties mounted, the Georgians' battle line began to waver. The observant Orr saw an opportunity to launch a counterattack and gave the order. An Indiana soldier recalled that the

---

12 Clayton, "Clayton's Battle Report"; Smith, "Hovey's Babies" *National Tribune*, December 29, 1897. Because Bvt. Maj. Gen. Alvin P. Hovey's XXIII Corps division fielded an unusually large number of young, unmarried men, it earned the nickname "Hovey's Babies."

13 *OR* 47, pt. 1, 978.

Hoosiers "climbed over their works, forded the creek, and then with a splendid line we made the charge, every man doing his duty nobly."[14]

As the Yankees surged forward, the demoralized Confederates panicked. Clayton looked on in horror as his brigades "gave way in confusion" before the onrushing 120th and 124th Indiana. Colonels Henry Kellogg and James Gordon tried in vain to rally their men, who fled to the rear. Orr's counterattack routed two Confederate brigades and created a gap between Pettus's and Walthall's commands.[15]

During the short but deadly engagement with the Hoosiers, Stovall's brigade suffered more than 40 casualties, the largest loss of an Army of Tennessee brigade at Wise's Forks. Though captured by Orr's Hoosiers, Pvt. George A. Knight of the 42nd Georgia had survived another brush with death. It seemed that neither Yankee bullets nor Mother Nature could claim the Rebel private. Eight months earlier, a bolt of lightning had struck Knight but failed to kill him.[16]

Clayton later described the conduct of the two Georgia brigades as "altogether unsatisfactory." He attributed the poor performance to their separation from the other units caused by Pettus's delay in the swamp and the continued forward movement by Walthall's command. Clayton reserved his most stinging criticism for the brigade commanders: "I deem it but just to the other officers and the men to say, it was not only due to the circumstance . . . but in a great manner to the want of proper management in the officers who happened to be in command." After the battle, Clayton relieved Colonel Gordon from command of Jackson's brigade, replacing him with Lt. Col. Osceola Kyle. Colonel Kellogg remained in command of Stovall's brigade, and exhibited excellent leadership nine days later at the battle of Bentonville.[17]

As the Georgians gave way under the Hoosiers' pressure, new Rebel lines suddenly appeared and succeeded in halting Orr's attack. Pettus's five Alabama regiments, totaling 350 men, had finally emerged from the swamp and threatened the 124th Indiana's right flank, forcing its men to retire to their

14 Smith, "Hovey's Babies" *National Tribune*, December 29, 1897; *OR* 47, pt. 1, 945.

15 Clayton, "Clayton's Battle Report."

16 Lillian Henderson, *Roster of the Confederate Soldiers of Georgia*, 6 vols. (Hapeville, GA, 1959-1960), vol. 4, 591-592.

17 Clayton, "Clayton's Battle Report."

Brig. Gen. Edmund W. Pettus
*Alabama Department of Archives and History,
Montgomery, Alabama*

entrenchments. "We had driven them nearly a half a mile," described a soldier in the 124th, "and the 120th had captured about 50 prisoners (with many more in our front ready to surrender), when we discovered we were being flanked."[18]

While Orr tried to cope with the threat posed by Pettus's Alabamians, Colonel Prather's 120th Indiana took fire from an advancing Confederate battle line along its flank and rear. The 128th Indiana on Orr's left had bogged down in a swamp, leaving the 120th's own left unsupported. To prevent the Confederates from cutting off his line of retreat, Prather ordered the left wing of the 120th to fall back, changing front to meet the advancing Southerners. Outnumbered by the approaching Confederates, Prather wisely ordered his regiment to retire, "bringing off some thirty-two prisoners and all my wounded."[19]

The Confederate force that drove back the Hoosiers belonged to Loring's division, commanded by Col. James Jackson of the 27th Alabama. Jackson's timing was superb. The 32-year-old was a planter from Florence, Alabama. Captured at Fort Donelson, Tennessee, in February 1862, Jackson spent seven months in a Yankee prison before gaining his parole. In June 1864, he lost an arm during the battle of Kennesaw Mountain and did not return to the regiment until after Hood's Tennessee campaign. Jackson assumed temporary command of the division on March 9 due to Maj. Gen. William W. Loring's illness, which had left him unable to travel beyond Charlotte.[20]

18 Davis, "Hovey's Babies," *National Tribune*, December 29, 1887.

19 Ibid.; *OR* 47, pt. 1, 945.

20 Albert Quincy Porter, diary, March 9, 1865, Miscellaneous Manuscript Collection, Library of Congress.

When Prather ordered the 120th Indiana's withdrawal, the color bearer, Cpl. James Davis, failed to hear the command. As the regiment began to fall back, Davis assumed that his comrades were retreating without orders. The brave soldier refused to budge and yelled, "Why will ye desert the flag of your country!"[21]

Sergeant Joseph Edmonds of Company F, 120th Indiana observed the "Johnnies come pouring on" to seize the colors—a Civil War regiment's most prized possession. Seeing a wave of Rebels converging on Corporal Davis, Capt. Benjamin F. Goe ordered Company F "to rally on the colors." Goe's men bought precious time as Lt. Col. Reuben C. Kise rushed into the fight with sword drawn and ordered the Hoosiers back to their works. According to Edmonds, "This act of bravery on the part of Lt. Col. Kise saved our colors and our scalps as well." An Indiana sergeant later wrote, "I do not claim for our flag that it was the first on all the courthouses and forts, but I do know, that just at this particular time we well-nigh placed it in the rebels' hands."[22]

Flushed with the success of having turned back Prather's Indiana regiment, Loring's division soon encountered Lt. Col. Jasper Packard's 128th Indiana, which anchored the left of Orr's brigade. A schoolteacher from LaPorte, Indiana, Packard was a veteran of numerous Western Theater campaigns. "We heard heavy firing on the skirmish line and every man was ordered to his post," recalled the 128th's Lt. Joshua Fraser. "In a few moments in came our skirmishers with the rebs after them. They [the enemy] charged our works with two rows of fight, but we repulsed them and drove them back."[23]

Lt. Col. Reuben C. Kise,
120th Indiana Infantry
Wade Sokolosky Collection

21 Joseph Edmonds, "The Late Col. R. C. Kise," *National Tribune*, November 29, 1883.

22 Ibid; Davis, "Hovey's Babies," *National Tribune*, December 29, 1887.

23 Joshua Fraser to brother and sister, March 13, 1865.

Packard then ordered three companies forward to recapture the rifle pits abandoned by his skirmishers. "I did not crave the job a bit," wrote an Indiana officer, "but we had to do it." The Hoosiers' charge forced the Confederates to relinquish the pits. Lieutenant Fraser described the fight as "the hottest place . . . worse than Franklin." Fraser's comparison is ironic, given that Featherston's and Scott's brigades of Loring's division had confronted the same three Indiana regiments at the battle of Franklin.[24]

On Orr's right, Colonel Henry Neff of the 124th Indiana also ordered his regiment to recapture their rifle pits. Neff's son, Capt. James L. Neff of Company H, and Capt. Asa Teal of Company G formed their two companies into line and advanced toward Pettus's waiting Confederates. The brave officers found the enemy "too strong for them" and "determined to hold" what little ground they had gained in the futile assault on the pits.[25]

As Captain Neff moved up and down the line encouraging his men, a Confederate bullet tore through the young officer's neck, killing him instantly. Despite heavy casualties, Captain Teal and his fellow Hoosiers remained steady and succeeded in holding their advanced position for the remainder of the day. A two-gun section from the 5th Illinois Independent Battery reported to Orr, who ordered the guns to deploy on his far right. Once unlimbered, the Illinois gunners began firing shot and shell into the woods, covering Orr's regiments as they advanced to retake their rifle pits.[26]

To the right of Loring's division, Brig. Gen. George D. Johnston led the depleted regiments from Quarles's brigade that formed Walthall's division. The 34-year-old Johnston was a North Carolinian by birth, but his mother raised him in Alabama. A member of the state legislature at the start of the war, Johnston abandoned politics for the Confederate army, receiving his baptism of fire at the battle of Manassas (Bull Run) in the first July of the war. He then served in the Army of Tennessee for the remainder of the war, despite a debilitating wound received during the Atlanta campaign that required him to use crutches. Following the defeat at Nashville, Johnston assumed command of Quarles's brigade.[27]

---

24 *OR* 47, pt. 1, 947; Joshua Fraser to brother and sister, March 13, 1865.

25 *OR* 47, pt. 1, 946.

26 Ibid.; 943.

27 Warner, *Generals in Gray*, 160-161.

Col. Jasper Packard, 128th Indiana Infantry
U.S. Army Military History Institute

Holding the extreme right of the Army of Tennessee's line, Quarles's brigade confronted Orr's brigade and Colonel Malloy's First Brigade of Carter's division. Malloy's defensive position stood just north of the Dover Road, where it connected with Orr's brigade on the right and Splaine's brigade on the left. Lieutenant Seymour placed his only remaining Napoleon in the road to contest a Confederate advance from the west. Malloy had occupied the position since the afternoon of March 7 and his men had constructed a formidable line of earthworks. As an added precaution, he established a second line of skirmishers. Malloy described the two skirmish lines as his "inner" and "outer" lines.[28]

Quarles's brigade brushed aside Malloy's outer-line skirmishers, but the Federal commander directed the artillery "to sweep the front of the command with shell," which halted the Confederate advance. During the assault, Johnston noted that his right flank came under an oblique fire, so he ordered his line to extend to the right until it reached the Dover Road. As Johnston adjusted his line, Captain Love observed "a heavy body of troops moving to the right, and almost in the rear of us." As Love turned to warn his commander, the 48th Tennessee received a heavy volley from the Federals, killing Sergeant Trousdale and Lt. Arthur H. Cranford of Company H.[29]

The 22year-old Trousdale had served in the 48th Tennessee since November 1861. The sergeant had just raised his rifle to fire when "a cruel wound to the neck" ended his life. Love witnessed his friend's "body drop to its

---

28 *OR* 47, pt. 1, 996.

29 Garrett and Lightfoot, *The Civil War in Maury County, Tennessee*, 230.

knees, falling back on his knapsack, hands across his chest, upon which his rifle rested." In making a rapid withdrawal, the Tennesseans had to abandon Trousdale and Cranford's bodies to the enemy.[30]

Johnston's second attack penetrated Malloy's inner and outer skirmish lines but the Federals once again responded with a lethal combination of musketry and artillery fire. The Federals Love had observed attempting to turn Quarles's right flank probably belonged to the 28th Michigan, which had just arrived with the 9th New Jersey from Palmer's division. Throughout the day, Col. William W. Wheeler's 28th Michigan had shifted from one critical point on the battlefield to another. In response to the attack on the Union center, Ruger had ordered the Wolverine regiment to reinforce Orr's brigade. [31]

Upon arriving, Orr assigned Wheeler a position along the main line. As his companies ocupied the entrenchments, Wheeler observed the right wing of the 28th Michigan—led by the unit's colors—vacate the works and attack. Unbeknownst to Wheeler, one of Orr's staff officers had ordered the right wing company commanders to seize the forward rifle-pits. The Michigan soldiers captured the pits and a dozen Confederate prisoners.[32]

One captive from Quarles's brigade, Pvt. John S. Haggard of the 48th Tennessee, stated that he was a U.S. soldier who had served in the 2nd Tennessee Mounted Rifles (Union). Haggard claimed that the Confederates had forced him to serve in the 48th Tennessee following his capture in October 1864. Haggard's story failed to convince Federal authorities in New Bern, who sent him and hundreds of other captives to the Union prison at Point Lookout, Maryland. He made a final appeal to the prison commandant, but it fell upon deaf ears. Much to his disappointment, Haggard received his parole around the same time as other Confederate prisoners.[33]

In the meantime, Walthall's attack had stalled. His outnumbered command now faced an enemy that extended well beyond his right and showed no

---

30 Ibid., 228, 230; According to the two soldiers' descendants, it is probable that Trousdale and Cranford lie in unmarked graves on the battlefield.

31 *OR* 47, pt. 1, 996.

32 Ibid., 953. In addition to the 28th Michigan, the 9th New Jersey of Palmer's division occupied the line vacated by McQuiston's brigade.

33 File of Pvt. John S. Haggard, *Records of Confederate Soldiers Who Served During the Civil War, Compiled Service Records of Confederate Soldiers Who Served in Organizations from the State of Tennessee,* M268, roll 313, Records Group 109, National Archives, Washington, DC.

Maj. Solomon Palmer, 19th Alabama Infantry
Millard Henderson Palmer III

hesitation in attacking. Worse, the untimely withdrawal of Jackson's and Stovall's brigades had created a gap between Walthall's command and Pettus's brigade to the north. Threatened on both flanks, Walthall recognized the futility of further assaults and wisely led his command to the rear.

Walthall's retreat prompted Clayton to halt Pettus's renewed advance and direct him "to push forward a strong skirmish line." Without Walthall on Pettus's right, an advance would have been risky at best. In addition to his endangered right, Pettus's oblique maneuver had created a gap of almost 600 yards between his brigade's left and the Confederate main line held by Colonel Coltart's command (Hill's division) along Mill Branch. Clayton recognized the danger posed by the separation and requested that Hill order Coltart to deploy his right regiment as skirmishers. Hill concurred and ordered Coltart to provide 300 men.[34]

Major Solomon Palmer, commanding the 19th Alabama of Deas's brigade, carried out Hill's order, aided by an injured Col. John C. Carter of Manigault's brigade. A tree had fallen on Carter the previous night. As Major Palmer deployed his skirmish line, it came under heavy fire from Claassen's brigade of General Palmer's Union division. Colonel Toulmin later reported that Deas's brigade suffered 17 men killed or wounded.[35]

Sergeant Calvin J. C. Munroe of the 25th Alabama received a severe wound in the right leg. The sergeant was the last of three Munroe brothers killed or wounded during the final months of the war. Munroe had buried his brother

---

34 Clayton, "Clayton's Battle Report."

35 OR 47, pt. 1, 1,088; Solomon Palmer, diary, n.d., March 1865, in Diary of Solomon Palmer 1852-1893, Palmer Family Papers, Alabama Department of Archives and History, Montgomery, Alabama; "Report of Casualties in Deas's Brigade, March 12, 1865," in Johnny B. Kerr Collection, North Carolina Department of Archives and History, Raleigh, North Carolina.

Pvt. Calvin J. C. Munroe,
Co. G, 25th Alabama
Alabama Department of Archives and History,
Montgomery, Alabama

William after the battle of Franklin, and then witnessed his brother Francis suffer from severe frostbite during the agonizing retreat from Nashville.[36]

Like Orr, Claassen had sent reinforcements to the far Union left during General Hoke's attack, leaving the 132nd New York thinly stretched along the brigade's front. The Army of Tennessee's oblique movement to the southeast initially drew the Southerners away from the New Yorkers' vulnerable position. However, the skirmishers Hill sent forward to support Pettus posed a late threat to Claassen's line. Lieutenant Col. Frank S. Curtiss's Provisional command had just returned from the Union left when Major Palmer's skirmishers made their initial push. Captain Andrew Wood's 5th Illinois Independent Battery arrived and deployed its guns between Orr's and Claassen's brigades.[37]

Major Palmer's skirmishers stubbornly pressed the Federals. Claassen later described the engagement as "very annoying and destructive," which "resulted in numerous casualties to the men of my command." As the afternoon wore on, Palmer gained possession of a portion of Claassen's skirmish line, inducing the colonel to reinforce the line with 50 men from the 132nd New York. Aided by Wood's guns, Claassen succeeded in retaking his skirmish line.[38]

Pettus's Alabamians held their advanced position "like a stone wall alone," marveled Hill. Observing Walthall's command retiring in "perfect order" and "a considerable Yankee force" massing before their works, Hill hesitated to

---

36 Calvin J. C. Munroe to Claudia F. Hefley, February 2, 1926, http://www.monroegen.org/ CJCMJLetter.htm; See also, *Western Enterprise*, Anson, Texas, September 12, 1913.

37 *OR* 47, pt. 1, 990.

38 Ibid.

renew the attack. By 3:30 p.m., the Army of Tennessee's assault had ended. Hill reported the situation to General Bragg, who ordered a withdrawal to the defensive works along the British Road.[39]

Bragg realized his attempt at another offensive victory had failed. At 3:45 p.m., he telegraphed General Johnston, apprising his commander of the defeat. "The enemy is strongly entrenched," wrote Bragg. "Yesterday and today, we have moved on his flanks, but without gaining a decided advantage. Prisoners report large reinforcements. . . . Under these conditions, I deem it best with the information you give, to join you, which I shall proceed to do."[40]

General Bragg's telegram to General Johnston effectively conceded the battlefield to Cox's Union army. The battle of Wise's Forks was over, at least from the Confederates' perspective. Cox would continue to maintain a defensive posture in anticipation of renewed assaults. For four days, Bragg had stalled the Federal advance and delayed the enemy occupation of Goldsboro. On March 8, he had captured an entire Federal brigade, and had come tantalizingly close to achieving a decisive victory, but ultimately failed to defeat Cox.

By the afternoon of March 10, General Bragg knew his position at Kinston was untenable and he readied his command to evacuate the town. He issued a congratulatory message to his troops, thanking them for "their gallantry in action," which had "won his gratitude." The message also explained the Confederate commander's decision to abandon Kinston. He failed, however, to mention the approach of General Sherman's Union army toward Fayetteville, noting only that duty called "a large portion of [his troops] to a distant field, and necessarily suspends offensive operations in this quarter."[41]

At least one Confederate officer did not look upon Bragg's withdrawal as an admission of defeat. Lieutenant James A. Hall of the 24th Alabama expressed quite the opposite attitude in a letter penned to his father on March 12. "Bragg came very near routing and capturing the whole Yankee force," explained Hall. "If he had had any cavalry he would have done so. We did not leave Kinston on account of the enemy in our front. I suffice we go again to confront Sherman." The Army of Tennessee veteran was correct. He and his

---

39 Ibid., 1,088.

40 Ibid., pt. 2, 1,364.

41 Ibid., 1,366.

men would oppose Sherman's army nine days later in the battle of Bentonville.[42]

Before Bragg shifted his headquarters across the Neuse River to Kinston, he directed the immediate transfer from Kinston to Goldsboro of "all the sick and wounded soldiers capable of being transported by railroad." As a large number of wounded Confederates remained on the battlefield and in temporary field hospitals, he directed his commanders to "put in motion for Kinston all trains, sick and wounded, and supplies not necessary for immediate use."[43]

Later that evening, Bragg issued Special Orders No. 59, directing a withdrawal toward Goldsboro, starting on the morning of March 11. The Army of Tennessee contingent would depart first, traveling on foot. Hoke's division and Baker's Junior Reserves brigade would cross the Neuse River, destroying the bridges behind them. As Bragg planned to move his headquarters to Goldsboro the next morning, he assigned Hoke command of the rear guard at Kinston. Hoke would ensure the evacuation of all wounded and critical materiel from Kinston by the morning of March 12. After that, he would oversee the destruction of all remaining supplies.[44]

To assist Hoke in covering the withdrawal, Bragg attached the 6th North Carolina Cavalry and a squadron of the 2nd South Carolina Cavalry to his division. The latter had moved north in front of the advancing Union columns from Wilmington. Bragg also requested the help of the Confederate ironclad gunboat CSS *Neuse*, anchored at Kinston and commanded by Wilmington native Capt. Joseph H. Price. Throughout the battle, the *Neuse* had remained inactive. However, its mere presence had deterred Federal naval support along the river. Expecting the gunboat to be scuttled before the Federals could capture it, Bragg asked Captain Price to create a diversion by moving the *Neuse* downriver, making the "loss of the vessel as costly to the enemy as possible.[45]

As the Confederates prepared to evacuate, Cox awaited the arrival of General Couch's Union column from Wilmington. Unsure of Bragg's next move, Cox advised General Palmer late that afternoon: "The rebels may, and

---

42 James A. Hall to father, March 12, 1865, in Bolling Family Papers, Alabama Department Archives and History, Montgomery, Alabama.

43 *OR* 47, pt. 2, 1,367.

44 Ibid., 1,366-1,367.

45 Ibid., 1,367; Captain John Chesnut commanded the squadron of the 2nd South Carolina Cavalry operating near Kinston.

probably will, try us again tomorrow." In explaining his decision not to go on the offensive, Cox recorded in his journal, "I do not feel strong enough to do so, and am satisfied with repulsing them, as it is clear that their force is very heavy." The presence of Confederate prisoners from various commands of the Army of Tennessee had greatly influenced his decision. Unbeknownst to Cox, these units were mere remnants of the force he had faced in Georgia and Tennessee.[46]

Both Cox and Schofield deemed the arrival of Couch's troops from Wilmington necessary to resuming offensive operations. Once again, Cox ordered his cavalry chief Colonel Savage to make contact with the approaching column: "You must get scouts through to General Couch at speed. . . . This word must go through to-night if horse flesh will carry it." Schofield's message to Couch exhibited a similar sense of urgency: "Move right for this place by the shortest route and by a force[d] march. Cox has been fighting heavily to-day and has repulsed the enemy so far."[47]

In response to Bragg's repeated attacks and continued intelligence reports indicating the arrival of Confederate reinforcements, Schofield issued orders directing the immediate transfer to the front of all available units at Morehead City—even those detailed to assist Gen. L. C. Easton, Sherman's chief quartermaster. Schofield went so far as to order Col. W. W. Wright to halt his railroad repairs for two days in order to allocate all available rolling stock to the transfer of men and materiel to the front.[48]

As night fell, Cox's weary soldiers huddled around campfires, exhausted from nearly four days of continuous combat. To add more misery to an already chilly winter night, a hard rain began around 10:00 p.m., extinguishing their fires and turning the ground into a sea of mud. "We were soon soaked from head to foot," recalled a Massachusetts soldier. "But even this condition of affairs did not prevent most of the men from getting that rest which soldiers secure often under the most trying conditions."[49]

In the waning hours of daylight, the Confederates began their retreat toward Kinston. The most pressing concern for Bragg was transferring the

---

46 OR 47, pt. 1, 933; pt. 2, 773.

47 Ibid.

48 Ibid., 767-769.

49 Kirwan, *Memorial History of the Seventeenth Regiment Massachusetts*, 353.

wounded across the Neuse River into town. Musician Albert Q. Porter of the 33rd Mississippi and his fellow band members were en route to Loring's division hospital. As Porter marched down the Dover Road, he observed an all-too-familiar sight—long columns of wounded men moving to the rear. "As we were going along out to the Division hospital," wrote Porter in his diary, "we met a great many wounded Southerners, some walking, others in ambulances on the way to town." After crossing the river, Porter and his comrades encountered "more wounded than ever, shot in every conceivable manner." At the hospital, "the surgeons [were] busy in preparing wounds and amputating fractured limbs."[50]

Bragg's weary foot soldiers used the cover of darkness to conceal their withdrawal. According to several sources, the Army of Tennessee brigades evacuated their positions first, followed by Hoke's division. A soldier from Stovall's brigade, Pvt. Francis H. Nash of the 42nd Georgia, noted his unit's evacuation and subsequent movement toward Goldsboro. "Left the line . . . at 9:00 p.m. and marched through town and camped 5 miles up R. R. on night [of] 10th," wrote Nash. "On morning [of] 11th marched 17 miles toward Goldsboro and camped." About midnight Hoke withdrew his brigades, with Hagood's serving as rear guard. "Roused at 3 a.m. and moved off on road to Kinston," Lieutenant Calder recorded in his diary. "It was evident we were evacuating our position. We bivouacked in a field near the town while the troops moved off on the road to Goldsboro."[51]

Musician Porter's duty at Loring's hospital proved brief. Within two hours, he had moved back to Kinston to assist in evacuating the wounded. "We worked hard until about 12 o'clock," wrote Porter. "There were four long trains full of wounded. When all were aboard, we were ordered to go along with them to Rawley [Raleigh] to assist in taking them off to the hospitals."[52]

Porter's reference to Raleigh rather than Goldsboro's military hospitals is significant, as it reveals the Confederates' strategic response to Bragg's withdrawal from Kinston. With the latter town all but in Union hands, Goldsboro was clearly the Federals' next major objective. In addition to its hospitals, Goldsboro was a key supply depot essential to sustaining military

---

50 Porter, diary, March 10, 1865; It was standard procedure during the Civil War for musicians to assist in evacuating and caring for the wounded.

51 Nash, diary, March 10, 1865; Calder, diary, March 10, 1865; Hagood, *Memoirs*, 355.

52 Porter, diary, March 10, 1865.

operations. Anticipating the worst, Bragg ordered Goldsboro's war materiel transferred west to Smithfield and Raleigh.[53]

By dawn on March 11, the Confederates had abandoned the battlefield to the Federals. In their haste, the Southerners had left many of their fallen comrades lying dead or severely wounded in front of the Union works—thus leaving them to the tender mercy of the enemy. Determining the total number of Confederate losses at Wise's Forks is problematic, owing to the scarcity of Confederate battle reports. Fifteen hundred casualties is the widely accepted figure, but the number is probably closer to 800.[54]

Hill reported the five brigades from Lee's Corps lost 134 men—11 killed, 107 wounded, and 16 missing. Based on a combined strength of 1,328 men, Hill suffered a loss of 10 percent. Hill did not report the losses of the brigades in Stewart's Corps, nor did Walthall provide the casualties for his command.[55]

The few Rebel sources available indicate that most of their casualties occurred on March 10. Bragg's lukewarm response to Governor Vance's offer of medical assistance prior to Hoke's disastrous attack on March 10 suggests the Confederates suffered few casualties up until then. Before Hoke's attack, Bragg had informed the governor that his loss was "so small" as to require no assistance.[56]

On the Union side, General Cox and his subordinates kept a meticulous record of their losses. Cox reported 1,337 total casualties—65 killed, 319 wounded, and 953 missing. Upham's brigade suffered 889 total losses, 828 of whom were captured or missing—the largest loss of any Federal unit at Wise's Forks. Carter's remaining two brigades, Malloy's and Splaine's, sustained a combined loss of 58—nine killed, 31 wounded, and 18 missing. Their loss reflects the predominantly defensive role the two brigades had assumed during the battle. The combined casualties in Palmer's division totaled 127—16 killed, 83 wounded, and 28 missing.[57]

---

53 *OR* 47, pt. 2, 1,368, 1,376-1,378.

54 http://www.nps.gov/abpp/battles/nc017.htm; Schofield estimated Bragg's total loss as 1,500 men. *OR* 47, pt. 1, 912. See Appendix C for the authors' analysis of Confederate losses.

55 *OR* 47, pt. 1, 1,089. We have documented 44 losses in Stewart's Corps.

56 Ibid., pt. 2, 1,363; Hagood described the Confederate losses up to March 10 as "inconsiderable." Hagood, *Memoirs*, 355.

57 *OR* 47, pt. 1, 61-62.

With the exception of Upham's brigade, Ruger's division suffered the greatest loss of the three divisions in the Provisional Corps. Ruger reported a total loss of 174—25 killed, 148 wounded, and one missing. Most occurred in Orr's brigade, which indicates the intensity of the fighting along his front. Orr reported a total loss of 103—12 killed, 90 wounded, and one missing.[58]

Although Bragg's determined resistance at Wise's Forks had briefly delayed Cox's advance on Goldsboro, Confederate President Jefferson Davis reflected that "it was on too small a scale to produce important results," as it did little to alter the strategic situation. However, the battle was a bright spot in an otherwise gloomy situation facing the Confederates in eastern North Carolina. Bragg's aggressive tactics dispelled the notion that the Rebels were beaten, teaching the Union Army in North Carolina a lesson repeated at Monroe's Crossroads, Averasboro, and Bentonville—that the "Confederate Army was still full of fight."[59]

---

58 Ibid.

59 Jefferson Davis, *Rise and Fall of the Confederate Government*, 2 vols. (Richmond, VA, 1938), vol. 2, 539; Barefoot, *General Robert F. Hoke*, 290-291.

Chapter 9

"I am straining every nerve to get the railroad completed"

— *Maj. Gen. John M. Schofield*

For Want of a Railroad

Nurse Kate Sperry arrived at Goldsboro's General Hospital No. 3 shortly after dawn on March 11, 1865, fully expecting to resume caring for the wounded and the sick. To her surprise, Sperry's husband, Surgeon Enoch Hunt, instructed her to "pack up—had orders to carry off all the Hospital stores that we could and burn the rest." Throughout the night Confederate medical officers in Goldsboro had loaded wounded soldiers aboard westbound trains for Raleigh. Since March 5, the medical director for North Carolina, Surgeon Peter E. Hines, had been planning to transfer the hospital to a point west of Raleigh, beyond the probable route of advancing Union forces. With Kinston's evacuation, Hines realized that he had to move it immediately.[1]

As state medical director, Hines faced a difficult task. He assumed that the casualties from Wise's Forks were just the beginning. Though unable to predict when or where the next battle would occur, Hines had to prepare for the worst. Medical personnel operating the Confederate hospital at Goldsboro were soon overwhelmed by the number of wounded, and the situation threatened to repeat itself at Raleigh. The capital city's three general hospitals—Nos. 7, 8, and

---

1 Peter E. Hines to W. A. Holt, March 5, 1865, in W. A. Holt Papers, Southern Historical Collection, University of North Carolina Library, Chapel Hill; Sperry, diary, March 13, 1865. Nurse Sperry noted that General Hospital No. 3 was relocated to the Barbee Hotel and the Female College in High Point, North Carolina.

Drawing General Hospital No. 13 (Pettigrew) Raleigh, North Carolina
State Archives of North Carolina

13—received wounded from Kinston. Nos. 7 and 8 could accommodate several hundred wounded, while No. 13, the newest and largest of the three, was a 400-bed facility.[2]

The sudden influx of casualties at Raleigh quickly overwhelmed the three hospitals. According to the Raleigh *Daily Confederate*, about 500 wounded were transferred from Kinston on March 11. Confederate surgeons in the capital city had no choice but to press local churches and private residences into service as temporary hospitals in order to accommodate the overflow. Raleigh resident Catherine Ann Devereux Edmondston noted in her diary that a Mrs. Miller "has cooking done for 280 patients in the Episcopal Church. These men were wounded in the battle below Kinston." To alleviate the overcrowding, several hundred of the injured were transferred farther west along the North Carolina Railroad to military hospitals located in High Point, Greensboro, Salisbury, and Charlotte.[3]

In addition to their own wounded, Confederate medical authorities made room on the westbound trains for a number of the injured Union prisoners. Confederate surgeon Simon Baruch was charged with caring for these unfortunates. A native of Prussia, Baruch's knowledge of German proved extremely useful in treating many of these Union soldiers. "They were raw

2   H. H. Cunningham, *Doctors in Gray*, 54; H. H. Cunningham, "Edmund Burke Haywood and Raleigh's Confederate Hospitals," in *North Carolina Historical Review* (April 1958), vol. 35, no. 2, 156.

3   *Daily Conservative* (Raleigh, NC) March 13, 1865; *Journal of a Secesh Lady*, 680.

Confederate Surgeon Simon Baruch
Confederate Veteran

Germans," was how Baruch recalled these injured men, "unable to speak English, and were delighted when I addressed them in their own language."[4]

Baruch's Federal patients included a "Col. Patterson" from Massachusetts, who was captured at Wise's Forks. The Union officer became extremely ill during the train ride and probably would have died without Baruch's treatment. Upon reaching High Point, the surgeon found a "more comfortable" location for Patterson to recover.[5]

In addition to removing the wounded from Goldsboro, the Confederates labored to relocate tons of critical war materiel essential to sustaining operations in North Carolina. The commissary department alone had about 200,000 rations stored at Goldsboro. General Johnston informed Bragg, "They are of great importance, so please have them brought away."[6]

While the Confederates evacuated Goldsboro, Federal soldiers at Wise's Forks found the battlefield strangely quiet on the morning of March 11. Just after sunrise, Union skirmishers reported that the Confederates had withdrawn. At 9:00 a.m., Palmer telegraphed Cox, "The enemy has evacuated his lines on

---

4   Ward, *Simon Baruch: Rebel in the Ranks of Medicine*, 58; Simon Baruch, "The Experiences of a Confederate Surgeon," *Civil War Times Illustrated*, (October 1965), vol. 4, no. 6, 46.

5   Ward, *Simon Baruch*, 58-59; Baruch, "The Experiences of a Confederate Surgeon," 46; The authors were unable to identify a Colonel Patterson from either of the three Massachusetts's regiments that fought at Wise's Forks. A Federal account suggests that this officer was Lt. Col. Walter G. Bartholomew of the 27th Massachusetts, who was admitted to a Confederate military hospital in High Point. Sergeant Henry C. Baldwin of the 15th Connecticut discovered Bartholomew and other wounded Union soldiers from Upham's brigade at the Masonic Hall in High Point. Thorpe, *The History of the Fifteenth Connecticut*, 253.

6   OR 47, pt. 2, 1,376-1,377. Johnston and Bragg were pressured by the Confederate War Department to ensure the safe evacuation of supplies. Interestingly, the War Department allocated the supplies solely for General Lee's Army of Northern Virginia. Johnston was ordered to procure his rations locally.

Southwest Creek, in front of the right, on the line of the railroad, as I presume he has on the whole line." Later, Palmer reported more information obtained from a New Jersey sergeant whose scout detail had ventured beyond Southwest Creek. During the reconnaissance, a local resident named John Jackson informed the sergeant that Bragg had evacuated Kinston and was moving toward Goldsboro.[7]

General Schofield telegraphed the important news of Bragg's withdrawal to his younger brother, Bvt. Brig. Gen. George W. Schofield, at New Bern, North Carolina. "The rebels seem satisfied with their pounding yesterday," he wrote, "and have disappeared, leaving their intrenching tools as well as their dead upon the field." With Bragg no longer a threat, Schofield instructed his brother to halt the movement of reinforcements from Morehead City. Colonel Wright was to push ahead with railroad repairs. More importantly, the Union commander directed that the pontoon bridge reportedly at Morehead City be sent forward at once.[8]

Later that day, Schofield returned to New Bern to refocus attention on solving the troublesome logistical issues hindering the army's movement to Goldsboro. The Federals could no longer advance without leaving the railroad—which was always a dangerous proposition. By the afternoon of March 11, the railroad had only been repaired to a point just a few miles east of Gum Swamp. As a result, General Cox's wagon trains had to make lengthy trips between the railhead and the front lines. With each passing day, resupply grew more difficult, as heavy rains made sections of the Dover Road nearly impassable.

Unable to supply his men with army rations, Cox had reached an impasse. The situation grew worse when General Couch arrived from Wilmington with 7,000 additional men. Resourceful Union soldiers quickly improvised, however, scouring the surrounding countryside for food. For the Yankee foragers, the Kinston area proved far more bountiful than the swampy region through which they had just traveled.

With control of the battlefield came the gruesome responsibility of burying the dead—friend and foe alike. Throughout the day, Union soldiers buried the remains in hastily dug trenches. "Cleared off the battlefield . . . burying the rebel

---

7   Ibid., 789; pt. 1, 986, 988, 993, 995.

8   Ibid., pt. 2, 788.

dead in deep trenches 5 to 10 in a place," wrote Capt. Henry J. Main of the 130th Indiana. "Such is the scenes of war and subjugation."[9]

At the site of Hoke's ill-fated assault, Federal soldiers found the dead "lying in every possible attitude, with every conceivable expression on their countenances." Thomas Kirwan, historian of the 17th Massachusetts, recalled the scene:

> The faces of these were frequently distorted, and gave every evidence of the mental and physical agony they had unconsciously passed through. At one place lay one of the dead, with legs nearly severed from the body, his plastic features plainly showing the anguish he had endured. Some had been killed by a single bullet, the wounds scarcely perceptible, and the features as placid as though the tired soldier had calmly laid down to rest.[10]

As burial details laid the dead to rest, Union doctors were still operating on the wounded—a monumental task that, according to Surgeon Alonzo Garwood of Ruger's division, lasted until the evening of March 12. As late as the thirteenth, Garwood recorded in his diary, "The sick and wounded have not all been sent off yet." Garwood's terse comment reveals the difficulty of transporting the wounded due to the shortage of wagons and the distance to the railhead.[11]

Nearly one-half of the Union soldiers wounded on March 10 did not reach Foster General Hospital at New Bern until three days after the fighting ended. The hospital records further indicate that 29 Confederates were admitted to the Foster facility, with all but one having been wounded and captured on March 10.[12]

The Federals also transported roughly 400 Confederate prisoners to New Bern. During the battle, the Union brigades turned over their prisoners to division provost marshals, who collected the Southerners in temporary

---

9   Henry J. Main, *Memoranda of 130th Indiana Vols.*, in Civil War Miscellaneous Collection, U.S. Army Military History Institute, Carlisle, Pennsylvania. Dead Union soldiers were later relocated to New Bern's Cedar Grove Cemetery. In February 1867, their remains were once more re-interred, this time in the newly established National Cemetery, which was also in New Bern.

10   Kirwan, *Memorial History of the Seventeenth Massachusetts*, 350.

11   Garwood, diary, March 11-13, 1865.

12   Foster General Hospital Registry, March 1865.

"bull-pens," where they awaited transfer to the rear. In Ruger's division alone, the provost marshal held a total of 235 Confederates.[13]

After marching to the railhead, the prisoners boarded trains bound for New Bern. At the port city, they embarked on ships destined for the North, where the Southerners spent the remainder of the war in Union prisons. Records indicate that most enlisted prisoners went to Point Lookout, Maryland, while officers went to either Fort Delaware, Delaware, or Johnson's Island, Ohio. At least one group of captives from Wise's Forks made the long journey from the battlefield to Point Lookout, Maryland, in just one week—a testament to the efficiency of the U.S. Army's transportation network in 1865. Those same Confederates, however, suffered a terrifying accident at sea in which several lost their lives.[14]

Meanwhile, Cox eagerly sought more information about the enemy. On the morning of March 12, he sent infantry and cavalry to reconnoiter toward the Neuse River. The Union soldiers confirmed that the Confederates had withdrawn across the Neuse River, leaving an infantry picket at the foot of the wagon bridge. Instead of burning the bridge, the Southerners had simply removed the center planks to disable the structure. On the opposite side, they manned a formidable line of rifle pits and artillery positions. As the Union reconnaissance party approached, sporadic gunfire erupted from Confederates defending the crossing, but the Federals withdrew down the Dover Road without pressing the issue.[15]

A detachment of Yankee cavalry was greeted with more than small arms fire. Captain Joseph Price and the ironclad gunboat CSS *Neuse* had steamed downriver from Kinston to aid in covering Hoke's withdrawal. Price and his 80-man crew fired several rounds of grape and canister from the gunboat's two 6.4-inch Brooke rifles before steaming upriver. After the crew had evacuated their personal belongings, Price ordered a powder charge detonated in the bow.

---

13 OR 47, pt. 1, 933, 941; *Old North State* (Beaufort, NC), March 14, 1865.

14 John K. Burlingame, *History of the Fifth Regiment of Rhode Island Heavy Artillery, During Three Years and A Half of Service in North Carolina* (Providence, RI, 1892), 252-253; Selected Records of the War Department Relating to Confederate Prisoners of War, M598, rolls 114 through 115, Records Group 109, National Archives, Washington, DC. See Appendix E, "Journey to Point Lookout, Maryland," for a detailed account of the hazardous journey experienced by one group of Confederate prisoners.

15 OR 47, pt. 2, 801.

The ensuing explosion blasted a nine-foot hole in the hull, sinking the *Neuse* to her deck line.[16]

The scuttling of the ironclad effectively ended the Confederate navy's presence on the Neuse River. During her brief two-year lifespan, the *Neuse* had not fired a hostile shot until March 1865. Lt. Richard H. Bacot, an officer aboard the *Neuse*, later wrote to his sister describing the vessel's final moments:

> My old home the 'Neuse,' is gone, all the troops had withdrawn from Kinston & the Yankees 18,000 strong came upon us & not having any prospect of being relieved before our provisions gave out & being in a narrow river where we could not work the ship under fire, after shelling the Yankee cavalry for a little while, we removed our powder & stores & burnt the vessel.[17]

Later that day, a Confederate officer sent by Hoke appeared across the river under a flag of truce, bearing a request to exchange prisoners. Unsure of his authority, Cox telegraphed Schofield in New Bern for guidance. Schofield denied the request but notified General Grant in Virginia, requesting clarification. Major Tristam T. Dow of Cox's staff delivered Schofield's response to Hoke's representative, who in the meantime had crossed the river by boat. Dow exploited the parley by assessing the Confederate defenses on the opposite bank and the condition of the wagon bridge.[18]

The motives for Hoke's request for a prisoner exchange remain unclear. Was he attempting to recover valuable manpower that General Kirkland had lost on March 10, or was his gesture purely humanitarian? By March 12, most of the Federal prisoners had already been evacuated. The few who remained in town were too weak to be moved.

Eager to resume operations, Schofield hurried to the front from New Bern. He agreed with Cox's suggestion to move immediately against Kinston and

---

16 Edwards and Rowland, *Through the Eyes of Soldiers: The Battle of Wyse Fork*, 100-101, 132; Leslie S. Bright, William H. Rowland, and James C. Bardon, *C.S.S. Neuse: A Question of Iron and Time* (Raleigh, NC, 1981), 17-19. The vessel was scuttled in a bend of the river near the terminus of Bright Street in Kinston.

17 Richard H. Bacot to sister, March 27, 1865, in Richard H. Bacot Papers, North Carolina Department of Archives and History, Raleigh, North Carolina.

18 *OR* 47, pt. 2, 801, 834; pt. 1, 933; pt. 2, 802; The Confederates had placed two 32-pound smoothbore cannons within the earthworks to protect the bridge from the Kinston side of the river. See, *OR* 43, ser. I, pt. 3, 1,321-1,322. The Confederates abandoned the guns during the withdrawal.

directed him to lead the advance with his corps, while Couch assumed a supporting role. Schofield instructed Cox to "effect a crossing of the Neuse" on the morning of March 14, "to secure possession of the wagon bridge [and] drive the enemy from the opposite bank"[19]

Fortunately for Cox, the Confederates offered little resistance. Bragg had ordered his remaining forces at Kinston to fall back on Goldsboro, where the majority of his command was encamped. All that remained at Kinston was a small contingent consisting of the 6th North Carolina Cavalry, Colquitt's brigade from Hoke's division, and the 67th and 68th North Carolina regiments.[20]

Bragg abandoned Kinston in response to General Johnston's decision to concentrate at Smithfield. Over the previous three days, the Confederate military situation in North Carolina had deteriorated considerably. Sherman's Union army had occupied Fayetteville on March 11, and after a brief respite was preparing to resume its advance toward Goldsboro. Unsure whether Sherman's destination was Goldsboro or Raleigh, Johnston ordered General Hardee to "impede" the Federal advance while he concentrated Confederate forces at Smithfield, roughly midway between the two towns. On March 13, Johnston ordered Bragg to move his command to Smithfield "with all promptness."[21]

Bragg instructed Colonel Zachry to "leave the cavalry to watch and obstruct the enemy," and to lead the rear guard infantry to Smithfield "without delay." He also ordered Colonel Whitford to proceed to Goldsboro and secure the town "until otherwise ordered, or driven away." At Goldsboro, the 67th and 68th North Carolina were combined to form a brigade under Whitford.[22]

---

19 OR 47, pt. 2, 814.

20 According to Capt. Thomas J. Marshall, Colquitt's brigade returned to Kinston on March 11, after marching six miles toward Goldsboro. Marshall gave no reason for the sudden about-face. On March 13, the Georgians evacuated Kinston and arrived at Goldsboro two days later. Marshall, diary, March 11-13, 1865.

21 OR 47, pt. 2, 1,363, 1,388.

22 Ibid., 1,389, 1,406; Official prisoner of war records indicate that a number of Rebels from Colquitt's and Hagood's brigades were captured at Kinston on March 14. It is unclear whether these men were malingerers or part of the rear guard. On March 18, Bragg ordered Colonel Whitford to Cox's Bridge (10 miles west of Goldsboro on the Neuse River) to destroy the span should the Federals advancing from Fayetteville attempt to cross there. OR 47, pt. 2, 1,436. On March 19, Whitford, reinforced by a four-gun battery, engaged an advance element from Sherman's army and set fire to the bridge. The Federals completed the destruction. Neither side wanted to leave the bridge standing. Manarin, et al., *North Carolina Troops*, vol. 15, 423-424.

Neuse River Bridge

William Garrison Reed Photo Album, New Bern-Craven County Public Library, New Bern, North Carolina

Colonel Malloy's brigade of Carter's division led the Union advance up the Dover Road toward Kinston. The Federals encountered no opposition until within three-quarters of a mile of the wagon bridge, where Confederate skirmishers were posted on the south side of the river. Malloy responded by sending out his own skirmishers and deploying for battle. The Southerners quickly withdrew to the Kinston side of the river and opened fire. Thirty minutes later, they fell back into town.[23]

Upon reaching the bridge, Malloy's men repaired the center section by felling a tree and placing it across the gap. Lieutenant Joseph B. Knox, Cox's chief signal corps officer, sat down on the tree and scooted across. He then proceeded into Kinston. Finding the town deserted, Knox established a signal station atop the cupola of the Saint James Hotel and sent a message across the river: "Place all quiet; no enemy in sight." Knox's station enabled him to communicate from Kinston to the railroad terminus several miles to the east.[24]

In response to Knox's all-clear signal, Malloy sent a battalion across the river. A delegation of civilians led by the mayor met the Federals at the bridge. "I am authorized to surrender the town," the mayor declared, "and claim

23 *New York Herald*, March 23, 1865.

24 OR 47, pt. 1, 918; Tyndall, *Threshold of Freedom*, 102.

protection for its inhabitants." Schofield himself was present and responded, "The protection will depend upon their behavior." The mayor reported that the only Confederates in town were rear-guard cavalry. After almost two weeks of campaigning, the Federals had at last seized Kinston.[25]

With Malloy's battalion in town, the rest of the Union army camped south of the river and awaited the pontoon bridge, which arrived later that day. From their campsites, Cox and his soldiers could see Kinston's tall church spires rising above the evergreens. By the afternoon of March 15, a pontoon bridge was finally completed. Schofield moved to consolidate his position, directing Cox to move his corps across the river that evening, while Couch's two divisions remained south of the river. Carter's division crossed first, followed by Ruger's and Palmer's. Once across, they moved to the outskirts of town and entrenched.[26]

Throughout the night, columns of infantry and artillery crossed the bridge and passed through town. "It is a novel sight to see cannons drawn by horses and troops of cavalry, the large loaded wagons and infantry passing over on a bridge of boats," wrote a greenhorn New York soldier. The 9th New Jersey of Palmer's division camped on Kinston's southeast side. The men discovered that their bivouac was located near several cemeteries with freshly-dug graves, most of which were unmarked. However, the graves of Col. James H. Neal of the 19th Georgia and his adjutant, Lt. Sterling G. Turner, were identified. Both men had been killed in battle. A year later, the families of the two fallen officers traveled to Kinston and recovered the remains for reburial back home in Georgia.[27]

By most accounts, Kinston's civilians accepted their fate—at least those who chose to stay. Although most businesses remained closed, women and children walked about town. In describing the general attitude of townspeople, a Union newspaper reported, "The inhabitants appear a little downcast, but are pleasant in their demeanor towards us." Private Thomas J. Davis of the 18th Wisconsin shared with his wife his mixed feelings toward the natives:

25 *Old North State* (Beaufort, NC), March 14, 1865.

26 *OR* 47, pt. 1, 934; pt. 2, 854.

27 Tournier, diary, March 14, 1865; Everts, *A Complete and Comprehensive History of the Ninth Regiment New Jersey Vols.*, 163; *Atlanta Intelligencer*, May 4, 1866; In 1892, the United Daughters of the Confederacy erected a monument in Kinston's Maplewood Cemetery honoring 44 unmarked Confederate graves. A short distance from the monument, a single grave marker identifies the final resting place of an unknown Union soldier who died in 1865.

Lt. Joseph B. Knox, U.S. Army Signal Corps
U.S. Army Signal School & Center, Fort Gordon, GA

I have been around town considerably . . .
and I find some folks that I really pitty
their condition. Some of them seem to be
good honest sort of people and say they
were always opposed to the war although
many were forced into it. Those rich
Rebels that have been broken up I cannot
cympathise with at all and I like to see
them brought to beggerry and I would
assist in the work if necessary.[28]

Soldiers like Sgt. Joseph Brown of
the 180th Ohio enjoyed ogling the
town's young women, but remained
suspicious of their deep-rooted hatred
of the Yankees. "I saw some pretty
good looking girls in town here," wrote Brown. "I expect they would like to
strike me if they had a chance and thought they dare to, they are all Rebels here .
. . . 'Secesh' as they can be."[29]

Due to the army's wagon shortage, Union soldiers confiscated anything
with wheels. As one described it, "Our boys take everything they can get their
fingers on." Private Sisco and a comrade from the 123rd Indiana ventured into
Kinston "to see what could be spared for the good of the military service of the
U.S." They located a carriage shop, and upon entering Sisco's "eye fell on a nice
appearing little wagon with a tongue, but only 3 wheels." The two Hoosiers
discovered a spare wheel a full two inches smaller than the other three. With a
little Yankee ingenuity, they soon mounted it. "A matter of 2 inches in height,
did not amount too much to the U.S. of America at that time," wrote Sisco.
Along with the wagon, they acquired a harness set made entirely of cotton
webbing except for the collars, which were constructed of corn shucks. After

---

28 *Old North State* (Beaufort, NC) March 16, 1865; Thomas P. Nanzig, ed., *The Badax Tigers:
From Shiloh to the Surrender with the 18th Wisconsin Volunteers* (Lanham, MD, 2002), 312-313.

29 Joseph J. Brown to Rosa, March 16, 1865.

Pvt. Moses A. Sisco,
Co. A, 123rd Indiana Infantry
Robert S. Matthews

hitching up a pair of mules, the two soldiers proudly "drove to the camp in style."[30]

The Federals found a number of wounded comrades left behind by their captors in the homes of Kinston residents. To provide for the sick and wounded, they established Lenoir General Hospital, a complex of makeshift wards located in the Episcopal and Methodist Churches, the Odd Fellows' Lodge, Riddles's Carriage Shop, and the Pavilion Hotel. Designed for 500 patients, the hospital held as many as 700 at one time.[31]

Although orders strictly forbade foraging or confiscating civilian property, the countryside around Kinston suffered greatly, as soldiers slipped out of their camps to augment their meager army rations. The *Old North State* reported that "due to the energy of the Western boys," Jackson's Mill had been repaired and was grinding corn brought in by the foragers. Enterprising soldiers also found an abundance of Lenoir County wine and applejack brandy to relieve the boredom of camp life. Surprisingly, no Federals were accused of violent crimes, but a number of inebriated soldiers committed misdemeanors and were put to work cutting railroad ties as punishment.[32]

Schofield had little inclination to celebrate Kinston's occupation, for the pressure to establish a forward supply base at Goldsboro before Sherman's arrival weighed heavily on the general's mind. His March 14 dispatch to Grant announcing the capture of Kinston also sought to justify his inability to push on to Goldsboro. "It is probable that I can occupy Goldsboro at any time when I can supply myself there," wrote Schofield. To do so, however, required a functioning railroad to that point—something he did not yet have. He

---

30 William Fifer to mother, March 17, 1865; Sisco, *Personal Memoirs*, 72-73.

31 *North Carolina Times*, March 28, 1865; Emmerton, *A Record of the Twenty-Third Regiment Mass.*, 247; Thorpe, *History of the Fifteenth Connecticut*, 106.

32 *Old North State* (Beaufort, NC), March 18, 1865; Tyndall, *Threshold of Freedom*, 121.

cautiously predicted that engineers would need at least a week to complete the railroad as far as Kinston. Until then, Schofield explained that his army could not move because "I have barely teams enough to haul supplies for my troops three or four miles."[33]

Schofield all but admitted to Grant that he had failed to accomplish the objectives the general-in-chief had tasked him with in January. "Under the circumstances it seems impossible to make my junction with Sherman," conceded Schofield, "and I think I am right in making the reconstruction of the road my primary object instead of trying to push forward my troops more rapidly than the road progresses." Schofield suggested making Kinston rather than Goldsboro a forward supply base, and that Sherman could send his wagons there for resupply. In a separate message to Sherman, Schofield added, "I am straining every nerve to get the railroad completed and supplying for you here" at Kinston.[34]

To Schofield's credit, he continued to work vigorously to find solutions to his logistical problems. With the railroad not yet operational beyond Dover Station, he sent infantry to assist Colonel Wright's repair crews. Schofield ordered Cox and Couch to provide 1,000 men each to cut and lay railroad ties. Cox's detail repaired the tracks between the Neuse River and Southwest Creek, while Couch's men worked from Southwest Creek back toward Wright's crew at Dover Station.[35]

To augment the railroad, Schofield directed that the Neuse River be used as a supply route from New Bern. On the evening of March 14, Cox telegraphed Capt. A. C. Rhind, commander of naval forces at New Bern, advising him that the Confederates had scuttled the CSS *Neuse*, leaving no significant threat on the river. Cox requested that Rhind dispatch a convoy of "steamers and flats, loaded with rations."[36]

The next morning, the four-gun paddlewheel steamer *Whitehead* escorted a six-vessel army convoy transporting more than 100,000 rations from New Bern—the gunboat *Shrapnel*, steamers *General Shepley* and *Ella May*, barges *Howlett* and *Cornelly*, and the flatboat *North State*. In compliance with Schofield's

---

33 *OR* 47, pt. 2, 833-834.

34 Ibid., 880.

35 Ibid., 836, 837, 839, 883.

36 Ibid., 836, 838; *ORN*, Ser. 1, vol. 12, 67.

Railroad Bridge over Little River. Colonel
Wright's engineers rebuilt 12 bridges
in eastern North Carolina.

U.S. Army Military History Institute

directive that a strong guard
accompany each convoy, the 13th
Connecticut Veteran Battalion, commanded by Capt. William E. Bradley,
boarded the *General Shepley* and *Ella May*.[37]

Forty-eight hours earlier, Bradley and his Connecticut soldiers had boarded
a transport at Savannah, Georgia, bound for North Carolina. Their steamer
arrived at Morehead City on the morning of March 14. Later that evening, the
battalion reached New Bern, where Bradley received orders to guard the
convoy steaming to Kinston.[38]

After a slow four-day journey, the convoy reached Kinston around noon
on March 18. The delivery of 100,000 rations filled Cox with confidence.
"Under these circumstances," he wrote in his diary on March 18, "it is probable
that we shall move soon for Goldsboro." A steady flow of convoys continued
for the next month, as steamers shuttled up and down the river with barges in
tow. The largest convoy, consisting of four steamers and five barges, departed
New Bern on March 26. The shortage of shallow-draft steamers and barges was
the greatest impediment to the amount of materiel reaching Kinston.
Nevertheless, the joint army-navy operation eventually succeeded in delivering
enough supplies to enable Schofield to resume his advance on Goldsboro.[39]

While the supply convoys plied the Neuse River, Wright's railroad
construction teams pushed their repairs forward. Working night and day, work
crews reached the Neuse River on the evening of March 20. However, one final

37 OR 47, pt. 2, 837; The March 15, 1865, New Bern port manifests for Kinston did not
mention the *Ella May*. However, one did list the *Sarah E. Brown* as part of the convoy. See, *New
Bern Times*, March 17, 1865. In December 1864, enlistments expired in the 13th Connecticut,
reducing the regiment to a battalion. Homer B. Sprague, *History of the Thirteenth Infantry Regiment
of Connecticut Volunteers during the Great Rebellion* (Hartford, CT, 1867), 243-244. The *Whitehead*
was unable to complete the journey because it drew too much water. *ORN*, Ser. I, vol. 12, 71.

38 OR 47, pt. 2, 837; Sprague, *History of the Thirteenth Connecticut Infantry*, 246-247.

39 OR 47, pt. 1, 934; *New Bern Times*, March 28, 1865; At the peak of operations, the army used
ten large barges, six steam tugs, and a dozen steamers. *OR*, 47, pt. 3, 5; The actual unloading site
for the supply barges is not known. Historian Cliff Tyndall believes the steamboat docks on the
west side of Kinston were probably the location. Tyndall, *Threshold of Freedom*, 118.

obstacle prevented the railroad from reaching Kinston—the river itself. The Confederates had so damaged the trestle that the entire structure had to be rebuilt. By March 23, Wright's engineers had finished the 863-foot span, completing the railroad from New Bern to Kinston.[40]

Schofield was eager to resume offensive operations now that his supply situation had improved. Because of Kinston's importance to future operations, Schofield left a sizeable security force there. General Harland and his brigade drew the assignment, joined by Battery G, 3rd New York Light Artillery and a cavalry detachment. Harland's orders were to garrison the town, guard the key railroad and wagon bridges in the area, and provide work details to build a temporary supply depot. With Colonel Savage's 12th New York Cavalry patrolling the routes running west of Kinston, Captain Graham's Company L, 1st North Carolina (Union) remained in town. The army also left a military hospital there for approximately 100 sick and wounded who were too weak to travel.[41]

On March 18, Schofield issued Special Orders No. 6, directing the march to commence at 6:00 a.m. the following morning. The order also specified several command changes. First, Palmer would return to New Bern and resume command of the District of Beaufort. Second, Palmer's and Carter's divisions were consolidated and renamed the division of the District of Beaufort, with General Carter taking command. Third, Brig. Gen. George S. Greene assumed command of the Provisional Division, which consisted of soldiers who, like Greene, were en route to Sherman's army.[42]

Schofield's decision to make so many command changes as operations resumed carried inherent risk, but given the circumstances, he felt the gamble was justified. The evidence suggests that both Schofield and Grant had lost confidence in Palmer. They believed his inaction the previous month was to blame for Schofield's difficulty in meeting Grant's objectives. On March 13, Grant had sent a message to Secretary of War Edwin M. Stanton placing the blame squarely on Palmer's shoulders: "Palmer was ordered and should have

40 OR, Ser. 3, vol. 5, 30, 33.

41 Ibid., 47, pt. 2, 881-882, 896, 911. Harland's reorganized brigade consisted of the 15th Connecticut, the 2nd Massachusetts Heavy Artillery, the 23rd Massachusetts, and Battery A, 3rd New York Light Artillery.

42 Ibid., 895-896; On March 23, Schofield officially disbanded General Greene's Provisional Division at Goldsboro. OR 47, pt. 2, 977.

taken Kinston while Hoke was at Wilmington. I have not yet learned his excuse for his failure."[43]

Although Schofield had ordered the army to advance on March 19, it failed to comply—likely due to ongoing supply problems and confusion arising from the reorganization of Cox's Provisional Corps. In any event, distant sounds of battle soon shattered the Sabbath stillness. The night before, Lieutenant Stewart—the commissary officer for Orr's brigade—had distributed rations in preparation for the march. After daybreak, he rode out to the brigade's advanced picket post. "It was very warm," Stewart wrote his wife. "[I] sat down on the ground in the shade of a large and beautiful pine tree to talk with the boys. We had not sat there long before the morning was broken by the roar of artillery in the distance."[44]

The noise originated from the vicinity of Bentonville, about 20 miles west of Goldsboro. General Johnston had led his hastily assembled Army of the South there, and in a skillful (and one of his few) offensive efforts struck the Left Wing of Sherman's army. In response, Sherman halted his army's movement toward Goldsboro and began a concentration against his old adversary. For three days, Johnston and Sherman fought the culminating battle of the Carolinas campaign. Finally, on the night of March 21-22, Johnston withdrew his army to Smithfield. Sherman opted not to pursue—for which he was later criticized—and chose instead to continue to Goldsboro for some much-needed rest and refitting.[45]

Reacting to Johnston's attack at Bentonville on March 19, Sherman had ordered Schofield to seize Goldsboro and thus prevent the Confederates from falling back upon the town. At dawn on March 20, Schofield's army began marching toward the city. Cox's Provisional Corps spearheaded the advance, with Ruger's division in front followed by Carter's and Greene's divisions.

---

43 Ibid., 806; General Cox's journal entry for March 20, 1865, stated that General Palmer had been ill since March 10. See, *OR* 47, pt. 1, 935.

44 Private Carey of the 15th Connecticut stated that "troops were under marching orders but will not go as supplies being wanting." Thomas J. Carey, diary, March 19, 1865, Southern Historical Collection, University of North Carolina, Chapel Hill, North Carolina; George F. Stewart to wife, March 19, 1865.

45 Sherman's decision to let Johnston escape was questioned by several of his senior subordinates. A detailed discussion of the battle of Bentonville goes far beyond the scope of this work. For the most complete treatment of the battle see, Bradley, *Last Stand in the Carolinas*. See also Nathaniel C. Hughes, *Bentonville: The Final Battle of Sherman and Johnston* (Chapel Hill, NC, 1996).

Couch's two divisions from the XXIII Corps were still camped south of the Neuse River and would bring up the rear. To allow for a rapid crossing of the river, all of Couch's wagons and artillery used the pontoon bridge while the infantry crossed on the repaired wagon bridge. Once Couch's command was over the river, the engineers dismantled the pontoon bridge and placed it in the column marching toward Goldsboro.[46]

An Ohioan from Ruger's division later described the straggling that resulted from the army's rapid march. "Next morning left Kinston about seven o'clock and marched very fast all day," he wrote his family, "so fast many were unable to keep along and stopped along the road. I was among the number, some have not yet caught up." By nightfall, Schofield's army was camped near Rockford along the north bank of the Neuse River, halfway between Kinston and Goldsboro.[47]

At dawn the next day, Schofield resumed the march, hell-bent on reaching Goldsboro before dark. With no Confederate force impeding them, the army made excellent time, reaching the city late that afternoon. As the lead units approached, the Federals encountered a small Confederate rear guard, which they quickly brushed aside, allowing the soldiers in blue to make a triumphant entry into Goldsboro.

Thirteen-year-old F. L. Castex vividly remembered the Union army's noisy arrival. From atop the Gregory Hotel, the boy observed the Union formations marching up the old stage road near Bissell's Mill. "In a short while they had covered every available space in and around the town," recalled Castex. "That night they encircled the entire town with a line of breastworks."[48]

Lieutenant Col. Samuel Hufty and his 9th New Jersey of Carter's division had the honor of leading the Union column into town. Mayor L. H. Privett and a deputation of citizens approached Hufty under a flag of truce to surrender the city. General Carter arrived soon thereafter to formally accept the mayor's surrender, and appointed Lieutenant Colonel Hufty and his regiment as the provost guard. Before assuming their duties, the New Jersey soldiers paraded through the streets "with flags flying, bands playing, and drums beating." When the regiment raised its national colors atop the courthouse, "cheer followed

46 OR 47, pt. 1, 910-911.

47 Joseph J. Brown to Rosa, March 2, 1865; OR 47, pt. 2, 922.

48 F. L. Castex, Sr., "Goldsboro during the Civil War," *Goldsboro News Argus*, April 4, 1976.

Wayne County Courthouse, Goldsboro
Wayne County Public Library, Goldsboro, North Carolina

cheer, and huzzah after huzzah." Hufty then ordered several companies to reconnoiter the town.[49]

While searching the former Confederate Wayside Hospital No. 4 at the fairgrounds, Hufty's men discovered 23 severely wounded comrades from the battle of Wise's Forks—all members of the 27th Massachusetts. The Confederates had abandoned the suffering Federals. Private Herman Everts of the 9th New Jersey found the conditions unspeakable: "The men, the beds, yea, even the building itself, was completely alive with lice, and other vermin."[50] To ensure that the wounded received adequate care, Surgeon D. W. Hand, the medical director from New Bern, seized the former Confederate General Hospital No. 3, as well as Griswold's and Grainger's hotels and several large private homes and put them to good use.[51]

49 Everts, *A Complete and Comprehensive History of the Ninth Regiment New Jersey Vols.*, 165.

50 Ibid.

51 Ibid., 165-166.

In the meantime, Schofield established his headquarters at the Borden house. That night he wrote to Grant, reporting that he had captured Goldsboro and that "General Terry's column from Wilmington . . . should be near [this] place to-night." He also reported on the condition of the railroad running back to Kinston. Aside from finding the bridges burned, the track was in good order and the warehouse facilities in town were "very fine."[52]

To the delight of Goldsboro's citizens, Schofield maintained strict discipline from the outset and published an order permitting the residents to apply for guards. The young Castex thought Schofield's no-nonsense approach later prevented wholesale "plundering by the gang of thieves" that traveled with General Sherman's army. Just two days after Schofield's arrival, Sherman entered Goldsboro on March 23. Battery I, 3rd New York Light Artillery fired a salute in honor of the commanding general and announcing his arrival. Schofield welcomed Sherman on the front porch of the Borden home. After exchanging pleasantries, the two generals entered the house to discuss matters in private.[53]

Sherman's army was in rough shape, having just completed a march of nearly 500 miles through hostile enemy territory. "Uncle Billy" was greatly disappointed to learn that the railroads from Morehead City and Wilmington were not yet fully repaired, and that there was no stockpile of supplies waiting at Goldsboro for his exhausted and battered army. He vented his frustration to chief quartermaster Langdon Easton:

> I have made junction of my armies at Goldsborough a few days later than I appointed, but I find neither railroad completed, nor have I a word or sign from you or General Beckwith of the vast store of supplies I hoped to meet here or hear of. We have sent wagons to Kinston in hopes to get something there, but at all events I should know what has been done and what is being done. I have constantly held out to the officers and men to bear patiently the want of clothing and other necessities, for at Goldsborough awaited us everything. If you can expedite the movement of stores from the sea to the army, do so, and don't stand on expenses.[54]

---

52 Castex, "Goldsboro During the Civil War," *Goldsboro News Argus*, April 4, 1976; *OR* 47, pt. 2, 941; Terry's Provisional Corps fielded about 10,000 men.

53 Hall and Hall, *Cayuga in the Field*, 282; Castex, "Goldsboro During the Civil War," *Goldsboro News Argus*, April 4, 1976.

54 *OR* 47, pt. 2, 970. Easton was not the only one to suffer General Sherman's displeasure. Colonel Wright received a similar chewing-out about the status of the railroad. *OR* 47, pt. 2, 970.

Sherman also shared his disappointment in a letter to his wife: "My army is dirty, ragged and saucy. I have promised them rest, clothing and food, but the railroads have not been completed as I expected and I fear we may be troubled thereby." Nor was Sherman the only general angry with Easton and Beckwith. The inability of the army's chief quartermaster and commissary officers to resupply the army as planned led the commanders of the XV and XVII corps to petition Sherman to replace them. Major Gen. Oliver O. Howard, the commander of the army's Right Wing, endorsed his corps commanders' request, adding that "there was a want of enlarged comprehension of and adequate provision for the wants of the army on the part of the chief quartermaster."[55]

Fortunately for Easton and Beckwith, Sherman's anger subsided once he gained a better understanding of the difficulties involved in transporting supplies from the coast. The suffering of the troops for want of shoes has not resulted from want of foresight or action on the part of the chief quartermaster or commissary of the army," Sherman explained to Howard. "All has been done that was possible, and I will not reflect on officers who have done so much, and done it well.[56]

In the meantime, Sherman directed the quartermasters in New Bern to forward up to 2,000 tons of materiel per week to Kinston by river. From there it would be transported to Goldsboro by wagon. To make every conveyance available, the army established temporary depots around Goldsboro where units emptied their wagons. Throughout the following week, an endless procession of wagon trains traveled back and forth between Goldsboro and Kinston. Each round trip totaled about 50 miles and required several days to complete.[57]

Near the wagon bridge at Kinston, the Federals had amassed great stores of materiel awaiting transportation to Sherman's army. A soldier from the 23rd Massachusetts on guard duty at the river crossing remembered, "The innumerable caravan of six-mule teams had filed, for days together, across the

55 *M. A. DeWolfe Howe, ed., Home Letters of General Sherman* (New York, NY, 1909), 335; OR 47, pt. 3, 28-29.

56 Ibid., 29.

57 Ibid., 4, 19.

bridge and followed the column in order to haul supplies from the end of the rail to the troops."[58]

By March 25, Wright's crews had finally completed repairs on the railroad from New Bern, and the first trainload of supplies arrived at Goldsboro. With a functional rail line stretching all the way back to Morehead City, Sherman's army no longer had to depend on wagon trains from Kinston. By the first week of April, dozens of railroad cars arrived daily loaded with rations, uniforms, shoes, and other essential supplies. The addition of Schofield's and Alfred Terry's commands increased the size of Sherman's army in North Carolina to more than 85,000 men. As the troops paused for a much needed rest and refitting, Sherman traveled north to City Point, Virginia, to confer with President Lincoln and General Grant on the closing operations of the war.[59]

For the Union and Confederate soldiers fighting in North Carolina, the end was near. On April 26, 1865, Johnston surrendered his forces to Sherman at the Bennett Place, near Durham Station. Sherman's victorious army then marched north to Washington, D.C., and participated in the Grand Review. The units comprising Schofield's Army of the Ohio remained in North Carolina on occupation duty, but the army rapidly drew down and most of the men had returned home by the end of the year.

The men of Johnston's former Confederate army received their paroles and began their journey home. In many cases, the trip took weeks or even months, especially for those who hailed from the Trans-Mississippi region.[60]

Sherman later commented on the public's fascination with his March to the Sea, to the neglect of the far more demanding Carolinas campaign. In December 1865, he wrote that "no one ever has and may not agree with me as to the very great importance of the march north from Savannah. The march to the sea seems to have captivated everybody, whereas it was child's play compared with the other."[61]

A similar neglect has also obscured the formidable challenges that Schofield, Cox, Easton, and Wright had to overcome to resupply Sherman's

---

58 Emmerton, *A Record of the Twenty-Third Regiment Mass.*, 248.

59 OR 47, pt. 1, 26; Sherman, *Memoirs*, 2, 324.

60 A detailed discussion of the surrender at Bennett Place is far beyond the scope of this work. For the best treatment of the surrender see, Mark L. Bradley, *This Astounding Close: The Road to Bennett Place* (Chapel Hill, NC, 2000).

61 Thorndike, *Sherman's Letters*, 260.

army at Goldsboro. In his report to Secretary of War Stanton, Union Quartermaster General Montgomery Meigs paid indirect tribute to those men and what they had accomplished:

> This army of nearly 100,000 men needed to be entirely reclad and reshod; the troops were to be fed while resting, for as soon as the army ceased its march it ceased to supply itself by foraging, and depended upon the supplies from the coast. Nevertheless, on the 7th of April I was able to inform General Sherman that the necessary supplies were in his camps. Every soldier had received a complete outfit of clothing and had been newly shod. The wagons were loaded with rations and forage.[62]

---

62 *OR*, Ser. 3, vol. 5, pt. 1, 227.

Chapter 10

Final Analysis

The battle of Wise's Forks is an interesting case study because its importance transcends the tactical level of warfare. Each side had distinct objectives that impacted both the operational and strategic levels. General Cox's primary objective was to open the coastal railroad to Goldsboro in order to resupply Sherman's army. Failing to do so would have affected Sherman's ability to continue his planned junction with the Union armies confronting Confederate General Robert E. Lee in Virginia. Uniquely, General Schofield's written orders to Cox specified only critical tasks necessary to achieve this outcome with no mention of direct action with the enemy. The success of Schofield's operations in meeting the greater strategic objective centered on repairing the railroad, not defeating Confederate forces.

Johnston's and Bragg's military objectives were quite different than those of the Federals. By the first week of March 1865, Johnston struggled with concentrating his widely dispersed and numerically inferior forces against multiple Union advances into the state's interior. To allow time to gather forces, the Southern generals sought to deny or delay the potential junction of Cox's smaller force with that of Sherman's massive army.

With the differing objectives, it is difficult to determine a victor based on the outcome of the battle at Wise's Forks. During the Civil War, the commander who controlled the battlefield at the end of the day earned the victory. In the traditional measure, by abandoning Wise's Forks on March 10, Bragg lost the battle. However, Bragg's objective was to either turn back or delay Cox. Delaying actions are intended to trade space for time, and in that sense Bragg succeeded. Between March 7 and March 10, the Confederates effectively halted the Union advance toward Goldsboro. Although Bragg conceded the battlefield to Cox, the Confederates were far from defeated—nine days later these same Southerners routed an entire Federal division at the battle of Bentonville.

Bragg's decision, with Johnston's consent, to delay Cox by conducting offensive operations carried extreme risk. From a tactical perspective, the battlefield's dense, swampy landscape greatly restricted maneuver and was more conducive to a primarily defensive strategy. Since 1862, the Confederates had maintained a line of earthworks with artillery along Southwest Creek. Several miles to west, the Neuse River presented a more formidable obstacle to a Federal advance. Staying on the defensive behind either of these natural obstacles would have been the prudent approach to achieving their objective. Bragg, through economy of force, could have delayed Cox's advance without risking the one thing Johnston could not replace—manpower.

In his memoirs, Sherman questioned why the Confederates on several occasions did not take advantage of natural obstacles during the Carolinas campaign. In Sherman's opinion, "a comparatively smaller force, well handled," could have significantly delayed the movement of the Union armies. Bragg's risky and bold course of action was not in keeping with his shaky command history.[1]

In response to Cox's advance from New Bern, and to bolster General Hoke's division at Kinston, Johnston concurred with Bragg's recommendation to concentrate his forces by dispatching Hill's Army of Tennessee troops. In doing so, Johnston deviated from his original plan to gather as much strength as possible at Smithfield. Two days later, Johnston—elated with Bragg's initial success against Cox—directed additional troops from Stewart's Corps sent to Kinston. Again, this was a risky decision by Johnston, as all indications pointed to Fayetteville as Sherman's next objective.

Two well-known historians have argued the wisdom of Johnston's decision to send more troops to Bragg. Thomas Connelly, author of *Autumn of Glory*, believed that Johnston's decision was "a fool hardy plan." Connelly noted that sending troops to Bragg moved valuable troops farther away from Sherman's army. Connelly further explained that the probability of Bragg achieving a

---

1 Sherman, *Memoirs*, vol. 2, 306-307.

decisive result was highly improbable, and nothing more than a "fruitless and wasteful" endeavor.[2]

Conversely, Mark Bradley, author of *Last Stand in the Carolinas*, argues that Johnston's decision to send troops to Bragg was prudent. Bradley notes that Johnston had several threats to contend with, Cox's advance being the most immediate. The railroad allowed Johnston to rapidly reposition his troops when the opportunity presented itself. At Wise's Forks, Bragg was able to mass enough troops and strike a blow against a more evenly matched Union force with a reasonable prospect of success. Bradley emphasizes that at this late stage in the war, Johnston had no other alternative but to take chances.[3]

Both historians' positions have merit. However, when taking a strategic look at the Carolinas campaign as it unfolded, Johnston realized he could not fight and defeat Sherman's united army. The Confederates lacked the manpower to fight Sherman on equal terms. Johnston's predicament brings to mind an old proverb that is applicable in this case: *When eating an elephant take one bite at a time.* Johnston's slim albeit best chance for victory was to fight the "elephant" while Sherman's forces were separated. Johnston needed to create his own opportunities or capitalize on the ones presented him. The authors agree with Mark Bradley's premise that Johnston had to take "long chances" to achieve some degree of success by capitalizing on opportunities presented by his enemy.[4]

Unfortunately for Johnston, he placed his faith and confidence in a controversial field commander with a less than admirable combat record. Throughout the war, Bragg's personality and indecisiveness caused a great rift between himself and the officers and men he led. One of Bragg's leadership flaws was that he "lacked imagination," which caused "inflexibility during a crisis." As history has demonstrated, Bragg remained true to character throughout his command tenure in 1865—from the loss of Fort Fisher and Wilmington to missed opportunities at Wise's Forks and Bentonville.

At times during battle, decisions and actions occur that change the outcome of the engagement in a significant way. Famed World War II commander Gen. George S. Patton was known to use a Rudyard Kipling quote

---

2 Connelly, *Autumn of Glory*, 524.

3 Bradley, *Last Stand in the Carolinas*, 75, 473-474.

4 Ibid.

to describe critical moments in battle that must be taken advantage of to ensure victory: "the unforgiving minute." At Wise's Forks, Bragg had two such moments: the halting of Hill's initial attack on March 8 and Hoke's unsupported attack on March 10.

In both instances, Bragg allowed potential success to slip away when his adversary was most vulnerable. On March 8, Bragg's failure to exploit initial success botched arguably his greatest opportunity. At that point in the battle, had Hoke and Hill been ordered to seize Wise's Forks, it is doubtful that General Carter's two remaining brigades would have fared any better than Colonel Upham's against a combined force of more than 6,000 veterans.[5]

Cox, the battle's victor in the traditional sense, actually failed in the broader context by not achieving his strategic objective—ensuring a functioning railroad to Goldsboro before Sherman's arrival. Bragg's aggressive tactics successfully checked the Federal advance for four days. However, beginning on March 11, Cox's inability to continue toward Goldsboro had more to do with logistics than Confederate resistance. From the onset of operations until military trains crossed over the Neuse River on March 23, the railroad was Schofield and Cox's true nemesis. Without the heavy lifting capability of the railroad to alleviate the critical shortage of wagons, Cox could not properly support any farther movement by his Provisional Corps.

As early as March 6, Cox's correspondence revealed a commander burdened by logistics, which required attention toward identifying solutions. On March 7, Cox was clearly distracted by these issues, as he remained in the rear and relied upon General Palmer to seize the crossings along Southwest Creek. Cox's absence from the front, coupled with Palmer's cautious leadership, contributed to the Federals' failure on March 7 to gain control of at least one of the three bridges over Southwest Creek. The loss of one bridge alone would have triggered a Confederate abandonment of the entire defensive line and subsequent withdrawal to Kinston.

After surviving the near disaster that befell his command on March 8, Cox demonstrated his battlefield savvy as a leader throughout the remaining two days of the battle. He wisely assumed the defensive, using the terrain and superior numbers to his advantage. Cox's use of interior lines to rapidly shift

---

5   Victor D. Hanson, "What would Patton Say about the Present War?" in *The National Speech Digest of Hillsdale College: Imprimis*, vol. 33, no. 10 (October 2004), 6; Hallock, *Braxton Bragg and Confederate Defeat*, vol. 2, 268.

artillery and infantry to threatened points along his front ensured success. In the end, however, the need for a railroad denied Cox the ability to rapidly transition back to the offensive and continue the advance toward Goldsboro.

Fortunately for Cox, the U.S. Navy was able to open a resupply line utilizing the Neuse River to help negate logistical shortcomings. Even so, it was not until March 18—eight days after Bragg's withdrawal—that sufficient supplies were available to enable a renewed advance. This delay proved valuable to the Confederates as Johnston was able to assemble a sizeable force that he would use against Sherman at Bentonville.

Schofield and Cox failed to meet Sherman's timeline at Goldsboro, where needed supplies were not on hand when his battered army arrived. Three days later on March 25, after overcoming numerous obstacles and working around the clock, Col. W. W. Wright finally established a functioning rail line from Goldsboro to the coast. Despite the grumblings of Sherman's corps commanders, what Schofield and Cox accomplished in the first weeks of March 1865 was nothing short of amazing. If not for their superior leadership, the three-day delay could have been weeks.

Despite the historical impact of the battle of Wise's Forks and the role it played in a larger context, it remained relatively forgotten for more than 150 years. Historians and students of the Carolinas campaign viewed it as an insignificant engagement, with relatively little impact on the overall outcome of the campaign. Hopefully, the authors have shed enough light on the battle to give it its proper standing in the poignant closing month of the war. Regardless, one cannot take away the courage and commitment of the officers and men of both sides who fought in the battle.

Appendix A

The Opposing Forces in the Battle of Wise's Forks, North Carolina

ORGANIZATION OF UNION FORCES

U.S. Army, Department of North Carolina
Maj. Gen. John M. Schofield

Cox's Provisional Corps
Maj. Gen. Jacob D. Cox

First Division, XXIII Army Corps
Bvt. Maj. Gen. Thomas H. Ruger

First Brigade
Col. John M. Orr
120th Indiana
124th Indiana
128th Indiana
180th Ohio

Second Brigade
Col. John C. McQuiston
123rd Indiana
129th Indiana

130th Indiana

28th Michigan[1]

Third Brigade
Col. Minor T. Thomas

174th Ohio

178th Ohio

8th Minnesota[2]

Artillery
5th Illinois Independent Battery, (Wood's)

1st Michigan Light Artillery, Battery F, (Paddock's)

First Division, District of Beaufort
Brig. Gen. Innis N. Palmer

First Brigade
Brig. Gen. Edward Harland

2nd Massachusetts Heavy Artillery (Cos. B, C, F, I, and M)

23rd Massachusetts

9th New Jersey

Second Brigade
Col. Peter J. Claassen

132nd New York (Cos. A and B, 99th New York attached)[3]

2nd Regiment Provisional Troops

---

1   Wise's Forks was the first battle for the newly mustered 28th Michigan. Formed in October 1864 with orders for assignment to the XXIII Corps, the regiment did not take an active part in the battle of Nashville. In January 1865, the 28th was assigned to the Second Brigade, First Division, XXIII Corps. During Wise's Forks, it was attached to three different brigades.

2   The 8th Minnesota remained at Gum Swamp throughout the battle.

3   In February 1865, all but two companies of the 99th New York mustered out of service in New Bern. Companies A and B remained in service due to enlistment obligations. During the battle these men were distributed throughout the 132nd New York.

Third Brigade
Col. Horace Boughton

18th Wisconsin[4]

1st Battalion Provisional Troops[5]

2nd Battalion Provisional Troops

Artillery
3rd New York Light Artillery, Battery C (Mercer's)

3rd New York Light Artillery, Battery D (Van Heusen's)

Second Division, District of Beaufort
Brig. Gen. Samuel P. Carter

First Brigade
Col. Adam G. Malloy

85th New York

1st Battalion Provisional Troops

2nd Battalion Provisional Troops

3rd Battalion Provisional Troops

Second Brigade
Col. Charles L. Upham

15th Connecticut[6]

27th Massachusetts

Battalion Provisional Troops[7]

---

4   In November 1864, the 18th Wisconsin granted furloughs to three-year service veterans who reenlisted. Upon their return from furlough, they assembled in Nashville and were forwarded to New Bern as part of Meagher's command.

5   Boughton's post-battle report stated that his organization included two Provisional Battalions, one of which was commanded by Maj. Theodore Stimming. See, *OR* 47, pt. 1, 991.

6   Company K of the 15th Connecticut arrived at Wise's Forks on the afternoon of March 9.

7   During the battle, the Provisional Troops battalion was dispersed and temporarily assigned to the 15th Connecticut and 27th Massachusetts.

Third Brigade
Lt. Col. Henry Splaine

17th Massachusetts

25th Massachusetts

3rd New York Light Artillery, Battery A, (dismounted) (Russell's)[8]

Battalion Provisional Troops[9]

Artillery
3rd New York Artillery, Battery G, (Kelsey's)

3rd New York Artillery, Battery I, (Kirby's)[10]

Cavalry
District of Beaufort, Department of North Carolina

12th New York Cavalry (Cos. A, B, C, F, G, and H)

23rd New York Cavalry (Cos. A and B attached to
12th New York Cavalry)[11]

Co. L, 1st North Carolina (Union)

---

8 Battery A served as infantry throughout the battle.

9 Regimental historian Denny wrote that "two hundred Indiana men," commanded by a captain, were organized as a battalion and attached to the 25th Massachusetts.

10 One section of Battery I remained in New Bern during the battle.

11 The 23rd New York Cavalry consisted of only two companies and served its entire term of service—July 1863 to July 1865—in the state of North Carolina attached to the 12th New York Cavalry.

ORGANIZATION OF CONFEDERATE FORCES[12]

Department of North Carolina
Gen. Braxton Bragg

Hoke's Division[13]
(From the Army of Northern Virginia)
Maj. Gen. Robert F. Hoke
Clingman's Brigade
Col. William S. Devane
8th North Carolina
31st North Carolina
51st North Carolina
61st North Carolina

Kirkland's Brigade
Brig. Gen. William W. Kirkland
17th North Carolina
42nd North Carolina
66th North Carolina

Hagood's Brigade
Brig. Gen. Johnson Hagood
Contingent of Lt. Col. James H. Rion
11th South Carolina
21st South Carolina
25th South Carolina
27th South Carolina
7th South Carolina Battalion
Contingent of Lt. Col. John D. Taylor

---

12 The Confederate Order of Battle lists regiments, battalions, and companies. By March 1865, attrition had reduced a number of the units significantly, some to as few as a dozen men.

13 Hoke's division was detached from the Army of Northern Virginia.

1st North Carolina Battalion Heavy Artillery

36th North Carolina (2nd Artillery)

Co. D, 13th Battalion North Carolina Light Artillery
(Adams's Battery)

Contingent of Col. John J. Hedrick (W)

40th North Carolina (3rd Artillery)

Colquitt's Brigade
Col. Charles T. Zachry

6th Georgia

19th Georgia

23rd Georgia

27th Georgia

28th Georgia

North Carolina Junior Reserves Brigade[14]
Brig. Gen. Laurence S. Baker

1st Junior Reserves (70th North Carolina)

2nd Junior Reserves (71st North Carolina)

3rd Junior Reserves (72nd North Carolina)

1st Battalion North Carolina Junior Reserves

2nd Sub-District, 2nd Military District, Department of North Carolina
Col. John N. Whitford

67th North Carolina

68th North Carolina

---

14 The unit designations 70th, 71st, and 72nd North Carolina are post-war identifications assigned by John W. Moore, ed. *Roster of North Carolina Troops in the War Between the States*, 4 vols. (Raleigh, NC, 1882). See Manarin et al., *North Carolina Troops*, vol. 17, 119.

Artillery

13th Battalion North Carolina Light Artillery

Lt. Col. Joseph B. Starr

Co. B (Atkins's Battery), Capt. George B. Atkins

Co. E (Dickson's Battery), Capt. Henry Dickson

Section, Co. C (Cummings's Battery), Lt. James M. Rowe (K)

Cavalry

2nd South Carolina Cavalry

6th North Carolina Cavalry

Co. G, 8th Georgia Cavalry

Army of Tennessee

S. D. Lee's Corps

Maj. Gen. Daniel Harvey Hill

Clayton's Division

Maj. Gen. Henry D. Clayton

Jackson's Brigade

Lt. Col. James C. Gordon

25th Georgia

29th/30th Georgia[15]

66th Georgia

1st Confederate

1st Battalion Georgia Sharpshooters

Stovall's Brigade

Col. Henry C. Kellogg

40th Georgia

41st Georgia

15 The two regiments were consolidated in the fall of 1861.

42nd Georgia

43rd Georgia

52nd Georgia[16]

Pettus's Brigade (Stevenson's Division)
Brig. Gen. Edmund W. Pettus

20th Alabama

23rd/31st Alabama[17]

30th Alabama

46th Alabama

D. H. Hill's Division
Col. John G. Coltart

Deas's Brigade
Col. Harry T. Toulmin

19th Alabama

22nd Alabama

25th Alabama

39th Alabama

26th-50th Alabama

16 Gary R. Goodson, *Georgia Confederate 7,000 Army of Tennessee Part II: Letters and Diaries. From Confederate Soldiers of Brigadier General Barton and Stovall's Georgia Infantry Brigade* (Shawnee, CO, 1997), 199-203. Not all members of the 42nd and 52nd Georgia were present during the battle. On January 3, 1865, elements from the two regiments were detached from Stovall's brigade at Rienzi, Mississippi, and tasked with guarding a wagon train bound for Columbus, Mississippi, under command of Col. Robert J. Henderson, 42nd Georgia. Upon arriving in Columbus, Henderson assumed command of Cumming's brigade, along with the detached men from the two regiments. Henderson's brigade arrived at Bentonville on March 20, 1865.

17 Rex Miller, *Hundley's Ragged Volunteers: A day-by-day account of the 31st Alabama Infantry Regiment, CSA* (1861-1865) (Depew, NY, 1991), 76. W. L. Roberts of Co. B, 31st Alabama recorded in his diary that the consolidation occurred prior to departing for the Carolinas, with Maj. J. T. Hester of the 23rd Alabama commanding.

Manigault's Brigade
Lt. Col. John C. Carter

24th Alabama

28th Alabama

34th Alabama

10th South Carolina

19th South Carolina

A. P. Stewart's Corps
Maj. Gen. Edward C. Walthall

Walthall's Division
Maj. Gen. Edward C. Walthall

Quarles's Brigade
Brig. Gen. George D. Johnston

1st Alabama

17th Alabama

29th Alabama

42nd/46th /49th/53rd/55th Tennessee[18]

48th Tennessee (Voorhies's)

Reynolds's Brigade
Col. Henry G. Bunn

1st Arkansas Mounted Infantry (dismounted)

4th Arkansas

18 On December 10, 1864, following the battle of Franklin, Quarles's brigade was reported as composed of the 1st Alabama, the 42nd/46th/49th/53rd/55th Tennessee consolidated, under Capt. A. M. Duncan, and the 48th Tennessee (Voorhies's), commanded by Capt. Joseph Love.

Loring's Division
Col. James Jackson

Adams's Brigade
Lt. Col. Robert J. Lawrence

6th Mississippi

14th Mississippi

15th Mississippi

20th Mississippi

23rd Mississippi

43rd Mississippi

Featherston's Brigade
Col. Wallace B. Colbert

1st Mississippi

3rd Mississippi

22nd Mississippi

31st Mississippi

33rd Mississippi

40th Mississippi

1st Mississippi Battalion Sharpshooters

Scott's Brigade
Capt. John A. Dixon

27th/35th/49th Alabama[19]

55th Alabama

57th Alabama

12th Louisiana

---

19 Clement A. Evans, ed., *Confederate Military History*, vol. 7, Alabama, 145, 207-208. In July 1864, the regiments were consolidated due to the 49th Alabama being "reduced to a paltry number," and the 27th and 35th Alabama being "reduced to mere squads." The consolidated regiment's commander, Col. S. S. Ives of the 35th Alabama, was absent during the Carolinas campaign due to a wound suffered at the battle of Franklin. Captain W. B. Beason commanded the consolidated regiment through the Carolinas campaign.

Appendix B

Confederate Strength at the Battle of Wise's Forks

Analyzing Confederate operations at Wise's Forks is a major challenge due to the lack of unit strength reports. Unfortunately, this paucity of information applies to the battle's two major participants: the Army of Tennessee and Hoke's division. General Hill's official battle report for Lee's Corps provides a figure for one of the two Army of Tennessee corps. In the case of Stewart's Corps, however, no known report exists.

Similar challenges arise in determining the strength of Hoke's division. Two separate returns dated February 10 and March 17, 1865, list the division's effective strength and that of other units from the Department of North Carolina. The February 10 return does not reflect the subsequent losses sustained by Hoke's division (most notably in Hagood's brigade) in the days leading up to Wilmington's evacuation. The March 17 return reflects a more probable effective strength, but fails to account for losses at Wise's Forks.[1]

For the purposes of this study (with the exception of Lee's Corps), the authors primarily used General Johnston's March 17 "Effective Total Present" as a baseline, and adjusted the number with documented battle losses to determine an estimated strength for Stewart's Corps, Hoke's division, and the Junior Reserves. *See* Appendix C, Documented Confederate Battle Losses for the sources used in compiling loss estimates.[2]

---

1   *OR* 47, pt. 1, 1,088-1,089; pt. 2, 1,154, 1,424.

2   "Effective Total Present," from March 17, 1865, field return, *OR* 47, pt. 2, 1,424.

Table A
Department of North Carolina

Unit	March 17 Strength	Documented Losses[3]	Adjusted Strength[4]
North Carolina Junior Reserves	1,135	29	1,164
67th North Carolina	700		700[5]
68th North Carolina	300		300
Total	2,135		2,164

Table B
Hoke's Division

Unit	March 17 Strength	Documented Losses	Adjusted Strength
Clingman's brigade	557	41	598
Colquitt's brigade	1,118	81	1,199
Hagood's brigade	949[6]	22	971
Kirkland's brigade	1,016	341	1,357
Total	3,640	485	4,125

3   Documented losses include killed, wounded, captured, and missing. See Appendix C.

4   Adjusted strength is the sum of the field return and documented losses.

5   Because the March 17 field return approximated the strengths for both the 67th and 68th North Carolina, documented losses were not included in the adjusted effective strength, OR 47, pt. 2, 1,424.

6   Hagood estimated that his brigade fielded about 1,150 men. Hagood, *Memoirs*, 351. The authors chose to use the March 17 field return.

Table C
Army of Tennessee

Unit	Reported Strength	Documented Losses	Adjusted Strength
Lee's Corps			
Hill's division	562		562
Clayton's division	416		416
Stevenson's division	350		350
Corps Total	1,328[7]		1,328
Stewart's Corps			
Loring's division	See note 8	40	
Walthall's division	See note 8	4	
Corps Total	890[8]	44	934
Aggregate	2,218	44	2,262

Table D
Total Confederate Forces

Unit	Strength
Department of North Carolina	
North Carolina Junior Reserves	1,164
67th North Carolina	700

7   Hill's official report for Lee's Corps, dated March 29, 1865, listed both effective strength and battle losses, OR 47, pt. 1, 1,088.

8   The March 17 field return for Stewart's Corps listed 890 effectives out of 1,349 present. The shortage of weapons and accoutrements negatively impacted the total number of men available, OR 47, pt. 2, 1,368, 1,408. The 44 documented losses from Stewart's Corps were added to the effective number. The individual strength of the two divisions in Stewart's Corps is undetermined. However, source material identifies Loring's division as fielding the greater number during the battle. A week later at the battle of Bentonville, Walthall's division fielded only 240 effectives—91 in Quarles's brigade and 150 in Reynolds's brigade, OR 47, pt. 1, 1,104-1,105.

Table D: Total Confederate Forces, continued	
Unit	Strength
68th North Carolina	300
Unit	Strength
Starr's Artillery	787
6th North Carolina Cavalry	484
Hoke's division	4,125
Army of Tennessee	2,262
Total	9,822

Table E
Estimated Infantry Strength by Day
Department of North Carolina and Hoke's Division

Unit	March 7	March 8	March 9	March 10
Colquitt's brigade	1,199	1,199	1,199	1,199
Clingman's brigade	598	973[9]	598	598
Hagood's brigade	See note[10]	321	971	971
Kirkland's brigade	1,357	1,357	1,357	1,357
67th North Carolina	700	700	700	700
68th North Carolina	300	300	300	300
North Carolina Junior Reserves	1,164[11]	1,439[12]	1,164	1,164
Total	5,318	6,289	6,289	6,289

9   Colonel Hedrick's 375-man battalion from Hagood's brigade was attached to Clingman's brigade during March 8 operation,. Hagood, *Memoirs*, 351.

10 Hagood's South Carolina contingent was delayed by a train wreck.

11 The North Carolina Junior Reserves were under Hoke's direction on March 7.

12 Colonel Taylor's 275-man battalion from Hagood's brigade was attached to the North Carolina Junior Reserves brigade during March 8 operations, Hagood, *Memoirs*, 351.

Table F
Estimated Infantry Strength by Day
Lee's Corps (Army of Tennessee)[13]

Unit	March 7	March 8	March 9	March 10
Hill's division				
Deas's brigade	277	277	277	277
Manigault's brigade	285	285	285	285
Clayton's division				
Jackson's brigade		76[14]	76	76
Stovall's brigade		340[15]	340	340
Stevenson's division				
Pettus's brigade	350	350	350	350
Total	912	1,328	1,328	1,328

Table G
Estimated Strength by Day
Stewart's Corps (Army of Tennessee)

Unit	March 8	March 9	March 10
Loring's division			
Adams's Brigade		arrived	
Featherston's Brigade	arrived		
Scott's Brigade		arrived	
Walthall's division			
Quarles's Brigade			arrived

13 *OR* 47, pt. 1, 1,088.

14 Jackson's brigade arrived at Kinston on the morning of March 8, but did not enter the fight until early afternoon.

15 Ibid.

Table G: Estimated Strength by Day, Stewart's Corps, (Army of Tennessee), continued			
Unit	March 8	March 9	March 10
Reynold's Brigade			arrived
Total	350[16]	584	934[17]

16 *OR* 47, pt. 2, 1,356.

17 *OR* 47, pt. 2, 1,368. General Walthall arrived the morning of March 10 with 354 men from Stewart's Corps. Quarles's and Reynold's brigades accompanied Walthall, but the strengths of these two brigades are undetermined.

Appendix C

Documented Confederate
Battle Losses

The documented losses in this appendix were determined in large part from the individual state sections of National Archives Records Group 109, Compiled Service Records of Confederate Soldiers, Prisoner of War Records, and Confederate Hospital Records. Material obtained from the National Archives was supplemented by information from other sources, such as Surgeon Isaac Tanner's record of wounded from Hoke's division, obituaries in wartime newspapers, the *Official Records*, Confederate pension applications filed by veterans and their wives, soldiers' letters, diaries, and journals, and postwar regimental histories. Invaluable sources for losses in Georgia and North Carolina units were *Roster of the Confederate Soldiers of Georgia* and *North Carolina Troops 1861-1865: A Roster*.

The figures listed in the tables below should not be interpreted as absolute, as the authors acknowledge the shortcomings of Confederate reporting during the final months of the war. However, the authors do question the validity of Maj. Gen. John M. Schofield's often quoted figure of "about 1,500" as the probable number of Confederate losses—a number derived not from Confederate reporting but from the general's own estimation.[1]

Bragg's assessment of the first two days of fighting was that his forces suffered minimal casualties. Early on March 10 (before Kirkland's costly attack), Bragg declined Governor Zebulon Vance's offer of additional medical personnel and supplies, giving the reason as "our loss is so small." Hagood supported Bragg's assessment of the early fighting, "the first day's loss of the Confederates having been very inconsiderable." Moreover, the Confederates evacuated almost 1,000 Union prisoners via the railroad from Kinston to Goldsboro late on March 8. If Bragg's army had suffered higher

---

1 *OR* 47, pt. 1, 912.

losses, evacuation of its own wounded would have taken priority and delayed the shipment of enemy prisoners.[2]

D. H. Hill reported that Lee's Corps sustained a total of 134 losses throughout the three days of fighting. In the absence of an official report from General Walthall, the authors documented a total of 44 losses in Stewart's Corps. It is important to note that the brigades from Stewart's corps did not begin arriving on the battlefield until the afternoon of March 9 and into the following morning.

Sufficient historical documentation exists to suggest that Hoke's division suffered the greatest number of casualties during the battle. If Schofield's estimated figure of 1,500 was correct, and the numbers for all Confederate units except Hoke's division are subtracted, then Hoke suffered about 1,200 casualties. If that was the case, in which brigades did the losses occur? Hagood reported minimal losses for the entire battle. The authors' documented figures, although slightly higher than Hagood's, corroborate the general's assessment. If Clingman's brigade had suffered heavy losses, for all practical purposes it would have ceased to exist, as it took only about 600 men into battle. Surgeon Tanner's medical registry for Hoke's division reported that Colquitt's brigade suffered only 46 killed or wounded, suggesting the unit escaped the battle with relatively few losses, as supported by the authors' research.

Kirkland's brigade suffered heavy losses, the majority of which occurred during its failed attack on March 10. In his memoirs, Hagood stated that "Kirkland's loss was about 300, and was the chief loss sustained." The authors documented a total of 341 casualties in Kirkland's brigade over the course of the entire battle—25 percent. On March 10, the 42nd North Carolina occupied the right flank of Kirkland's brigade, where it absorbed the initial shock of the Union counterattack. The authors documented a total of 166 losses in the 42nd—the highest number for any Confederate regiment during the battle.

A list of casualties printed in the *Carolina Watchman* suggests that the 42nd North Carolina did not sustain terrific losses as post-war accounts have indicated. During the Civil War, families were often notified of casualties through newspaper listings. In the *Watchman*, Capt. James A. Blackwelder of the 42nd's Company F listed 19 casualties during the entire battle—one killed, three wounded, and 15 captured. Blackwelder's numbers are consistent with documented losses from other companies in the regiment.[3]

As the following tables illustrate, Hoke's division suffered the greatest losses during the battle, followed by Lee's Corps from the Army of Tennessee. In Bragg's command as a whole, 716 casualties have been documented. When Schofield's estimate

---

2   Ibid., pt. 2, 1,363; Hagood, *Memoirs*, 355.

3   *Carolina Watchman* (Salisbury, NC), March 13, 1865.

of 1,500 is compared to the documented figure, there is a 48 percent discrepancy of 784 losses.

The lack of official Confederate reporting from the time of the battle remains problematic. However, it is unlikely—based on ten years of research utilizing numerous sources—that such a large discrepancy is correct. To account for potentially undocumented losses, and to determine a more probable estimation, a 15 percent error rate (107) was factored into the documented number of 716. Thus, an adjusted figure of 823 is the approximate number of Confederate losses in the battle of Wise's Forks.

Table A
Confederate Forces

Unit	Killed	Wounded	Captured	Unit Total
Department of North Carolina	1	41	6	48
Hoke's division	14	154	317	485
Army of Tennessee	15	137	26	178
Total	30	336	350	716

Table B
Department of North Carolina

Unit	Killed	Wounded	Captured	Unit Total
North Carolina Junior Reserves	0	29	0	29
67th North Carolina	0	4	2	6
68th North Carolina	0	5	0	5
Starr's artillery battalion	1	2	2	5
6th North Carolina Cavalry	0	0	2	2
Total	1	41	6	48

Table C
Hoke's Division

Unit	Killed	Wounded	Captured	Unit Total
Clingman's brigade	0	21	20	41
Colquitt's brigade	5	46	30	81
Hagood's brigade	4	18	0	22
Kirkland's brigade	5	69	267	341
Total	14	154	317	485

Table D
Kirkland's Brigade (Hoke's Division)

Unit	Killed	Wounded	Captured	Unit Total
Brigade Staff	0	0	1	1
17th North Carolina	1	30	50	81
42nd North Carolina	4	22	140	166
66th North Carolina	0	17	76	93
Total	5	69	267	341

Table E
Army of Tennessee

Unit	Killed	Wounded	Captured	Unit Total
Lee's Corps				
Hill's division	7	34	0	41
Clayton's division	3	42	15	70
Pettus's brigade	1	21	1	23
Total[4]	11	107	16	134

4   Ibid., 1,089.

Table E: Army of Tennessee, continued			
Unit	Killed	Wounded	Captured	Unit Total
Stewart's Corps				
Loring's division	2	29	9	40
Walthall's division	2	1	1	4
Total	4	30	10	44
Army of Tennessee Total	15	137	26	178

Appendix D

The Return of
Capt. Julius Bassett's Sword

In the aftermath of the fighting on March 8, Capt. Robert A Carter of the 42nd North Carolina had ordered his men to bury the dead around the Cobb house. The body of Capt. Julius Bassett of the 15th Connecticut was discovered near one of the home's outbuildings. "The Captain, who was buried by the rebels, was wearing a long red and white scarf and a handsome sword engraved with his name," wrote Carter's wife Elizabeth, who shared the story as told by her husband. Engraved on the Federal captain's sword were the words, "Capt. Julius Basset–Meridan. Conn." Carter claimed Bassett's personal items only after his men insisted that he take them. Carter draped his personal sash over Bassett's body, and in a gesture of respect marked the fallen enemy's grave with his own sword.[1]

Years later, Carter decided to locate Bassett's family, return the items, and relate to them the circumstances of his demise. Carter wrote a detailed letter to the governor of Connecticut describing the incident leading to the Yankee officer's death. Weeks later, Bassett's grateful sons

Capt. Robert A. Carter
Jodi Gee

---

1 Lilly Bassett Carter Hoffman, Notebooks of Lilly Bassett Carter Hoffman, in Private Collection of Jodie Gee.

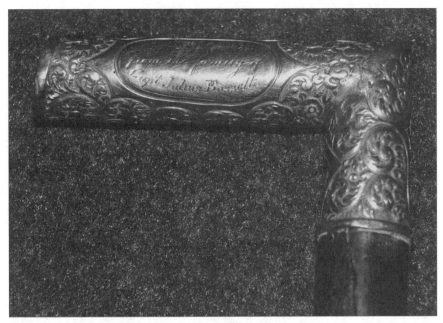

Engraving
Museum of the Cape Fear, Fayetteville, N.C.

replied to Carter that "they had never until this time, been able to learn anything at all about their father's death."

Soon thereafter, Carter presented Bassett's sword and sash to the family. The sons, impressed with the thoughtful and compassionate spirit of the Southerner, rewarded Carter with a handsome gold-headed ebony walking stick, capped at the bottom with silver. The inscription on the stick read, "Capt. Robert Allen Carter from the family of Capt. Julius Bassett." This cane is currently on display at the Museum of the Cape Fear, on loan from the North Carolina Museum of History.[2]

2   Ibid.

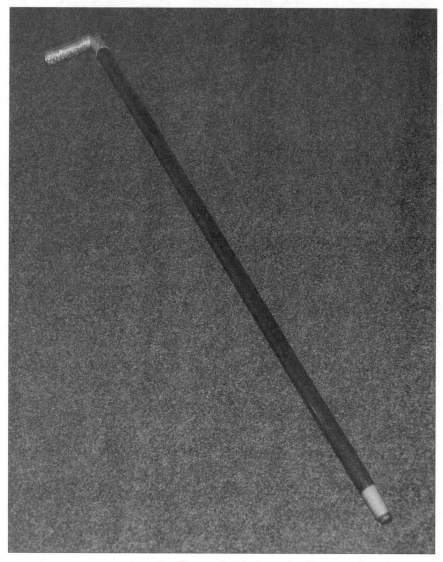

Presentation Cane

Museum of the Cape Fear, Fayetteville, N.C.

Appendix E

Journey to Point Lookout, Maryland

I n the days following the battle, captured Rebel soldiers were transported to Northern prison camps where they spent the remainder of the war. The majority of these men were eventually paroled. Some, however, still lie in Northern cemeteries having succumbed to disease or wounds. For one group of Confederate prisoners, the journey north was as horrifying as anything experienced thus far in the war.

On March 12, the first group of Confederate prisoners arrived at New Bern from Wise's Forks. The following day, 352 captives boarded the steamer *S. R. Spaulding* bound for Fort Monroe, Virginia. Lieutenant Christopher W. Howland and a detail of 13 soldiers from the 5th Rhode Island Heavy Artillery accompanied the prisoners as

guards throughout the voyage. Unfortunately for the prisoners, the ship's cargo hold reeked of fresh manure and urine, as the vessel had just delivered a load of beef cattle. The *S. R. Spaulding* required slightly more than 30 hours' travel to complete its trip to Virginia, arriving at Fort Monroe the morning of March 15. In Virginia, the prisoners were segregated into groups for officers and enlisted men.[1]

Lt. Christopher W. Howland, Co. A,
5th Rhode Island Heavy Artillery
History of the Fifth Regiment of
Rhode Island Heavy Artillery

1 John K. Burlingame, *History of the Fifth Regiment of Rhode Island Heavy Artillery, During Three Years and A Half of Service in North Carolina* (Providence, RI, 1892), 252-253. The *Morning Leader* stated the Confederate prisoners captured at Wise's Forks arrived at Fort Monroe from New Bern onboard the *Rebecca Clyde, Morning Leader* (Cleveland, OH), March 17, 1865.

Steamer Transport *S. R. Spaulding*
Library of Congress

The following morning, enlisted soldiers boarded the steamer *Clyde* en route to Point Lookout, Maryland. Lieutenant Howland remembered that "All went well until about ten o'clock [p.m.], when we were within a mile or two of Point Lookout light . . . when suddenly I was flung against the door . . . with such force that it was thrown open." The gunboat *Western World* had struck the *Clyde* in her starboard side, tearing through the planking below the water line. Hundreds of Confederates were below decks when seawater poured into the vessel. Four soldiers were sucked out of the ship and never seen again.[2]

Throughout the remainder of the night, as the *Clyde's* captain and crew fought to repair the damaged hull, Howland and his guards transferred their prisoners to the *Western World*. If the collision was not bad enough, gale-force winds and strong seas further compounded the desperate situation. Howland left a graphic account of that tragic night:

> The guard came over first. One of the officers stood on one side and I on the other, with sailors holding us so we would not go overboard, then when the surf-boat would rise on a wave we would reach out and grasp a man by the shoulders and pull him in. The marines were formed in open ranks with cutlasses drawn and revolvers in hand, while the prisoners were marched below. When the hold was filled, those remaining on deck were chained, handcuffed, and strapped to the guns in every conceivable way. This was done for our own safety. One poor fellow had his head crushed between the

2   Ibid.

guard of the surf-boat and side of the gunboat, killing him instantly, and we dropped the body overboard."[3]

Howland arrived at Point Lookout shortly after sunrise the next morning and turned his captives over to authorities. Howland's group of Confederates was the largest sent to Point Lookout from the battle of Wise's Forks. Two other smaller contingents arrived at the prison on March 30 and April 3, 1865.[4]

---

3   Ibid.

4   Selected Records of the War Department Relating to Confederate Prisoners of War, M598, rolls 114 through 115, Records Group 109, National Archives, Washington, DC.

Bibliography

Primary Sources

Newspapers

Atlanta Weekly Intelligencer
Carolina Watchman (Salisbury, NC)
Charlotte News & Courier
Daily Confederate (Raleigh, NC)
Daily Constitutionalist (Augusta, GA)
Daily Journal (New Bern, NC)
Evening Times (Trenton, NJ)
Goldsboro News Argus
Hutchinson News (Hutchinson, KS)
Jones Journal (Trenton, NC)
Morning Ledger (Cleveland, OH)
National Tribune (Washington, D.C.)
New Bern Times
New York Herald
New York Times
North Carolina Standard (Raleigh, NC)
Salem Register (Salem, MA)
Old North State (Beaufort, NC)
Republican (Springfield, MA)
The Sunny South (Atlanta, GA)
Weekly Sumter Republican (Americus, GA)
Western Enterprise (Anson, TX)

Manuscripts and Collections

Alabama Department of Archives & History, Montgomery, Alabama
    Samuel Camp Kelly Letters
    Civil War Soldier's Letter
      M. J. Blackwell Letters
      Bolling Hall Family Papers
      William P. Howell Manuscript
      Palmer Family Papers
      R. R. Smyrl Civil Letters
University of Alabama, Tuscaloosa, Alabama, William Stanley Hoole Special Collections Library
    Henry De Lamar Clayton, Sr. Papers

Auburn University, Auburn, Alabama, Special Collections and Archives, Ralph B. Draughon
  Library
      Martin Link Diary
Duke University, Durham, North Carolina, Special Manuscripts Department, William R. Perkins
  Library
      Catherine Jane Buie Papers
      H. J. H. Thompson Diary
Indiana Historical Society, Manuscripts & Archives, Indianapolis, Indiana
      Dwight and Joshua Fraser Letters
      Kidd Family Papers
      Timothy A. Rardin Letters
      George F. Stewart Autobiography and Letters
East Carolina University, East Carolina Manuscripts Collection, J. Y. Joyner Library, Greenville,
  North Carolina
      Sarah Holt Arthur Collection
      Henry T. King Collection
      Charles V. Peery Collection
      Nicholas W. Schenck Journal
      Charles A. Tournier Diary
      Johnny Craig Young Papers
High Point Public Library, North Carolina Collection, High Point, North Carolina
      Barbee Hotel Confederate Hospital Registry
Library of Congress, Washington, DC, Manuscripts Reading Room, Madison Building
      Edward Pendleton Papers
      Albert Quincy Porter Collection
      Patrick Ryan Diary
Minnesota Historical Society, St. Paul, Minnesota
      Leonard Aldrich Papers
Museum of the Confederacy, Richmond, Virginia, Eleanor S. Brockenbrough Library
      Halcott Pride Jones Diary
      Isaac S. Tanner Collection
National Archives, Washington, D.C.
      Record Group 94, Office of the Adjutant General; Volunteer Organizations of the Civil
      War, Various Regimental Returns for March 1865
          Record Group 94, Field Records of Hospitals, 1821-1912
          Record Group 109: War Department Collection of Confederate Records, 1825-1927
North Carolina Division of Archives and History, Raleigh, North Carolina
      R. H. Bacot Letters
      Mary Gash Papers
      Johnny B. Kerr Collection
      John Douglas Taylor Papers
      Henry C. Whitehurst Reminiscence
University of North Carolina at Chapel Hill, Southern Historical Collection, Louis Round Wilson
  Library
      Calder Family Papers
      Thomas J. Carey Diary
      Henderson Dean Reminiscences
      James Clarence Harper Papers
      W. A. Holt Papers
University of Michigan, Bentley Historical Library, University of Michigan, Ann Arbor, Michigan

Edwin R. Farmer Papers
William Fifer Papers
University of Texas at Austin, Texas, Dolph Briscoe Center of American History
    Francis H. Nash Civil War Diary
United States Army Military Heritage Institute, Carlisle Barracks, Pennsylvania
    Civil War Miscellaneous Collection
        Harvey Brooks Letters
        David J. Hussey Letter
        Henry J. Main Memoranda
        Edwin Williams Letters
        John T. Wood Letters
    Civil War Times, Illustrated Collection
        Corporal W. J. Abernathy Collection, Diary
        Sergeant Joseph J. Brown
Virginia Public Library, Richmond, Virginia
    Personal Papers Collection
        Kate S. Sperry
Private Collections
    Jodie Gee—Notebooks of Lilly Bassett Carter Hoffman
    Gary Ezzard—James O'Keel Civil War Letters
    Linda W. Meadows—Cannon Civil War Letters
    Douglas W. Reynolds, Jr.—Horace F. Farnsworth Civil War Letters

Government Publications

Surgeon General's Office, United States Army, *The Medical and Surgical History of the Civil War*, 6 volumes. Wilmington, NC: Broadfoot Publishing Company, 1990-1992.
Supplement to the Official Records of the Union and Confederate Armies. 100 volumes. Wilmington, NC: Broadfoot Publishing Company, 1994-1999.
United States Navy Department. *Official Records of the Union and Confederate Navies in the War of the Rebellion.* 30 volumes. Washington, D.C.: Government Printing Office, 1900-1901.
United States War Department. Atlas to *Accompany the Official Records of the Union and Confederate Armies.* Washington, D.C.: Government Printing Office, 1891-1895.
_____. *The War of the Rebellion: A Compilation of the Official Records of the Union and Confederate Armies.* 128 volumes. Washington, D.C.: Government Printing Office, 1880-1891.

Published Primary Sources

(Includes Autobiographies, Diaries, Journals, Memoirs, Reminiscences and Unit Histories)

Bartholomew, W. G. "Battling Against Heavy Odds," *National Tribune*, August 7, 1902.
Benson, William C. "Civil War Diary of William C. Benson," *Indiana Magazine of History*, vol. 23, no. 3 (September 1927), 333-364.
Brogden, John V. and Crowson, Noel, eds. *Bloody Banners and Barefoot Boys: "A History of the 27th Regiment Alabama Infantry CSA": The Civil War Memoirs and Diary Entries of J.P. Cannon M.D.* Shippensburg, PA: White Mane Publishing, 1997.
Browning, Judkin and Smith, Michael Thomas, eds. *Letters from a North Carolina Unionist—John A. Hedrick to Benjamin P. Hedrick 1862-1865.* Raleigh: N. C. Division of Archives and History, 2001.

Browning, Judkin. *The Southern Mind under Union Rule: The Diary of James Rumley, Beaufort, North Carolina, 1862-1865.* Gainesville, FL: University Press Florida, 2009.

Burlingame, John K. *History of the Fifth Regiment of Rhode Island Heavy Artillery, During Three Years and A Half of Service in North Carolina.* Providence, RI: Snow and Farnham, 1892.

Clark, Walter, ed. *Histories of the Several Regiments and Battalions from North Carolina in the Great War 1861-'65. Written by members of the Respective Commands.* 5 vols. Goldsboro, NC: Nash Brothers, 1901.

Cox, Jacob D. *Military Reminiscences of the Civil War.* 2 vols. New York: Charles Scribner's Sons, 1900.

Crabtree, Beth G. and Patton, James W., eds. *Journal of a Secesh Lady: The Diary of Catherine Ann Devereaux Edmondston 1860-1865*, eds. Raleigh, NC: North Carolina Division of Archives and History, 1979.

Cummings, Charles L. *The Great War Relic, Valuable as a Curiosity of the Rebellion, Together With A Sketch of My Life, Service in the Army, and How I Lost My Feet Since the War; Also, Many Interesting Incidents Illustrative of the Life of a Soldier.* Harrisonburg, PA: n.p., 188-.

Davis, Jefferson. *The Rise and Fall of the Confederate Government.* 2 vols. New York: D. Appleton and Company, 1881.

Derby, W. P. *Bearing Arms in the Twenty-Seventh Massachusetts Regiment of Volunteer Infantry During the Civil War 1861-1865.* Boston, MA: Wright & Potter Printing Co., 1883.

Dennis, G. T. "Wise's Forks: What a Comrade of the 85th N.Y. Saw at the Fight," *National Tribune*, August 31, 1893.

Denny, Joseph W. *Wearing the Blue in the Twenty-fifth Mass. Volunteer Infantry, with Burnside's Coast Division, 18th Army Corps, and Army of the James.* Worcester, MA: Putnam & Davis, 1879.

Drake, James M. *The History of the Ninth New Jersey Veteran Vols.: A Record of Its Service from Sept. 13th, 1861, to July 12th 1865, With a Complete Official Roster and Sketches of Prominent Member.* Elizabeth, NJ: Journal Printing House, 1889.

Elliot, Charles G. Elliott. "Kirkland's Brigade, Hoke's Division, 1864-'65," *Southern Historical Society Papers*, vol. 23 (1895), 169-170.

Emmerton, James A. *A Record of the Twenty-Third Regiment Mass. Vol. Infantry in the War of the Rebellion 1861-1865.* Boston, MA: William Ware & Co., 1886.

Everts, Hermann, *A Complete and Comprehensive History of the Ninth Regiment New Jersey Vols. Infantry, from Its First Organization to Its Final Muster Out.* Newark, NJ: A. Stephen Holbrook, 1865.

Fish, Daniel. *The Forty-Fifth Illinois, a Souvenir of the Re-Union Held at Rockford, On the Fortieth Anniversary of its March in the Grand Review.* Minneapolis: Byron & Willard, 1905.

Goodloe, Albert Theodore. *Confederate Echoes: A Soldier's Personal Story of Life in the Confederate Army from Mississippi to the Carolinas.* Washington, D.C.: Zenger Publishing Co. Inc., 1893.

Grant, Ulysses S. *Personal Memoirs of Ulysses S. Grant,* 2 vols. New York, NY: Charles L. Webster & Co., 1885.

Hagood, Johnson. *Memoirs of the War of Secession, from the Original Manuscripts of Johnson Hagood, Brigadier General, C.S.A.* Columbia, SC: The State Company, 1910.

Hall, Henry and Hall, James. *Cayuga in the Field: A Record of the 19th N. Y. Volunteers, All the Batteries of the 3d New York Artillery and 75th New York Volunteers.* Auburn, NY: Truair, Smith & Co., 1873.

Hauptman, Laurence M., ed. *A Seneca Indian in the Union Army: The Civil War Letters of Sergeant Isaac Newton Parker, 1861-1865.* Shippenburg, PA: Burd Street Press, 1995.

Houts, Joseph K., Jr., ed *A Darkness Ablaze: The Civil War Medical Diary and Wartime Experiences of Dr. John Hendricks Kinyoun, Sixty-Sixth North Carolina Infantry Regiment.* St. Joseph, MO: Platte Purchase Publishers, 2005.

Howe, M. A. DeWolfe, ed., *Home Letters of General Sherman.* New York, NY: Scribner's Sons, 1909.

Hunt, Roger D. *A Civil War Biographical Dictionary, Colonels in Blue: Indiana, Kentucky and Tennessee,* McFarland & Company, Inc., Jefferson: NC, 2014.

Jones, John S. *History of the 174th O.V.I. and Roster of the Regiment.* Marysville, OH: Journal Print, 1894.

Kaler, William S. *Roster and History of the One Hundred Twenty-Third Regiment, I. V. I. in the War of the Rebellion.* Rushville, IN: Press of the American, 1899.

Kirwan, Thomas. *Memorial History of the Seventeenth Regiment Massachusetts Volunteer Infantry in the Civil War from 1861-1865.* Salem, MA: Committee on History, 1911.

Lawrence, Thomas L., ed. *Grandfather's Civil War Diary: A Biography.* Buffalo, WY: T. L. Lawrence, 1994.

M'Gee, E. E. "Last Days as a Confederate Soldier," *Confederate Veteran,* vol. 22, no. 5 (May 1914), 213.

Marshall, Thomas J. *"Diary of Thomas Jefferson Marshall from June 1863 to May 1865", Confederate Reminiscences and Letters 1861-1865,* vol. 20, Georgia Division United Daughters of the Confederacy, 2001.

Munroe, James Phinney, ed. *Adventures of an Army Nurse in Two Wars: Edited from the Diary and Correspondences of Mary Phinney Baroness von Olnhausen.* Boston, MA: Little, Brown, and Company, 1903.

Nanzig, Thomas P., ed. *The Badax Tigers: From Shiloh to the Surrender with the 18th Wisconsin Volunteers.* Lanham, MD: Rowman & Littlefield Publishers, 2002.

Neighbors, J. W. *Neighbors Home Mail: The Ex-Soldiers' Reunion and National Camp-fire,* Issue 2, Princeton, NJ: n.p., 1874.

Sherman, William T. *Memoirs of W. T. Sherman by Himself,* 2 vols. New York: Scribner, 1891.

Sprague, Homer B. *History of the Thirteenth Infantry Regiment of Connecticut Volunteers During the Great Rebellion.* Hartford, CT: Case, Lockwood & Co., 1867.

Thorpe, Sheldon B. *The History of the Fifteenth Connecticut Volunteers in the War for the Defense of the Union.* New Haven, CT: The Price, Lee & Adkins Co., 1893.

Tonnoffski, G. L. "My Last Days as a Confederate Soldier," *Confederate Veteran,* vol. 22, no. 2 (February 1914), 68-69.

Troxler, Beverly Barrier & Auciello, Billy Dawn Barrier, eds. *"Dear Father" Confederate Letters Never Before Published.* n.p.: privately published by the editors, 1990.

Valentine, Herbert E. *Story of Company F, 23d Massachusetts Volunteers in the War for the Union, 1861-1865.* Boston, MA: W. B. Clarke, 1896.

Walker, Cornelius I. *Rolls and Historical Sketch of the Tenth Regiment, So. Ca. Volunteers, in the Army of the Confederate States.* Alexandria, VA: Stonewall House, 1885.

White, William L. and Runion, Charles D., eds. *Great Things Are Expected of Us: The Letters of Colonel C. Irvine Walker, 10th South Carolina Infantry, C.S.A.* Knoxville, TN: University of Tennessee Press, 2009.

Published Secondary Sources

Allardice, Bruce S. *More Generals in Gray: A Biographical Register.* Baton Rouge, LA: Louisiana State University Press, 1995.

———. *Confederate Colonels.* Columbia, MO: University of Missouri Press, 2008.

Auten, Timothy. *The Battle of Wyse Fork: North Carolina's Forgotten Battle.* Wilmington, NC: Broadfoot, 2008.

Barefoot, Daniel W. *General Robert F. Hoke: Lee's Modest Warrior.* Winston Salem, N.C.: John F. Blair Publisher, 1996.

Barnard, Harry V. *Tattered Volunteers: The Twenty-Seventh Alabama Infantry Regiment, C.S.A.* Northport, AL: Hermitage Press, 1965.

Barrett, John G. *Sherman's March Through the Carolinas.* Chapel Hill: University of North Carolina Press, 1956.

———. *The Civil War in North Carolina.* Chapel Hill, NC: University of North Carolina Press, 1963.

Bender, Robert P. ed. *Worthy of the Cause for Which They Fought: The Civil War Diary of Brigadier General Daniel Harris Reynolds, 1861-1865.* Fayetteville, AR: University of Arkansas Press, 2011.

Black, III, Robert C. *The Railroads of the Confederacy.* Chapel Hill, NC: University North Carolina Press, 1952.

Bradley, Mark L. *Last Stand in the Carolinas: The Battle of Bentonville.* Mason City, IA: Savas Publishing, 1996.

Branch, Paul. *Fort Macon: A History.* Charleston, SC: Nautical & Aviation Publishing Co. of America, 1999.

Bright, Leslie S, Rowland, William H., and Bardon, James C. *C.S.S. Neuse A Question of Iron and Time.* Raleigh, NC: North Carolina Department of Cultural Resources, 1981.

Bridges, Hal. *Lee's Maverick General: Daniel Harvey Hill.* Lincoln, NE: University of Nebraska Press, 1961.

Cochran, William C. *General Jacob Dolson Cox, Early Life and Military Service.* Oberlin, OH: Bibliotheca Sacra Co., 1901.

Connelly, Donald B. *John M. Schofield & the Politics of Generalship.* Chapel Hill, NC: University of North Carolina Press, 2006.

Connelly, Thomas A. *Autumn of Glory: The Army of Tennessee, 1862-1865.* Baton Rouge, LA: Louisiana State University Press, 1971.

Cunningham, H. H. *Doctors in Gray: The Confederate Medical Service.* Baton Rouge, LA: Louisiana State University Press, 1958, 1986.

———. "Edmund Burke Haywood and Raleigh's Confederate Hospitals," *North Carolina Historical Review*, vol. 35, no. 2 (April 1958).

Daniel, Larry J. *Cannoneers in Gray: The Field Artillery of the Army of Tennessee, 1861-1865.* Tuscaloosa, AL: University of Alabama Press, 1984.

Edwards, Tom J. and William H. Rowland. *Through the Eyes of Soldiers: The Battle of Wyse Fork, Kinston, North Carolina March 7-10, 1865.* Kinston, NC: Lenoir County Historical Association, 2006.

Fonvielle, Chris, Jr. *The Wilmington Campaign: Last Rays of Departing Hope.* Campbell, CA: Savas Publishing, 1997.

Gabel, Christopher R. *Rails to Oblivion: The Decline of Confederate Railroads in the Civil War.* Fort Leavenworth, KS: U. S. Army Command and General Staff College Press, 2002.

Garrett, Jill K. and Lightfoot, Marise P. *The Civil War in Maury County Tennessee.* Columbia, TN: n.p., 1966.

Gatze, Hans W., ed. *Principles of War, 1812.* 1942; reprint Mineola, NY: Dover, 2003.

Goodson, Gary R. *Georgia Confederate 7,000 Army of Tennessee Part II: Letters and Diaries. From Confederate Soldiers of Brigadier General Barton ad Stovall's Georgia Infantry Brigade.* Shawnee, CO: Goodson Enterprises, 1997.

Grimsley, Mark. *The Hard Hand of War: Union Military Policy Toward Southern Civilians 1861-1865*, New York: Cambridge University Press, 1995.

Hallock, Judith L. *Braxton Bragg and Confederate Defeat*, 2 vols. Tuscaloosa, AL: University of Alabama Press, 1991.

Hanson, Victor D. "What would Patton Say about the Present War?" *The National Speech Digest of Hillsdale College: Imprimis*, vol. 33, no. 10, (October 2004), 6.

Henderson, Lillian, comp. *Roster of the Confederate Soldiers of Georgia*, 6 vols. Hapeville, GA: Longina & Porter, Inc., 1959-1964.

Huston, James. *The Sinews of War: Army Logistics 1775-1953.* Washington, D. C.: U.S. Government Printing Office, 1966.

Hood, Stephen E. John Bell Hood: *The Rise, Fall and Resurrection of a Confederate General.* El Dorado Hills, CA: Savas Beatie, 2013.

Howell, H. Grady, Jr. *To Live and Die in Dixie: A History of the Third Regiment Mississippi Volunteer Infantry, C.S.A.* Jackson, MS: Chickasaw Bayou Press, 1991.

Johnson, Crisfield. *History of Branch County, Michigan, with Illustrations and Bibliographical Sketches of Some of its Prominent Men and Pioneers.* Philadelphia, PA: Everts & Abbott Publishing Company, 1879.

Kelly, William M. "A History of the Thirtieth Alabama Volunteers (Infantry) Confederate States Army," *Alabama Historical Quarterly,* vol. 9, no. 1 (Spring 1947), 115-189.

McRae, Cameron F. *History of Seneca County New York With Illustrations, 1786-1876.* Philadelphia, PA: Ensign & Everts, 1876.

McWhiney, Grady. *Braxton Bragg and Confederate Defeat.* 2 vols. Tuscaloosa, AL: University of Alabama Press, 1991.

Mahood, Wayne. *The Plymouth Pilgrims: A History of the Eighty-Fifth New York Infantry in the Civil War.* Hightstown, NJ: Longstreet House, 1991.

Manarin, Louis H., Weymouth T. Jordan, Jr., Matthew M. Brown, and Michael W. Coffey, comps. *North Carolina Troops 1861-1865 A Roster, 19 vols. to date.* Raleigh, NC: 1966-.

Miller, Rex. *Hundley's Ragged Volunteers: A day-by-day account of the 31st Alabama Infantry Regiment, CSA (1861-1865).* Depew, NY: Patrex Press, 1991.

Perry, Aldo S. *Civil War Court Martials of North Carolina Troops.* Jefferson, NC: McFarland Publishing, 2012.

Pohoresky, W. L. *The Notorious George W. Graham During the Civil War.* Havelock, NC: The Print Shop, 1982.

Price, Charles L. "The United States Military Railroads in North Carolina, 1862-1865," *North Carolina Historical Review,* vol. 53, no. 3 (July 1976).

Scaife, William R. *The Campaign for Atlanta.* Cartersville, GA: Scaife Publications, 1993.

Simmons, R. Hugh. "The 12th Louisiana Infantry in North Carolina, January—April, 1865," *Louisiana History: The Journal of the Louisiana Historical Association,* vol. 36, no. 1 (Winter, 1995), 77-108.

Smith, Mark A. and Sokolosky, Wade. *No Such Army Since the Days of Julius Caesar, Sherman's Carolinas Campaign: Fayetteville to Averasboro.* Ft. Mitchell, KY: Ironclad Publishing, 2005.

Tolson, Mrs. Charles (Eva Mae Hardesty). "History of Morehead City," *Researcher,* vol. 17, no. 1 (Spring 2001), 19.

Tyndall, Cliff. *Threshold of Freedom: Lenoir County, NC During the Civil War.* Kinston, NC: Lenoir County Historical Association, 2003.

Ward, Patricia S. Simon Baruch: *Rebel in the Ranks of Medicine, 1840-1921.* Tuscaloosa, AL: University of Alabama Press, 1994.

Warner, Ezra J. *Generals in Blue: The Lives of the Union Commanders.* Baton Rouge, LA: Louisiana State University Press, 1964.

———. *Generals in Gray: The Lives of the Confederate Commanders.* Baton Rouge, LA: Louisiana State University Press, 1959.

Watford, Christopher M. ed. *The Civil War in North Carolina: Soldiers' and Civilians' Letters and Diaries, 1861-1865, Vol. I: The Piedmont.* Jefferson, NC: McFarland & Company, Inc., 2003.

———. *The Civil War in North Carolina: Soldiers' and Civilians' Letters and Diaries, 1861-1865, Vol. II: The Mountains.* Jefferson, NC: McFarland & Company, Inc., 2003.

Wynne, Ben. *A Hard Trip: A History of the 15th Mississippi Infantry, CSA.* Macon, GA: Mercer University Press, 2003.

Zorn, William A. *Hold At All Hazards: The Story of the 29th Alabama Infantry Regiment, 1861-1865.* Jesup, GA: W. A. Zorn, 1987.

Theses and Dissertations

Kincaid, Gerald A., Jr., Major, U.S. Army. *"The Confederate Army, A Regiment: An Analysis of the Forty-Eighth Tennessee Volunteer Infantry Regiment, 1861-1865."* Master's thesis, U.S. Army Command and General Staff College, Fort Leavenworth, Kansas, 1995.

Sokolosky, Johnny W., Major, U.S. Army. "The Role of Union Logistics: Sherman's Carolinas Campaign of 1865." Master's thesis, U. S. Army Command and General Staff College, Fort Leavenworth, Kansas, 2000.

Unpublished Special Studies

Material on File at Bentonville Battleground State Historic Site, Newton Grove, North Carolina.

Index

144, 153-154, 157, 175, 178, 180-180n,
191-194, 197-198, 200, 202-203, 204n,
205-213, 220, 241
Kirby, William M., 161, 228
Kirkland, William W. and his brigade, 12, 36,
73, 229, 236, 238, 244; Wise's Forks,
March 8, 90, 96, 98, 112, 141; Wise's
Forks, March 10, 160, 163-164, 167-
167n, 168-174; aftermath, 203; losses,
242; *photo*, 163
Kirwan, Thomas, 65, 94, 201
Kise, Reuben C., 149-150, 176, 185; *photo*,
185
Knight, George A., 183
Knox, Joseph B., 205; *photo*, 207
Kyle, Osceola, 183
Lamb, Wilson G., 90n, 167
Lawrence, Robert J., 144, 233
Lee, Robert E., 1-3, 12, 17n, 32, 45, 78, 125,
131, 199n, 219
Lee, Stephen D., and his division, 47, 50, 52,
85, 108, 147, 149, 178, 182, 195, 231,
235, 237, 239, 242, 244
Lenoir General Hospital, 208
Lincoln, Abraham, 2, 11, 217
Lineberry, Edwin C., 108; *photo* 108
Link, Martin, 112
Linsley, Soloman F., 102, 108
Lipscomb, Thomas J., 40
Little Miami Railroad, 25
Loftin, William "Bill," 90
Loring, William W., 142-142n, 176-177,
184-186, 194, 233, 237, 239, 245
Louisiana units
12th Infantry, 49, 144, 234
Love, Joseph, 178, 180, 187-188, 233n
Lower Trent Road, 72, 82, 84-85, 89, 91,
106-107, 109, 118-119, 122-123, 130,
140-141, 147, 158, 160-161, 163, 165,
167, 168-169, 171, 174, 180-181
Main, Henry J., 201
Mallory, Stephen, 15n
Malloy, Adam G., 80, 82, 95n, 141, 147,
149n, 151-152, 187-188,195, 205, 227;
photo 152

Manigault's brigade, 86, 108, 142, 155, 189,
239
Mansfield General Hospital, 22-23
Manville, George W., 102, 133
Marshall, Thomas J., 163, 204n
Marvin, George, 110; *photo* 110
Massachusetts units
2nd Heavy Artillery, 58-59, 67, 82, 84, 91,
107-119, 140-140n, 211n, 226
17th Infantry, 58-59, 65, 67, 92, 94, 112-113,
115-116, 141, 162-163, 173, 201, 228
23rd Infantry, 60, 67, 77, 82, 91-92, 107,
118-119, 140, 211n, 216, 226
25th Infantry, 67, 141, 162-163, 228
27th Infantry, 58, 81-82, 92, 99-100, 102-
103, 109n, 129n, 133, 137, 199n, 214,
227-227n
McAlpine, Charles L., 20
McCourt, Patrick, 93
McGeachy, John D., 39
McKay, Hiram, 150
McQuiston, John C., 122, 140, 147n,
166-167, 171, 181, 188n, 225; *photo*, 166
McRae, Alexander, 104, 106
Meagher, Thomas F., 17, 25, 27, 29, 57-59,
60-60n, 61, 227n; *photo*, 61
Medlock, John O., 155
Meigs, Montgomery, 17-18, 21, 218
Mercer, William E., 76-77, 119-120, 150,
227; *photo*, 151
Michigan units
1st Artillery, Battery F, 165, 226
28th Infantry, 70, 147-147n, 165n, 188-
188n, 226-226n
Mill Branch, 164, 178, 142, 155, 157, 161,
176, 180-181, 189
Miller, John R., 122
Minnesota units
8th Infantry, 226-226n
Mississippi units
1st Battalion Sharpshooters, 234
3rd Infantry, 50-51, 234
6th Infantry, 233
14th Infantry, 144, 233
15th Infantry, 177, 233
20th Infantry, 233-234
23rd Infantry, 233

author

About the Author

Colonel (Ret) Wade Sokolosky is a graduate of East Carolina University and a 25-year veteran of the U.S. Army. He leads tours of Civil War battlefields and is a popular speaker on the Civil War circuit.

Wade is the co-author (with Mark A. Smith) of *"No Such Army Since the Days of Julius Caesar": Sherman's Carolinas Campaign from Fayetteville to Averasboro* (forthcoming in an expanded revised edition by Savas Beatie in 2016), and the author of *Final Roll Call: Confederate Losses during the Carolinas Campaign* (2013).

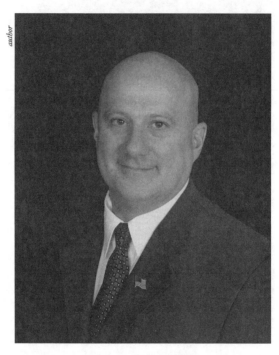

author

About the Author

Major (Ret) Mark A. Smith, who holds a Masters in Military Studies, is a U.S. Army veteran with 21 years of service. Mark served in various positions including Scout Platoon Leader, Three Company Commands, Battalion Executive Officer, Brigade and Battalion S-4, and was an Army ROTC Instructor at Virginia Tech.

Mark is the co-author (with Wade Sokolosky) of *"No Such Army Since the Days of Julius Caesar": Sherman's Carolinas Campaign from Fayetteville to Averasboro* (forthcoming in an expanded revised edition by Savas Beatie in 2016).